WORKS ISSUED BY
THE HAKLUYT SOCIETY

———————

Series Editors
Gloria Clifton
Joyce Lorimer

———————

THE VOYAGES AND MANIFESTO OF
WILLIAM FERGUSSON,
A SURGEON OF THE EAST INDIA COMPANY
1731–1739

THIRD SERIES
NO. 37

INTERNATIONAL REPRESENTATIVES OF THE HAKLUYT SOCIETY

Receipt book from the *Britannia* showing Fergusson's signature (third entry) with two s's in his name and the wages he earned as Surgeon's Mate on his voyage to Calcutta. Reproduced courtesy of the Trustees of the British Library.

THE VOYAGES AND MANIFESTO OF WILLIAM FERGUSSON, A SURGEON OF THE EAST INDIA COMPANY 1731–1739

Edited by
DEREK L. ELLIOTT

Published by
Routledge
for
THE HAKLUYT SOCIETY
LONDON
2021

First published 2021 for the Hakluyt Society by
Routledge
2 Park Square, Milton Park, Abingdon, Oxon OX14 4RN

and by Routledge
711 Third Avenue, New York, NY 10017
Routledge is an imprint of the Taylor & Francis Group, an Informa business

British Library Cataloguing in Publication Data
A catalogue record for this book is available from the British Library

Library of Congress Cataloguing in Publication Data
Names: Fergusson, William, approximately 1710–approximately 1776, author. |
Elliott, Derek L., editor. | Hakluyt Society, issuing body.
Title: The voyages and manifesto of William Fergusson, a surgeon of the
East India Company 1731–1739 / edited by Derek L. Elliott.
Description: London : Routledge for the Hakluyt Society, 2021. | Includes
bibliographical references and index.
Identifiers: LCCN 2020044193 (print) | LCCN 2020044194 (ebook)
Subjects: LCSH: Fergusson, William, approximately 1710–approximately 1776.
Fergusson, William, approximately 1710-approximately
1776—Travel—Indian Ocean Region. | East India Company. | Ship
physicians—Scotland—Biography. | Medicine, Naval—Great
Britain—History—18th century. | British—Indian Ocean Region. |
Natural theology. | Enlightenment. | Indian Ocean Region—Description
and travel.
Classification: LCC R489.F45 A3 2021 (print) | LCC R489.F45 (ebook) | DDC
610.92 [B]—dc23
LC record available at https://lccn.loc.gov/2020044193
LC ebook record available at https://lccn.loc.gov/2020044194

ISBN: 978–0–367–71391–1 (hbk)
ISBN: 978–1–003–15065–7 (ebk)

Typeset in Garamond Premier Pro
by Waveney Typesetters, Wymondham, Norfolk

Routledge website: www.routledge.com
Hakuyt Society website: www.hakluyt.com

For Katja and Phinn

CONTENTS

LIST OF MAPS AND ILLUSTRATIONS

Frontispiece

Receipt book from the *Britannia* showing Fergusson's signature with two s's in his name and the wages he earned as Surgeon's Mate on his voyage to Calcutta. Reproduced courtesy of the Trustees of the British Library (BL, IOR/L/MAR/B/285a).

Maps

Colour Plates

See separate plate section between pages 78 and 79.

Figures

PREFACE AND ACKNOWLEDGEMENTS

This volume brings to publication the eighteenth-century manuscript of Scottish ship's surgeon William Fergusson. Between the years 1731 and 1739, Fergusson made one voyage from Scotland to London, stopping in Ireland, and three voyages from England to the East Indies, calling at ports in the Atlantic, Africa, Arabia, India, South East Asia, and China.

In a series of twenty-three small notebooks, or fascicles, Fergusson wrote what he titled the 'Journals of my Voyages & Manifesto 1767', indicating that he recorded the memories of his youth while in retirement. There is no way of knowing what Fergusson intended to do with his manuscript. He may have sought a publisher, though as the introduction will explain, it is more likely a private journal written for himself or his descendants. Upon Fergusson's death in 1776, the journals passed into the hands of his eldest daughter Elizabeth, and then, upon her marriage in 1780, into the private papers of the Fleming of Barochan family.[1] Two generations later, Elizabeth's grandson William Fleming died without issue, and the Barochan estate, along with Fergusson's journals, were passed to a third cousin named William Hamilton (d. 1931). His grandson, Andrew Gladstone, is the current custodian of the Fleming of Barochan papers. Fergusson's journals today remain a part of this collection and are kept by the family at a private estate near Kirkcowan, Scotland. Twice, however, the Gladstones have kindly entrusted Fergusson's diaries to the Centre of South Asian Studies (CSAS) at the University of Cambridge, where copies were produced and are available for viewing by researchers.

When I was a doctoral student in 2012, I came across Fergusson's journals while examining the eighteenth-century holdings of the CSAS archive. Enthused by a prospective project other than my dissertation, I immediately took an interest in the journals and soon became engrossed in reading them. When I had finished, I found at the bottom of the collection the correspondence between CSAS archivist Mary Thatcher and Andrew's father, John Gladstone, who in 1974 was custodian of the journals. In one letter Thatcher expressed how it was 'unusual to find anything written so early <u>about</u> India', and that one of the research fellows at CSAS thought the journals should be published, ideally with the Hakluyt Society. John Gladstone was very interested in pursuing the project, and I too agreed with him and that anonymous fellow.[2] This volume realizes our shared sentiment, however many years later.

It is true that newly discovered early eighteenth-century first-person accounts of India are rare. Since being made available to the public Fergusson's manuscript has remained

---

[1] Paterson, *History of the County of Ayr*, I, p. 203.

[2] Underlined in original. Cambridge, Centre of South Asian Studies, Ferguson Papers (hereafter CSAS: FP), Letter of Thatcher to Gladstone, 30 April 1974; CSAS: FP, Letter of Gladstone to Thatcher, 2 May 1974.

virtually ignored, only being cited in one article in a now defunct academic journal.[1] This is unfortunate as there are many insights into the history of science and medicine, early-modern economies and trade networks, and the main subject of Fergusson's manifesto, the prevailing notions of Enlightenment thought. In his account, Fergusson reveals himself to be a conduit in the global exchange of ideas that shaped early modern European thought. His memoir demonstrates how his experiences in the world both confirmed and challenged the universalist beliefs popular during his lifetime. For these reasons, and many others to be discussed in the introduction, these diaries have been made available to a wider audience.

Fergusson's three voyages to Africa and Asia were aboard two ships sailing under contract with the British East India Company (EIC), the *Britannia* and the *Godolphin*. His diaries have been referenced with the official logbooks of the ships he travelled in, and any inconsistencies have been noted. The ships' records also provided the data used to plot Fergusson's voyages on the maps included in this volume. The maps use both the historical names as Fergusson knew them and present-day place names following in parentheses. With the exception of European states, which simply will not fit on maps of this scale, all other geographical place names mentioned in the diaries are shown on the maps. The countries that Fergusson knows about, the cities he mentions, the places he recalls, are all elements of the worldview or cosmography of an eighteenth-century educated British man like Fergusson. These are the places of the world that composed the common geographical knowledge of the time. Some were important trade entrepôts or political centres like Canton, Manila, or Batavia. Some were fabled ports then closed to European commerce, like Amoy. Others were places that made European seafarers cautious, like Morocco with its captive-taking corsairs.[2] Fergusson's worldview also includes regions about which little was known, such as Abyssinia and Manchuria. Additional place names mentioned by Fergusson are found in the two maps provided for each voyage. The first provides an overview of the entire route, and another details the ports or region of the destination, usually with insets. The maps also reveal that by the 1730s, while the sea was still a dangerous place, plying the merchant trade routes was relatively routine. The latitudes and longitudes of the fairest wind patterns and currents were well understood, and each voyage followed more or less the same path outbound and return. Thanks are due to Eric Ross at Al Akhawayn University who graciously drafted early versions of these maps and provided excellent cartographical advice from a geographer's perspective, and to David Cox who drew the final versions.

Further thanks are extended to the many people without whom this project would not have been possible. The staff and researchers of the CSAS at Cambridge provided a wonderful environment for study and intellectual exploration. Among them in particular the late and dearly missed Chris Bayly, as well as Sujit Sivasundaram, for their early backing of this project in its current form; Rachel Rowe always helped with the stacks and sources and Barbara Roe provided support and kindness when needed most; Kevin

[1] Stuart, 'Scots in India I: With the *Britannia* and the *Hindoostan*', pp. 315–23. This article appeared in the official journal of the Royal India, Pakistan, and Ceylon Society, the *South Asian Review*, both of which no longer exist. It should not be confused with the current academic journal of the same name established in 1976, by the South Asian Literary Association.

[2] For a contemporary account of a British woman held in captivity at the Moroccan Sultan's court, see the wonderful, Colley, *The Ordeal of Elizabeth Marsh*.

Greenbank was truly instrumental in lifting the project off the ground by arranging the digital preservation of the Fergusson Diaries with the Gladstone family. The current custodian of Fergusson's manuscript, Andrew Gladstone, granted permission for the project and was kind enough to send the journals to Cambridge so it could get underway. He also offered crucial information on the bibliographic history of the journals. Robert Gladstone facilitated communication at key stages, without which this volume would not have seen the light of day. Patrick Wallis at the London School of Economics and Nancy Um at State University of New York at Binghamton were gracious enough to provide valuable comments and explanations on their areas of expertise. Colleagues at my home institution, the School of Humanities and Social Sciences at Al Akhawayn University in Ifrane, have been subjected to many conversations about Fergusson and the eighteenth-century intellectual world of a ship's surgeon. Among them are Katja Žvan Elliott and John Shoup. Paul Love read drafts of the introduction and identified the ream wrapper on fascicle 12. Back in Britain, I would like to thank the staff of the British Library (BL) and the Caird Library at the National Maritime Museum, Greenwich (NMM), for their always courteous and helpful assistance. Mark Condos and Brigid Ward helped facilitate logistical issues and have long been good friends and colleagues. Of course, this volume would never have happened without the support of the Hakluyt Society; Jim Bennett's invitations to the Editor's Workshops were gratefully received and the experience there proved very useful in preparing this volume; Katherine Parker proved a most friendly correspondent over the years; and last, though certainly not least, Gloria Clifton has been a patient and thorough editor. Fergusson and I owe her a debt of gratitude for her keen eye and constructive commentaries.

LIST OF ABBREVIATIONS

&.C.	et cetera
BL	British Library
CSAS	Centre of South Asian Studies, University of Cambridge
EIC	British East India Company
f.	folio
fasc.	fascicle
HEIC	Honourable East India Company
HEICS	Honourable East India Company ship
IOR	Indian Office Records
NMM	National Maritime Museum, Greenwich, London
OREAH	*Oxford Research Encyclopaedia of African History*
r.	reigned
ref.	library or museum object reference number
SEP	*Stanford Encyclopedia of Philosophy*
TNA	The National Archives, Kew, London
Viz(.)	namely, or that is to say, from the Latin 'videlicet'
VOC	Vereenigde Oostindische Compagnie (Dutch East India Company)

WEIGHTS, MEASURES, AND CURRENCY

Weights and Measures

Fergusson used both imperial and foreign weights and measurements. The list below includes all such terms found in the manuscript, along with their modern equivalencies in both imperial and metric systems, even if they may be familiar to many readers.

Catty	A Chinese unit of measurement, commonly used for weighing food and grocery items, which is equivalent to 1.33 lbs (604 grams).
Gallon	Imperial measure of volume equivalent to 3.7 litres.
Hogshead	Old British unit of volume that has fluctuated since its first standardization by Parliament in 1423, though generally referring to large casks of roughly 79 gallons (300 litres).
League	Here used to measure distance at sea, where it is equivalent to 3 nautical miles (3.452 imperial miles or 5.556 kilometres).
Mile	Imperial length of distance equal to 1.61 kilometres.
Pound	Imperial unit of weight equivalent to 453.59 grams.

Currency

In the early eighteenth century, the British pound (£) was divided into 20 shillings (s) with each shilling consisting of 12 pence (d), or 240 pence to the pound. A guinea was worth 21 shillings.

Dollar	Either the Dutch lion dollar (*leeuwendaler*) or the Spanish silver dollar, which in the 1730s was in the process of overtaking the former as the major Indian Ocean trade currency. The Spanish silver dollar was worth about 4s 6d in eighteenth-century British coinage, in which a shilling contained 5.6 grams of silver.
Fanam	A currency used along the Coromandel Coast that was minted by Indian sovereigns and the British in Madras. The currency was divided into pagoda, fanam, and cash. 80 cash = 1 fanam, 36 fanams = 1 pagoda.
Pagoda	See entry for fanam above.
Tael	A tael was a Chinese weight and currency system based upon the value of silver. Under the Qing, the Canton tael weighed 37.5 grams.

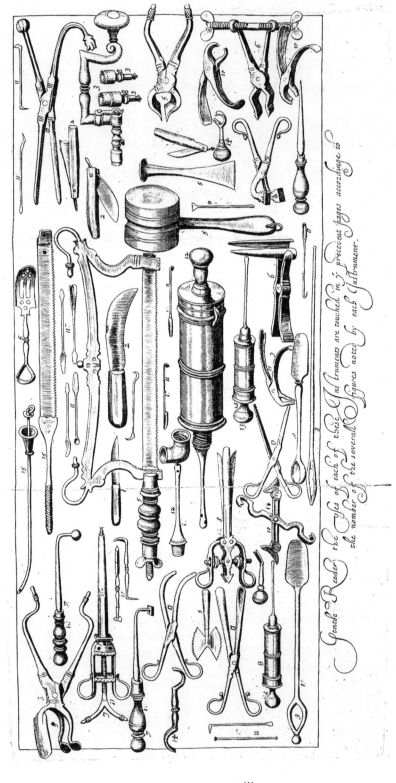

Figure 1. 'EIC Ship Surgeon's Tools', plate from John Woodall, *The Surgeons Mate*, 1617. Woodall was made Surgeon General of the EIC in 1613. His text went through multiple editions and became the standard for EIC ship's surgeons. By the time of his third voyage Fergusson would have had a similar set of instruments. Image provided courtesy of the Wellcome Collection under CC BY licensing (https://wellcomecollection.org/works/gsmgt63).

INTRODUCTION

What shall I say? this is not all
the Chymist must abide
This Labyrinth out, his glasse then breaks,
his patience there is tride.

Yet grant to this although twere more
there's no man never knew,
A work so slight and cheape as this,
such rare effects to shew

In gaining health to sicke and sore,
preserving men from woe:
Yea sundry waies expelling greefes,
which in mans body grow.

'Certaine Chimicall Verses, or Good Will to Young Artists [Surgeons]'.
John Woodall, *The Surgions Mate*.[1]

1. Ship's Surgeons of the Early Modern Era

As these lines demonstrate, the job of an early modern ship's surgeon was tireless and often thankless. Surgeons like William Fergusson bore close witness to disease and death. If a ship was blown off course or supplies were lost or ran low, then illnesses like scurvy could quickly overflow the sick bay with ill men. Meanwhile, a storm or a violent altercation at sea could lead to more fractures, amputations, and open wounds than the single ship's surgeon or his mate could treat. Even when a voyage went smoothly the ship's surgeon was not idle. He was doctor, surgeon, apothecary, and dentist to the entire crew. No small feat considering long-distance European merchant ships of the age required many hands to sail. For example, on Fergusson's final voyage East aboard the *Godolphin*, he cared for some 117 men.[2] Of course, not all lives can be saved, and in the language of one of the lines above, seven sailors perished from 'greefes' along this journey.

Indeed, the maritime world of the eighteenth century was fraught with dangers. As these diaries attest, even relatively routine voyages, like those of Fergusson's, could experience strife. As a surgeon's mate, Fergusson would have seen the worst that could happen to men voyaging for the East India Company. Disease, shipboard accidents, and

---

[1] Woodall, *The Surgions Mate*, pp. 336–7 (pages are mis-numbered in volume as 343–4).

[2] London, British Library: Asia, Pacific, and Africa Collections, India Office Records, Marine Department Records, B/594C (hereafter BL: IOR L/MAR/B/594C), *Godolphin* Ship's Log.

violence were all part of life at sea, and it was up to the surgeon and his mate to tend to ailing and injured men. The job also offered the opportunity to see distant lands and experience foreign cultures at a time when knowledge and imagery of the world were growing but still limited. Fergusson was an educated man of the Enlightenment, an era when European medicine, science, and thought were rapidly developing. He entitled his manuscript 'Journals of my Voyages & Manifesto', which reflects a dual aspect of the diaries. The journals record what Fergusson experienced on his voyages, offer local anecdotes and descriptions of landscapes, places, and religious ceremonies. They also offer, as their manifesto, impassioned polemics on natural religion, together with his thoughts on devotional 'enthusiasm' and just governance, while they implore the principles of rationality and reason. Fergusson viewed the world through the universalist assumptions of the Enlightenment and his manuscript demonstrates that, when Europeans took their ideas out into the world, they also brought others back. Fergusson eagerly engages with and seeks to understand the foreign cultures with which he comes in contact. He does not always find accordance with everyone he meets, nonetheless he reveals himself an empathetic interlocuter. These issues will be returned to at the end of the introduction. First, the state of early modern European medicine and the duties of EIC ship's surgeons are described below. A biography then introduces William Fergusson's life, focusing on his London years whilst an apprentice apothecary. To place the contents of the diaries within their various local contexts, the penultimate section then explains how European surgeons like Fergusson fitted within the healing practices, host-societies, and state-politics of the Indian Ocean trading world.

The poem above is from *The Surgions Mate*, a medical manual for use at sea written in 1617 by the first official surgeon-general of the EIC, John Woodall. Contrary to the sentiments of the excerpted stanzas, the poem's main subject, as its name suggests, is the uses of chemicals in preparing medicines. It was one of several lyrical verses included by Woodall as mnemonic devices to aid Company surgeons in remembering the vast materia medica, or the corpus of botanical and medical knowledge, that their profession demanded. Woodall's book also included a pharmacopeia of medicinal ingredients and instructions on how to treat any variety of ailments, from poulticing a rash to trepanning a skull. It set the standard for medical manuals at sea and went through several editions.

The text reveals a seventeenth-century medical world that was as much alchemy as science. One indicator of this is to be found in the poem's subtitle, where it refers to surgeons as 'Artists'. Woodall does this throughout *The Surgions Mate* demonstrating a rather metaphysical approach to medicine. If the surgeon was artist, then the body and its ailments were the canvases to work upon, a place where science had yet to claim a monopoly. The progress that European medical knowledge had made in the century between Woodall and Fergusson can be seen by examining what practices included in the manual were still in use during the 1730s, and what were not. For example, treatments that 'doth much availe in the cure of the flix', such as having the afflicted sufferer inhale 'the steeme of wine vinegar sprinkled on a hot bricke', were no longer used by Fergusson's day, at least not for 'curing' dysentery.[1] Other sections of the book discuss the elemental properties of planets and their associated materia medica and group treatments and cures around these shared attributes. Saturn, for example, is associated with lead, which was

---

[1] Woodall, *The Surgions Mate*, p. 39.

used in medicines treating the spleen, while Mercury, and the toxic liquid-metal that shares its name, was used with disorders of the lung.[1] Fergusson lived in an era when European medicine was in transition from a practical art to science. His diary shows how he was a proponent of the new empirical method that was helping to bring about a Scientific Revolution and propel the Enlightenment forward in Europe. However, it also shows he was still informed by the medical theories of the ancient Greeks. After curing a group of sailors from scurvy on St Helena, Fergusson implores the use of empirical observation by men like him:

> the attention that ought to be given by Physicians & others who undertake the Care of Peoples health, to discover that Method of Cure that the peculiar nature of Each different Disease requires; which no theory can discover, but a judicious & patient observation of what does hurt & what does good in the affective Dissorders, [*sic*] agreably [*sic*] to the Plan followed & prescrib'd by Hippocrates[.][2]

Eventually the application of empirical scientific standards to theories of healing would lead to a revolution in European medicine. However, for the moment, Fergusson used both observation and centuries-old theories. The fact that Fergusson wrote his diaries in the 1760s shows both how far European medical knowledge advanced during the early Enlightenment, and the distance it still had to go to develop away from ideas first put forward in antiquity.

While by Fergusson's day European medicine had lost many of its cosmological elements, and its practitioners were certainly no longer referred to as artists, it was still humoral in theory and practice, and would remain so until the next century. Articulated first in the ancient Eastern Mediterranean, humoralism viewed disease and illness as the result of the body's fluids, or humours, being out of balance. Treatments sought to restore order to the four humours – blood, phlegm, and yellow and black bile – by adding to or purging the body of any of these excess liquids. Medicines too, as we saw, were associated with attributes relative to the humours and were administered to help increase or decrease their levels in the sufferer. This is why enemas, inducing vomiting, and bloodletting were common treatments. For example, as a humour, blood was associated with the qualities of warmth and heat. Thus, when a patient came down with fever the prescribed remedy was to drain blood from the sufferer, either through the application of leeches, or through cupping, or lancing. The idea was to relieve the patient of enough of the problematic humour to bring the body back into equilibrium, thus restoring health and order. In one of the few sections where Fergusson discusses his professional duties, he tells us that, when men aboard the *Britannia* became feverish on the way out to India, he treated them through 'bleeding and Vomitting with a cool regimen'.[3] Such treatments further demonstrate the logic of the humoralist theory of medicine. Hot fevers required cooling medicines to be administered and the body drained of its excess 'hot' fluid to cool it down and alleviate the fever. Fergusson claims that his treatment worked, and perhaps it did. Of course, we now know that, for most patients, they survived in spite of, rather than because of, these kinds of medical interventions. The dangers of bloodletting were well known even in Woodall's day. In *The Surgions Mate* he cautions that when 'at sea [...] it

---

[1] Ibid. pp. 308–9, 312–13.
[2] See, p. 170.
[3] See p. 46.

is good to be sparing in the quantitie of blood to be taken away, and rather often take blood away, then [sic] too much at once'.[1] European medical knowledge certainly advanced in the hundred years separating Woodall's and Fergusson's lives, yet much also remained familiar. Most of Fergusson's methods would have been as recognizable to Woodall as would the contents of his medical chest. Woodall established the first official inventory regulating what EIC surgeons took with them to sea, which, like much medical practice of his day, remained in use by ship's surgeons like Fergusson, as seen in Figure 1.

The eighteenth century also witnessed the increasing professionalization of the medical trades in Britain. When Fergusson's diary takes place, many practising barber-surgeons and apothecaries were not even members of their respective guilds. As the middle of the century drew nearer, however, regulation for surgeons increased, and many non-guild practitioners were shut down or fined. Training for apothecaries was even more unregulated during the entire eighteenth century, and only came under official oversight in 1815 with the passing of the Apothecaries Act. As we will explore in the next section below, Fergusson's own career corresponds to these changes, as he likely spent his apprenticeship outside of his guild, the Worshipful Society of Apothecaries. However, by the early 1740s, probably when he was establishing his own practice, Fergusson became a member of the Society after paying to take its examination, granting him licence to practise legally as an apothecary. The risk of operating professionally outside the guilds was becoming increasingly untenable as the century progressed, even if training remained rather ad hoc. For surgeons, a further mark of distinction for their profession was that they were shedding from their duties and title the appellation 'barber'. Throughout the seventeenth and into the early eighteenth century, EIC ship's surgeons also performed this task for their ship's crew. In fact, even Woodall as surgeon-general was required to trim the hair of the workmen in the EIC shipyard.[2] Nonetheless, by the 1730s cutting the hair and shaving the beards of the men on board was no longer part of the surgeon's duties, as evidenced by the fact that the company-lists of the ships Fergusson sailed in all included barbers.[3]

It is unfortunate that Fergusson does not spend more time in his diary describing his duties as a ship's surgeon. To date there has been no study of EIC ship's surgeons as a historical group of subjects. They have appeared and are featured in several works examining colonial medicine, early imperial knowledge networks, and even in their capacity as diplomats. While illuminating in their own ways, none of these works deals with surgeons as medical practitioners.[4] This leaves much of what is known about their shipboard lives obscure. Iris Bruijn's exhaustive study of Dutch East India Company (VOC) ship's surgeons helps to reveal some of what their British counterparts experienced.[5] However, there is still much to know about EIC ship's surgeons, and it is hoped that this volume may inspire further work on the subject. Fergusson does shed some light on the professional activities of early modern ship's surgeons in his journal.

---

[1] Woodall, *The Surgions Mate*, p. 29.

[2] Foster, *John Company*, p. 78.

[3] BL: IOR/L/MAR/B/285AA, *Britannia* Ship's Log, 1734; BL: IOR L/MAR/B/285BB, *Britannia* Ship's Log, 1737; BL: IOR L/MAR/B/594C, *Godolphin* Ship's Log, 1739.

[4] Examples include works cited elsewhere in this volume, such as: Arnold, *Science, Technology, and Medicine in Colonial India*; Winterbottom, *Hybrid Knowledge*; Um, *Shipped but Not Sold*.

[5] Bruijn, *Ship's Surgeons of the Dutch East India Company*.

On his second *Britannia* voyage, whilst in Mocha purchasing coffee, Fergusson relates how he treated, probably for syphilis, a Yemeni dignitary. As we shall see below, this brief tryst with medical diplomacy left him disillusioned.[1] He also makes the occasional reference to local medicinal plants he noticed along his journeys. His most detailed descriptions of treating patients is during his first *Britannia* voyage, already quoted in part above, and aboard the *Godolphin* during the homeward journey. He describes treating sailors suffering fevers, pains, and scurvy, sometimes in grisly detail. He explains the symptoms of the afflicted, what medications he prepared, and how they were administered. He also reveals something else; a rare glimpse into the emotional. He ends his brief, most illuminating account of eighteenth-century medicine at sea, appropriately perhaps, detailing the caring for scurvy patients, and ending with an admission of helplessness. The men were so stricken with vitamin C deficiency they were 'emaciat'd & breathless', with their teeth falling out of their swollen gums and their limbs covered with painful ulcers. '[A]s long as we continu'd at Sea', he wrote, there was 'no hope of being able to cure' the poor sufferers.[2] Fergusson bares his humanity with these words and says little else about practising medicine. Fortunately, the *Godolphin* arrived at St Helena in time so that only one of the sick sailors' lives was lost.

Most of what is known about early modern British ship's surgeons comes from the history of the Royal Navy, where regulations were somewhat stricter on who could qualify. For example, since 1629 all surgeons in the Royal Navy had to be approved for service by the Worshipful Company of Barbers in London. Similar regulations for EIC vessels did not arrive until more than a century later. Despite the name of their guild, even in the seventeenth century Royal Navy surgeons were considered too specialized to attend to the menial task of cutting hair, a service that instead went to the ship's specifically appointed barber.[3] As we saw above, the literal appellation of the early modern professional title 'barber-surgeon', still applied to their colleagues in the EIC into the eighteenth century. Of course, the main purpose of surgeons on both merchant and naval vessels was to be responsible for attending to the illnesses and injuries of everyone onboard. As we know, ships of the eighteenth century were dangerous places and injuries and loss of life were common. On Fergusson's final voyage the *Godolphin* was battered by the seas and almost sank twice, leaving our narrator surprised they were 'delivered without losing or much hurting one man'.[4] This was quite the stricken voyage as on their way out to India's Coromandel Coast, the ship was blown off course, causing them to sail in the opposite direction for twenty days. During the return voyage another ship in their company barely made it into St Helena, which would have caused disaster for the crew had they missed the important revictualling station. If any of the sailors been hurt in the storms or began showing signs of dietary deficiencies as a result of the extended sailings, it was Fergusson's responsibility to care for them. Ship's surgeons had to be ready to deal with any variety of healthcare needs and would have administered enemas, drawn blood, dressed wounds, set bones, practised dentistry, and treated fevers and illnesses such as scurvy. They also had extensive pharmaceutical knowledge and would have mixed many of their own medicines, tinctures, and ointments, and made compresses to treat a variety

---

[1] See, p. 91.
[2] See, pp. 46–7, 169–70. Quotation is on p. 47.
[3] Rodger, *The Wooden World*, p. 26.
[4] See, p. 168.

of internal and topical ailments. Surgeons were also the chief officers in charge of ship sanitation, meaning Fergusson likely also monitored drinking water contamination and carried out and scheduled cleaning for the ship and its men.

EIC ship's surgeons were required to keep an onboard medical journal or surgeon's log. Very few of these have survived, suggesting that if regulations existed requiring ship's surgeons to submit their logbooks, they were not enforced.[1] Those that have been preserved do not differ greatly in the kind of information usually recorded in the official logbooks of voyages, although there are some key differences. Examples from 1789 and 1834 begin with a list of the ship's company followed by a log of each day's reckoning, course, and weather.[2] They also contain any noteworthy activities carried out by the surgeon, such as when clothes washing day for the sailors was held on deck, fumigating the hull, and of course, the illnesses, recoveries, and deaths of any crew members. Like other ships' logs, they also recorded any out of the ordinary incidents and punishments carried out on board. Fergusson's medical journal would have contained similar information. In the diaries of the present volume, Fergusson mentions the dates and times of weighing anchor, setting sail, and the coordinates of places passed along the way. Fergusson's manuscript was written some thirty years after the events recorded took place and few would be able to recall such detailed information after so many decades. He probably kept his surgeon's journals and used them to draw upon the details of his voyages. However, like most surgeon's journals, his too are now lost to time. Fortunately, the logbooks of the *Britannia* and *Godolphin* have survived to corroborate most of these details. The same cannot be said for most information on the life of William Fergusson.

2.   William Fergusson, Apprentice Apothecary-Surgeon

There is indeed little information to begin with and even less to offer in the way of verifying the details of Fergusson's life. Nonetheless, his major movements can be traced from the scattered fragments left behind in the historical archives. Mystery surrounds his childhood as there is no clear record of his birthdate, or even place. He was probably born in Ayrshire sometime around 1710, growing up and living there until he set sail from the city of Ayr in 1731, when his journals begin. Fergusson returned home in 1755 to live out the last twenty years of his life. When the reader first meets Fergusson, he was about to embark on that early voyage leaving Scotland one afternoon in June 1731, aboard the *Adventure* sailing for London. Fergusson offered nothing by way of introduction to his younger self, a man probably between fifteen and twenty years. Nor did he say why he was going to England. It is only upon arrival that any clues were offered. The end of the narrative of his voyage south finally reveals that when in London he stayed at 'Mr Gilletts', an apothecary in Grosvenor Street.[3] Fergusson says he lived there for the next year and a half, adding that his last weeks in the city were spent residing somewhere else to prepare

---

[1] Bruijn, *Ship's Surgeons of the Dutch East India Company*, p. 71.

[2] London, National Maritime Museum, Caird Library, Logs, 81, (hereafter NMM: LOG 81), G. Parr, Surgeon's Journal on the HEICS *Ocean*, 1798–1800; NMM, Journals and Diaries, 289/1 and 289/2 (hereafter JOD 289), A. Coventry, Journal of the Proceedings (1) and Medical Journal (2) on the HEIC ship *Warren Hastings*, 1833–4.

[3] Fergusson has omitted a possessive apostrophe in Gillet's name.

to ship out aboard the *Britannia* in January 1733 as a surgeon's mate.[1] He revealed nothing else of his months in the city, not what he did nor whom he met, and Fergusson's following entry in the journals began his next voyage.

From the scant clues left behind we can piece together that Fergusson went to London to pursue a medical career. It is likely that he went to train with Gillet as an apprentice apothecary. Records confirm that at the time a 'William Gillet' rented a house at the location Fergusson gave and that a 'Will. Gillet' who lived in the same parish, registered an apprentice with the rather memorable name of 'Botoler Bamford' in September 1732, a few weeks before Fergusson shipped out in the *Britannia*.[2] If this is the same Gillet, and it likely is, then about the same time Fergusson wrote that he left his house, a new apprentice was brought in. As there is no record of Fergusson ever having been similarly registered, he probably paid no fee to his master and was already planning to spend much of his apprenticeship at sea. Usually, those learning a trade lived within their master's household, just as Fergusson did for his year and half in London. But, no records confirm that either Gillet or Fergusson were free or indentured members of any medical guild in the city during the 1720s and 1730s. At the time the usual course to a medical profession other than for physicians, who went to university, was through the guilds. However, as we saw above, it is also true that many early eighteenth-century apothecaries were not members of their professional society. By then the enforcement of guild monopolies over practising traders was spottily applied. This was especially true for practitioners like Gillet, who lived outside the boundaries of the City of London, and thus outside the jurisdiction of the guild. Even though Fergusson was not apprenticed through an official guild-sanctioned agreement of indenture, his life very likely resembled that of an apprentice. He was of the age appropriate to begin such training and his further professional milestones align with the dates when the historical evidence of his life surfaces.

One such clue in the archival record that helps piece together Fergusson's professional life is that in 1741 a 'William Ferguson' was examined and made a freeman of the Worshipful Society of Apothecaries, after having 'paid a fyne of 20 guineas and 40 [pence]'.[3] As this is the only such reference to any man of that name in the relevant London livery company records, it is probably our Fergusson. It appears that after he returned from his final voyage on the *Godolphin* in 1739, he spent the next two years completing his training and probably working awhile to save for the fee to sit the apothecary examination. This means that Fergusson spent about a decade training, not an unusually long time, and only a couple of years longer than the minimum seven that official guild apprentices spent. By 1741, Fergusson must have decided he wanted to practise medicine as a qualified freeman of the Society of Apothecaries, and he took its examination. This gave him membership in his guild and the official licence to practise his trade for the rest of his medical career.

---

[1] See, p. 41.

[2] The National Archives, Kew (hereafter TNA), IR 1/13, Board of Stamps: Register of Duties Paid for Apprentices' Indentures, 1710-1811. Entry for 19 September 1732; Sheppard, ed., 'Appendix 1', pp. 172–95. I am grateful to Gloria Clifton for finding Gillet in the apprentice registry records. Both sources cited here have the spelling as 'Gillet', and this has been adopted here as opposed to Fergusson's 'Gillett'.

[3] London, Guildhall Library: City Livery Company Records, Society of Apothecaries, Freedom Registers 1725–85, CLC/L/AA: MS 8206/2 (hereafter CLC/L/AA: MS 8206/2), f. 67r.

The year and a half that Fergusson spent with Gillet was just long enough to gain the experience he needed to be eligible for a position on board a ship as a surgeon's mate. An unapprenticed man without qualifications would simply not have been hired, even by the most unscrupulous of ship's captains. Fergusson's first months in London were probably spent becoming familiar with the basics, beginning with cleaning and stocking the apothecary shop, moving on to mixing remedies, applying treatments, and even letting blood if his master also practised surgery.

Apprentices had to be prepared to begin training with their masters immediately upon indenture. As was expected of prospective apprentice apothecary-surgeons, Fergusson would have come to London with some education. He was literate and trained in Latin, knowledge of which he retained throughout his life, as his diaries reveal. For the previous 170 years the Barber-Surgeons' Company, the oldest medical guild in the country, had required Latin for apprentices as it was still the language of the materia medica.[1] Such basic skills were expected to be in place before specialized training in a profession could begin, even for those not officially apprenticed. The fact that Fergusson was educated and could afford to go to England for his professional training suggests that he came from a family with some means. Research on VOC ship's surgeons has revealed that most apothecaries and barber-surgeons came from middle-class families, though where they stood within society depended upon where they were located. In a place like London, apothecary-surgeons were part of the class of middling merchants and tradesmen. In smaller cities like Ayr, or in rural locations, they could be counted amongst the upper classes or even the village elite.[2] Considering the education Fergusson already had when he left Scotland and carried with him for the remainder of his life, he probably came from a well-off family.

The life of an indentured man was regimented. Even though Fergusson was not himself an officially bound apprentice of the guild, he would still have been expected to behave in a similar manner. His contemporaries would have found little to distinguish his situation from that of a guild member's apprentice. A rather preachy manual published in 1725 called *The Servant's Calling* set out the ideal qualities of an apprentice. It emphasized what it declared were the Christian values of obedience, chastity, humility, honesty, sobriety, and above-all, of knowing one's place in the master's household. While this may have been the ideal, the reality was, as usual, far more complex. Indenture lasted years and the apprentices were young men, after all. Nonetheless, there were some clear expectations of behaviour and men not willing to abide by a master's rules often never finished their training. Apprentices lived under their master's roof and had to 'duly and truly' serve.[3] Masters demanded secrecy over their trade's skills and that apprentices should be chaste, and certainly unmarried. Neither did many masters tolerate gambling or time spent in public houses and theatres. The master controlled how the apprentice lived, ate, and took leisure. For some men, abiding by these kinds of strictures was simply too much. Desertion and running away was a common strategy for apprentices who did not get along well with or suffered abuse from their masters. However, breaking the terms of indenture came with potential fines for both parties. Apprentices were warned that

---

[1] Lane, 'The Role of Apprenticeship in Eighteenth-Century Medical Education in England', p. 65.
[2] Bruijn, *Ship's Surgeons of the Dutch East India Company*, pp. 170–71.
[3] Quoted in ibid., pp. 58–9.

that if they were not willing to abide by their master's rules then they ought to pursue other lines of work. Another manual for aspiring tradesmen suggested exactly that when it offered advice for 'such bold and daring Spirits, as would think themselves above being confin'd to the necessary Rules of an orderly Family'.[1] The *Apprentice's Vade Mecum* was written by Samuel Richardson originally as an advice letter to his soon-to-be apprentice nephew. It was published in early 1734 while Fergusson was returning from his first voyage to Calcutta.[2] Cautioning that 'The SEA [is] the best choice for such as cannot comport to orderly rules', Richardson reasoned that shipboard life, despite its heavy regimentation, offered far more in the prospect of adventure for lads not meant for the more mundane pursuits of a structured life on land.[3] Whether or not to pursue the life of a tar was best decided before 'the Youth [is] to be bound 'Prentice' because young men who went to sea of their own accord gained shipboard experience earlier and kept the wages they earned. This was not the case for apprentices who were sent to sea by angry masters, as we will see below.

Figure 2.   'The Idle 'Prentice turn'd away, and sent to Sea', engraving by Thomas Cook after William Hogarth, 1795. A later rendition of Plate 5 of William Hogarth's *Industry and Idleness* series, showing the unwanted apprentice sent out to sea, with his crying mother by his side. Image provided courtesy of The Wellcome Collection under CC BY licensing (https://wellcomecollection.org/works/ y6b3ry2f).

[1] Richardson, *The Apprentice's Vade Mecum*, pp. 51–2.
[2] In 2001, Calcutta changed its name to Kolkata.
[3] Ibid., pp. i, 51–2.

Some apprentices did not have a choice in whether or not they went to sea. They were sent as punishment. Maybe they broke the master's rules or committed other transgressions. Perhaps it was a simple matter of clashing personalities. In general apprentices had a bad reputation. The era's tropes described them as lazy, recalcitrant, and unruly. Of course, the reality was far more complex. Some apprentices were indeed bad sorts. So too, were some masters. Abuse was commonplace and apprentices often had little legal recourse if indentured under a tyrant.[1] Nonetheless, the image of the lazy apprentice was popular enough by 1747, that William Hogarth satirized the 'Idle 'Prentice' in a twelve-part series titled *Industry and Idleness*. One of the plates even depicts an apprentice being sent out to sea (see Figure 2). In it several figures are in a boat, including a poor mother weeping into her handkerchief for her son the Idle 'Prentice, who cowers while his master leers over him, taunting and laughing as he points to the waiting ship they are rowing towards. This was a common method of getting rid of unwanted apprentices, made all the more popular by the fact that, under the terms of indenture, masters maintained rights over the labour of their charges. Thus, they were entitled to almost all of their apprentice's wages while at sea. If Gillet was indeed Fergusson's master, he too could have retained most of Fergusson's wages earned aboard the *Britannia* and *Godolphin* to make up for his lost labourer. This was an ideal situation for Gillet and explains how he was able to bring another apprentice into his home after Fergusson changed residences to prepare for his first EIC voyage. With an unofficial apprentice at sea, and an officially registered one under his roof, Gillet was probably keeping the wages of one while maintaining the labour of another, it seems, to the benefit of all parties involved. To be clear, there is nothing to indicate that Fergusson was sent or went to sea as a result of running afoul of his master. Indeed, from what we can conjecture from his diary and know about his later life's successes, Fergusson was anything but an idle apprentice. In fact, going to sea was common for apprentice apothecaries and surgeons, no matter how they got on with their masters.

Generally speaking, apprentices in all trades often spent much of their time indentured away from their masters. The strict rules of indenture disguised a system of training that was actually much more adaptable to the realities of life.[2] This was especially true of apprentice surgeons and apothecaries of the sort Fergusson may have been. Medical knowledge was always in demand at sea, and the shipboard conditions made it difficult to attract well-established or even fully qualified medical practitioners, such as university-educated physicians. These men did go to sea, though if they worked on board a vessel it was only as ship's surgeons on their way out to a more senior position in one of the Company's trade settlements. Barber-surgeons and apothecaries with surgical training were hired as the ship's surgeons and mates and were often the cheapest source of labour for the job. With experience they could rise to become full ship's surgeon before their apprenticeship was over. Certification of EIC surgeons by the guild in London began only in 1745, after Fergusson was already a full member of the Worshipful Society of Apothecaries. Before then it was the EIC surgeon-general who oversaw the qualifications of its medical officers. Considering that John Woodall was himself appointed examiner of the barber-surgeon's guild in 1626, and the Royal Navy

---

[1] Levene, "'Honesty, sobriety and diligence'", pp. 186, 196–8.
[2] Minns and Wallis, 'Rules and Reality', p. 558.

in 1641, there were probably few practical differences in quality between Royal Navy and EIC surgeons at the time.[1]

As Fergusson's own experience shows, one single voyage was enough to qualify a mate as full ship's surgeon. By his second trip East on the *Britannia*, Fergusson had his own surgeon's mate assisting him. While this may seem odd at first, the dangers of life at sea necessitated immediate medical care by the best available individual, even if they were short on experience. As a result, many surgeon's mates were promoted early, some even during their first voyage, especially if the full ship's surgeon happened to die along the way. Thus, the sea offered young apprentices the opportunity to rise quickly through the ranks and come to know a greater variety of illnesses and afflictions in a short amount of time. This system also contributed to the poor reputation of ship's surgeons as under-qualified at best and butchers at worst. In the words of one historian, 'the universally shared opinion in the history of the European seafaring countries', was that the ship's surgeon was considered 'a mere village barber, a good-for-nothing and an illiterate by his contemporaries'.[2] In *The Surgions Mate*, Woodall addressed the stigma of those disreputable surgeons who bring 'disgrace to themselves and a great scandall to their calling', and implored his readers to be 'dutifull, diligent, willing, [and] careful' in their profession.[3] Though there were plenty of surgeons like Fergusson who, as his diary reveals, were careful and learned practitioners, their poor reputation persisted. As one mid-nineteenth-century Briton in India recalled:

> In former times, so little care was taken about the selection of the medical officers of the East India Company, that it was facetiously said, a man need only sleep upon a medicine chest for a single night to become perfectly qualified for the office.[4]

As we have seen, apprentices that were hired aboard merchant vessels received a small stipend, with most of their wages going to their masters as recompense for the lost hand. Not only were apprentices a cheaper source of labour, they were also deemed more likely to put up with the difficult conditions of life at sea and be more amenable to a captain's orders. In return, the apprentices received on-the-job training with a variety of ailments and injuries that they never would have come across working in a shop in a city like London. Furthermore, sailing to the East also meant adventure and the opportunity for private trade. Such practices were common among the chartered companies of the mercantilist era and Fergusson describes how VOC officials in Malacca enriched themselves through the perquisites of their offices.[5] EIC employees also were notorious for private trading. Fergusson never mentions if he took advantage of the opportunity to make extra money on his voyages, though he did go 'ashore to do some business' of an undisclosed nature near Madras during his first trip to India.[6] Regardless of the difficulties and poor pay, an apprenticeship at sea for potential apothecary-surgeons offered clear professional advantages, an opportunity for adventure, and the potential for extra income. Unfortunately, we will never know which of these most persuaded Fergusson to enlist

[1] Longfield-Jones, 'John Woodall, Surgeon General of the East India Company', pp. 12–13.
[2] Bruijn, *Ship's Surgeons of the Dutch East India Company*, p. 15.
[3] Woodall, *The Surgions Mate*, ff. 7v–8r.
[4] Stocqueler, *The Oriental Interpreter*, p. 297.
[5] See, p. 135.
[6] See, p. 61.

on the *Britannia* in early 1733 to set sail for Calcutta, since his diaries simply do not tell us.

What is clear is that Fergusson made his voyages when he was a young man in his late teens and early twenties, during his period of training to become an apothecary. He made two voyages aboard the *Britannia*, going as far as Calcutta. After his third voyage travelling to Canton[1] aboard the *Godolphin*, he returned to London in 1739 and gained his professional qualification two years later. Once Fergusson had paid to take his examination with the Worshipful Society of Apothecaries in 1741, his presence in the historical record again vanished. All we know is that he went on to establish his own successful medical practice in London. He was probably never a surgeon at sea again.

Fergusson next resurfaced in the historical record upon his return to Ayr in 1755. A nineteenth-century local history described him as a gentleman who 'had spent the greater part of his life – as a medical practitioner – in London, where he realised a considerable fortune'.[2] It seems that, after more than a decade of success in London, Fergusson returned to Scotland for unknown reasons. In his diaries Fergusson quotes Virgil, praising the values of the 'quiet life' and longingly describes his desire for 'Tranquillity & retirement'.[3] Considering that Fergusson wrote the diaries while enjoying the very life he extols, perhaps this was his goal in going to London: to make his fortune and return home to a peaceful life of rural retirement. If it was, he surely found it. In the countryside just south of the city of Ayr, Fergusson used his wealth to purchase an estate from a merchant, on which he soon built a manor house and gardens. He named the estate Doonholm and raised his family there. Records confirm Fergusson had three daughters, Jane, Elizabeth, and Susanna, who were married in 1773, 1780, and 1783 respectively, to various gentlemen of good social standing.[4] Nothing else is known about Fergusson's family or personal life.

Fergusson lived at Doonholm until his death in 1776. It is uncertain what exactly he did with his time in Ayrshire. We know he was active in his community, serving for a number of years as Ayr's town clerk and later provost, a position in Scotland similar to mayor. There is one source that claims Fergusson had a son named James who took over the position of town clerk and also later became provost.[5] However, this is probably a confusion with his nephew James, since it is unlikely Fergusson had a son, as upon his death his estate went to his daughters Elizabeth and Jane. They co-inherited Doonholm along with the diaries, which eventually came into Elizabeth's sole possession. If Fergusson had a son, then he would have inherited his father's property, not his sisters. There is no record of whether Fergusson continued a medical practice while conducting his civic duties. Maybe he dispensed his specialized knowledge only amongst friends when asked. Or, perhaps he left his profession completely behind in London and enjoyed a sort of retirement as a public official.

One interesting anecdote about Fergusson that has emerged is that, from 1757 until his death almost twenty years later, he employed a man named William Burnes as head

---

[1] Today's Guangzhou.

[2] Paterson, *History of the County of Ayr*, I, pp. 202–3.

[3] Amongst the vineyards of Cape Town, Fergusson was struck by the happy retirement of a minister who had a lovely home and garden, though his young wife was, by our surgeon's account, less enthusiastic about such a tranquil existence. See, pp. 124–5.

[4] Burke and Burke, *A Genealogical and Heraldic Dictionary*, pp. 419, 620, 668.

[5] Ferguson and Fergusson, eds, *Records of the Clan*, p. 77.

gardener and overseer at Doonholm. Burnes and his wife lived on a small farm leased from Fergusson's estate. By all accounts the men got along very well, with Fergusson playing the role of 'benefactor' and Burnes the honest and faithful overseer, though this may have been a Romanticist interpretation of their relationship.[1] Regardless, in 1759 Burnes's wife gave birth to their first son whom they named Robert. In time, long after having left his childhood home on Fergusson's estate, this boy would drop the Scottish 'e' from the spelling of his last name and go on to become one of the Romantic era's most important poets, familiarly known as Rabbie Burns. The future Bard of Scotland spent his early years growing up at Doonholm with Fergusson as his father's employer and friend. This was Fergusson's closest brush with fame, though he would not live to see young Robert Burns become a national figure.

Indeed, Fergusson himself was never famous, nor was he a member of a famous expedition or voyage. This sets him apart from most subjects of Hakluyt volumes, including that of fellow ship's surgeon and naturalist Lionel Wafer, who died just a few years before Fergusson was born. Wafer became well known through the publication of a picaresque narrative of his explorations of Panama's Darien isthmus and other buccaneering adventures, sometimes in company with William Dampier.[2] His book was translated into several European languages and read widely in the eighteenth century. Fergusson, however, was not an adventurer – at least not one who lived at the edge of the law and known world like Wafer. Fergusson was a ship's surgeon who sailed the well-plied trade routes of the EIC. His diaries preserve only the part of his life he spent voyaging to Asia, and no other writings of his are known to survive. Through his journals he proves himself a curious observer of the world and its people. He does not seem, however, overly intrepid. Had he grown tired of life at sea and visited enough of the world by 1739? Perhaps. After all, life at sea was harsh and Fergusson spent the better part of a decade voyaging. He eventually returned to his native Ayr to live out his last decades at home in Scotland. If he ever entertained the idea of leaving Britain to take up an adventurous residence abroad in one of the Company's settlements, it was certainly never acted upon. Should he have wished, his experience would more than have qualified him for a post in India. Many surgeons took up positions in the East looking for further adventures or even the possibility of riches.

3.   European Medicine and the Indian Ocean World

Much medical practice in the Indian Ocean world was informed by the same sources as in Europe. Descended from the ideas of ancient Greek medical physicians like Galen and Hippocrates, this knowledge was significantly improved upon in the medieval period, most famously by Ibn Sina, known to Europeans in his Latinized appellation, Avicenna. He was an Abbasid-era Persian physician whose *Canon of Medicine* formed the basis of most healing practices in both the Christian and Muslim worlds of the Mediterranean and Indian Ocean. Originally written in 1085, it remained the standard general medical textbook published in Latin throughout Fergusson's lifetime. Like in

---

[1] Currie, *The Complete Works of Robert Burns*, pp. xxxiii–iv; Rogers, *Genealogical Memoirs*, pp. 36–7.
[2] Joyce, ed., *A New Voyage and Description of the Isthmus of America by Lionel Wafer*.

13

Europe, eighteenth-century medical practice in much of the Indian Ocean was humoralist in approach. Thus, it viewed disease and illness as a result of the body being out of balance. Despite these shared scientific origins and common practices, the trade ships of Europe did bring disparate worlds of medical knowledge together. Europeans both introduced and were introduced to a wide variety of afflictions, botanicals, treatments, and remedies that were unknown or uncommon in other regions of the world.

As the medical officers stationed in foreign ports and sailing the seas aboard merchant vessels, surgeons like Fergusson were at the forefront of expanding Europe's knowledge of medical science. In the VOC, 'medical surgeons were responsible for knowledge of both bodily and botanical systems', and the expectations were similar for surgeons employed by the EIC.[1] Engaged in that Enlightenment-era activity of collecting useful knowledge, apothecaries, botanists, surgeons, and others eagerly sought out unfamiliar species of plants for study and propagation.[2] They brought these to gardens set up expressly for this purpose in the settlements of the European trading companies. Such gardens were precursors to the establishment of similar enterprises back home, such as the Royal Botanic Gardens at Kew, created in 1759. Over the course of the eighteenth century and into the next, these practices effectively globalized the specialized local knowledge of the Indian Ocean world's materia medica, and in so doing, greatly expanded European medical science.[3] Fergusson was probably too junior in his career to participate in specimen collection, however, he favourably remarks on the VOC garden in Cape Town, which at the time was almost as large as the town itself.[4] The size of this impressive garden was not unexpected considering the settlement's importance as a revictualling station for passing ships. Fergusson commented on the numbers of fruit and shade trees, and how it was full of 'all Manner of pott and Physical Herbs', things of particular interest to any apothecary and ship's surgeon.[5]

The Indian Ocean was, and remains, home to a great diversity of societies and cultures, many of them having their own medical philosophies and practices different from European and Perso-Arab understandings. To varying degrees these also came under increasing study by Europeans in the early modern period. Japan was closed off to all but the Dutch, limiting information on its particular approach to medicine. China, too, was difficult to study. The movement of outsiders was restricted in the country and Europeans were generally allowed only within the port city of Canton. A few exceptions were made for individual missionaries who were working scattered throughout the country. By Fergusson's time, however, these privileges were also curtailed. These missionaries regularly sent reports back to Europe and Paris-based Jesuit and scholar Jean-Baptiste Du Halde compiled these accounts to create eighteenth-century Europe's most authoritative source of information on the country. His four-volume *The General History of China* was originally published in French and soon appeared in English in 1736. Fergusson says he read it but does not say when. He could have picked it up in London between voyages when it was printed. Perhaps he purchased the tomes knowing he was

---

[1] Grove, *Green Imperialism*, p. 108

[2] Arnold, *Science, Technology, and Medicine*, p. 49.

[3] I borrow this idea of 'globalising local knowledge' from Winterbottom, *Hybrid Knowledge*, p. 131.

[4] See Figure 5, p. 67, and the description in Voyage 3 below, p. 68.

[5] See, p. 68.

soon to set sail for Canton aboard the *Godolphin*. Having the volumes on the voyage would mean that he could have it in hand as he sailed up the Pearl River, pausing to contemplate views of the Chinese countryside passing alongshore. Considering that Fergusson wrote his diaries some thirty years after his voyages, we have no way of knowing when he actually read Du Halde, only that he did. *The General History of China* was quite favourable in its treatment of the history, science, and politics of the country, however, when it came to the topic of medicine, Du Halde was less than enthusiastic. What he had to say is worth quoting:

> It cannot be said that the Art of Medicine has been neglected by the Chinese; they have a great number of ancient Authors who treat of it, and they have applied themselves to it from the Establishment of the Empire.
>
> But as they have but little Skill in natural Philosophy, and are not at all versed in Anatomy, they never knew the Uses of the Parts of the Human Body, nor consequently the Causes of Distempers, their whole Knowledge entirely depending upon a doubtful System of the Structure of the Human Body; it is therefore not at all surprising that they have not made the same Progress in this Science as our Physicians in Europe.[1]

At the root of the problem were fundamental differences between European and Chinese understandings of anatomy and the workings of the body. Such reports from an authoritative source, like Du Halde, served to discourage Europeans from attempting to overcome the difficulties and potential dangers of gaining access to further study Chinese medicine.[2] As a result, most of China's healing practices largely remained an enigma to Europeans until the early nineteenth century.

India was a completely different environment. Europeans were well-established all along the coasts, with individuals and groups frequently travelling inland. By the time of Fergusson's arrival in Madras in 1731, the relationship between Indians and Europeans was already over two centuries old. Europeans were really only the latest participants in a long-standing cross-cultural exchange of scientific and medical knowledge centred around Indian Ocean trade. India's geographical position in the middle of the Indian Ocean brought it into contact with many different ideas and practices. As a result, its medicine had influences from the ancient eastern Mediterranean and was essentially also humoral in its approach. Even so, Indian practices also maintained distinct elements, the best-known of which is Ayurvedic medicine. Eighteenth-century European apothecaries and surgeons borrowed elements of the materia medica of Ayurveda and incorporated it into their own healing practices. However, as in China, intense scholarly understanding of Ayurveda would not occur until the early nineteenth century when its study by Europeans was greatly facilitated by British rule.[3] By the mid-nineteenth century Europeans would come to look down upon Ayurvedic medicine, but in Fergusson's day it was common for them to be treated by local practitioners when they fell ill, reasoning that Indian ailments needed Indian treatments.[4] Of course Indians also learned from Europeans who brought new medical practices and botanical knowledge to Asia and offered some novelty. European surgeons

---

[1] Du Halde, *The General History of China*, III, p. 356.
[2] Bivins, 'Expectations and Expertise', pp. 463–6.
[3] Arnold, *Science, Technology, and Medicine*, pp. 66–7.
[4] Arnold, *Colonizing the Body*, p. 11.

were often asked by foreign rulers for treatments and cures. This was a potentially dangerous and costly undertaking if the cure failed, though one that could also reap great reward for European surgeons in Asian courts.

It was not unusual for ship's surgeons to stay on in Asian ports as medical practitioners serving the EIC trade factories. Several early European barber-surgeons, physicians, and apothecaries in India received their appointments after serving as surgeons aboard vessels on their way East. Some even became quite well-known in their day, forming the basis for origin stories of the British empire in India that took on mythical elements, the most famous of which was the legend of Gabriel Broughton. He sailed out to India as ship's surgeon aboard the *Hopewell* in the early seventeenth century. Upon arrival in Surat he was asked by the EIC council to venture into the interior above the hills onto the Deccan Plateau to meet the Mughal court at their camp on campaign. When they arrived, they discovered that the favourite daughter of Emperor Shah Jahan had had a terrible accident. She was retiring for the night in her quarters when her clothes had caught alight on a candle flame. The fire engulfed her leaving her body badly burned as a result. The story goes that local doctors were unable to treat the girl, so an English surgeon was sent for. Broughton was successful in 'curing the Princess, and was desired by the grateful Emperor to name his reward'.[1] What really turns this story into legend is that for his reward Broughton eschewed all thought of personal gain and instead asked that his masters, the Honourable Company, be allowed to establish trade factories in Bengal. Shah Jahan granted him his reward and the EIC began building trading factories along the Hooghly River in competition with the other Europeans already established there.

Broughton's story was one of the most popular told in the eighteenth and nineteenth centuries about the early Company days. In nineteenth-century versions, Broughton is cast as the ideal servant of the EIC. He is loyal, thinks of his employer first, and uses his personal talents in furthering the Company's, and ultimately, the nation's ends. Broughton's sacrifice was recognized as responsible for opening the path to British rule over India. That path led to conflict in the 1750s between the EIC trade factory at Fort William (today's Kolkata), and the ruler of Bengal, Siraj ud-Daulah, at the Battle of Plassey, precipitating the Company's direct control over Bengal itself by 1765. Bengal was the 'bridgehead' that led to the creation of British territorial empire in India, which by the mid-nineteenth century stretched across the subcontinent.[2] Indeed, according to one twentieth-century version of this story, 'Broughton's influence in high places' with the Mughal court led the EIC to get 'a secure footing in India and laid the foundation for the mighty empire we see'.[3] However, more than a century separates Broughton's lifetime from the time when the EIC came to rule over Bengal and his actions were certainly not responsible for it, whatever they actually were. In fact, some elements of the story are outright false. There is enough historical evidence in both Mughal and European sources to confirm that a daughter of Shah Jahan was indeed badly burned; however, she was successfully treated by local medical practitioners, not Europeans. Broughton did go to the emperor's court and travelled overland to Agra and Bengal, before dying in the interior sometime around 1656. It seems that though he was held in high esteem by many

---

[1] Chevers quoted in Crawford, 'The Legend of Gabriel Boughton', p. 3.
[2] Marshall, *Bengal: The British Bridgehead*.
[3] Anon., 'British Medicine in India', p. 1248.

Mughal officials, he did not secure any privileges for the Company in Bengal.[1] Though Broughton's story took on new meanings in the later eighteenth century the fantastical elements of it were already in place by Fergusson's day, and it was a popular tale even then. Fergusson surely would have heard it, if not in London, then certainly on his voyages. He also would have heard the story of his contemporary William Hamilton.

Like Broughton, Hamilton was another ship's surgeon who was said to have been handsomely rewarded at the Mughal court for his medical services. However, unlike the previous story this one was true. William Hamilton went to India in 1709 aboard the *Sherborne*. He jumped ship to flee an 'unpopular' captain in the Coromandel port of Cuddalore, and then made his way to Calcutta. His desertion was seemingly considered not very serious by Company officials there and he was appointed second surgeon at Fort William in 1711. A few years later he was invited to join the Company's embassy travelling to Delhi to visit the Mughal court. When they arrived, they found that Emperor Farrukhsiyar was suffering from 'swellings in his groin'.[2] Hamilton began treatment at great risk to himself and the embassy should he fail. Luckily, he was able to cure the Emperor's maladies and as a result was largely credited for the success of the diplomatic mission. In gratitude Farrukhsiyar held a public ceremony wherein he showered Hamilton with rewards that included: clothes, jewels, gold ornaments, diamond rings, 5,000 rupees, a horse, and even an elephant. The Emperor was so pleased with Hamilton that he attempted to retain him as his own personal court physician. At length, Hamilton and the rest of the embassy were permitted to depart upon promise of Hamilton's return to Delhi. Soon after the embassy made its way back to Calcutta in 1717, Hamilton died. When word of what had happened was sent to Farrukhsiyar, he so valued Hamilton's return that he sent officials to verify the surgeon's death, making sure the Company was true to its word and was not trying to prevent Hamilton from going back to his court.

Hamilton's story differs from that of Broughton largely in that he makes no sacrifice for the benefit of his employer the Company. Instead, Hamilton was enriched personally and became a nabob who did not survive long enough to live the part. In the early 1700s the term 'nabob' was not the caricature or slander that it would become by the end of the century, when Burke used it to vilify types such as Clive and Hastings.[3] A nabob is exactly what Hamilton would have been had he survived to return to Britain, another EIC servant enriched through his Indian adventures. This was indeed the dream of many who went to India. The lure of private trade on the Company's ships was considered a perquisite, even as officials continued to regulate against it. The favour of foreign courts and their rich rewards was the romantic legendary element of Hamilton's story – one where dreams became a reality, even if Hamilton's was tragically cut short by death. This story was popularized almost immediately, and surely would also have found Fergusson's ear.

Both of these stories do share one common element, and that is the importance of medical diplomacy in the early modern Indian Ocean world. At the time, the British EIC was one of many European trading companies competing for local political influence and

---

[1] Crawford, 'The Legend of Gabriel Boughton', pp. 6–7.
[2] Anon., 'British Medicine in India', pp. 1248–9.
[3] Lawson and Philips, '"Our execrable Banditti"', pp. 225–6.

profits in the lucrative markets of Asia. The Company of the early eighteenth century was not the territorial behemoth it would later become. Instead, it was a series of trading factories and fledgling settlements scattered across the Indian Ocean littoral. Trading factories in Canton and Malacca connected the silks and porcelains of the Far East with the cottons and calicoes of India through the trade outposts scattered up and down the Malabar and Coromandel Coasts to Bengal, across to the coffee port of Mocha in Arabia. The Company's most important centres in India were Madras, Bombay, and Calcutta, which served as regional centres of government and settlement.[1] In most of these locations the EIC established its presence through the permission of local rulers. By the time of Fergusson's visits in the 1730s, the central authority of the Mughal Empire had largely collapsed into regional successor states. Local princes, or more properly nawabs, localized power across India turning the Mughal provinces into virtually independent kingdoms. Many of these nawabs acknowledged fealty to the Emperor in Delhi, though they were, for all intents and purposes, sovereign over their own affairs. Leaders of the various successor states often entered alliances with vying European powers in order to shore themselves up against enemies, both foreign and Indian. The best example of this would come mid-century when the French and British Companies, under the respective leadership of Dupleix and Clive, famously supported rival sides in mid-century succession struggles in Hyderabad and the Carnatic.

Each of the EIC's trading factories existed through the goodwill of the local government. This was something the British Company was starkly reminded of at the end of the seventeenth century. In 1686, the EIC, at the behest of one of its governors in London, Sir Josiah Child, declared war on the Mughal Empire after the failure of an EIC diplomatic mission to Emperor Aurangzeb's court. Child's War, as it became known, was disastrous for the Company and almost cost them their trade rights in India at a time when Mughal power was at its height. Woefully underprepared for war, the EIC attempted to attack Chittagong in Bengal but were routed and scattered. Aurangzeb ordered a counterattack against the Company's possessions and had all EIC goods seized and their trading privileges revoked. This left Madras and Bombay as the only settlements that could reasonably be defended. Aurangzeb turned his attention to the west, where Bombay had some initial successes against Mughal shipping in the Arabian Sea during the early stages of the war. Now, however, the EIC found their island blockaded by the Mughal fleet. Soon troops were landed, and Bombay Fort was besieged, while the Company's other possessions were burned. The loss of life and trade revenue forced the EIC to sue for peace in 1690. This was accepted on the condition that the Company send a delegation to the Mughal court to personally beg forgiveness, including the Bombay governor who was spared this obsequious embassy by his own death, which came shortly before the delegation departed. After receiving profuse apologies and over a half a million rupees paid as indemnity, Emperor Aurangzeb restored the Company's privileges.[2] The EIC learned that, for the moment, diplomacy rather than war was more profitable.

The dissolution of Mughal power in India following Aurangzeb's death increased the opportunities for European diplomatic missions. The myriad states that established themselves as sovereign by the time of Fergusson's visits in the 1730s meant that there

---

[1] In 1996, Madras and Bombay changed their names to Chennai and Mumbai, respectively.
[2] Stern, *The Company-State*, pp. 121–4.

were more courts from which to gain favour and keep pleased. A European apothecary's or surgeon's knowledge and novel treatments could play a role in helping an embassy achieve its objectives, as the stories of Broughton and Hamilton attest. Indeed, medicine was 'crucial to diplomatic relations' across the early modern Indian Ocean.[1] As we saw above, Fergusson only used his talents for this purpose once while in Yemen, and the experience left him sour. He wrote in his diary that he was asked 'to give advice in their Diseases' and wound up treating a local high-ranking official, the admiral of Mocha.[2] Fergusson happily obliged but when the time came to be paid for his services, he received only declarations of eternal friendship, rather than his expected handsome reward. Of course, due to the admiral's lofty status, there was no one to whom he could complain without risking the Company's position in the city. It is possible that Fergusson's actions paid off in in the long run in the form of some favour granted to the next arriving British ship. He himself though, was left out of pocket for the used medical supplies. The kind of medical diplomacy that Fergusson unexpectedly found himself taking part in fitted within a larger pattern of gift-giving that was common in Yemen. Treatment by foreign surgeons was probably among the favours local elites expected to glean from the Europeans trading in their port.[3] This was Fergusson's first and only time in the region and he was unaccustomed to local social practices and the culture of trade in the Arabian Sea. Whatever the case, Fergusson never again reports of treating any other locals in any other ports for the rest of his voyages. He seems to have learned that doing so simply was not worth the risk.

4.   A Manifesto of the Enlightenment

Few new European sources on Asia from the early eighteenth century come to light, but Fergusson's journals and manifesto are important for more than this reason alone. Crucially, they offer a perspective on the world before the Great Divergence.[4] This is the moment, sometime around 1750, when European states overtook China and other Asian economies as the world's wealthiest region. This was the result of the unprecedented technological and intensive economic growth Europe began experiencing during the early modern period, which eventually brought about the Industrial Revolution and its rise to global prominence. Fergusson was born into and travelled a world on the cusp of this transition and his perspective is heavily influenced by the prevailing ideas of Enlightenment thought. The philosophical and scientific advancements made in Europe that now stand as hallmarks of the scientific revolution were recent achievements in Fergusson's day. So recent, in fact, that Isaac Newton personally oversaw the publication of a new edition of his revolutionary *Principia* in 1726, only five years before Fergusson left his childhood home in Scotland. Even as late as 1767, when Fergusson penned his diaries, he was still able to comment on how new the rise of European science was. For example, in a passage evaluating 'Knowledge in

---

[1] Winterbottom, *Hybrid Knowledge*, p. 112.

[2] See, p. 91.

[3] Um, *Shipped but not Sold*, p. 124.

[4] The term was originally coined in Pomeranz, *The Great Divergence*, p. 44; other historians put the date as late as the early 19th century, Darwin, *After Tamerlane*, p. 187.

Mathematicks', he proclaimed Chinese understanding as 'Superficial', but only 'when compar'd with the late Improvements made in these Sciences in Europe'.[1] The fact that Europe had not yet reached the zenith of its global political, economic, and cultural influence was also reflected in how Fergusson offered a worldview devoid of the civilizational hubris that tainted later European colonial-era views of local peoples. Moreover, the pages here reveal that though Fergusson approached the world firmly through the lens of the Enlightenment, he also found accordance with the principles of reason and rationality throughout his travels, whether in Africa, India, China, or elsewhere. He did not seem to believe himself superior to the non-European peoples he met and even admonished the bigotry of Dutch settlers against the indigenous Khoikhoi at the Cape of Good Hope.[2] Fergusson's manuscript thus offers far more than a travelogue of voyages with exotic anecdotes. Uniquely, it is also a manifesto of the Enlightenment. It presents an example of how the ideas of early modern Europe were incorporated into the worldview of an educated man of his era, who was, for all other intents and purposes, rather ordinary. It shows how Enlightenment thought was engaged with and carried into the extra-European world where it was confronted with, and renegotiated through, foreign contexts and ways of thinking by the ordinary individuals who sailed for the EIC. The remainder of this introduction will examine the text and draw a few examples of how Fergusson interpreted what he saw on his travels through the prevailing ideas of his time.

Fergusson's journal demonstrates how different his world was from the one that emerged by the end of the century. When the *Britannia* departed London in 1732 with Fergusson aboard, it was one of only thirteen vessels sent that trading season to the EIC's scattered settlements in the East. When he went out again on the same ship in 1735, fifteen other vessels were contracted by the EIC, and by the time of his final voyage in the *Godolphin* during the 1738–9 season, the total number of ships sent was eighteen.[3] This number would not rise substantially until the end of the century, before reaching a peak of fifty-four vessels sent in both 1802 and 1803.[4] By that time British power already extended across large swathes of India and would continue to expand well into the modern era. However, it is worth remembering that Fergusson sailed the coasts of India only fifty years after the EIC's embarrassing defeat in Child's War, and though by then the Mughals' power was fractured, they were still not to be trifled with. Neither were the regional successor states, as Fergusson makes clear when he arrived in Bombay in 1736. He tells of how local powers like the Marathas were 'formidable to Europeans', and had seized 'many of their Ships with rich cargos as well as exceeding many Moremen's Ships'.[5] While the naval or military capabilities of these groups lagged behind those of European forces, they did present an unyielding opposition that could not be removed by the EIC for another twenty years. Until that time, as Fergusson confessed, these powers were able to 'stagnate the present Trade of Bombay and partly of all India'.[6] Successor states were

---

[1] See, p. 166.

[2] See, p. 71.

[3] Hardy, *Register of Ships* [...] *to 1760*, pp. 9–12.

[4] Hardy, *Register of Ships* [...] *to 1819*, pp. 222–4.

[5] Like most Europeans of his era Fergusson refers to the Marathas by the term 'Suviaja', a variation of the name of dynasty-founder Shivaji Bhosale (d. 1680). See, p. 95.

[6] Loc. cit.

also able to coerce the EIC into entering into regional conflicts against their interests. For instance, our surgeon reported from along the Malabar Coast that the British were drawn into a war because their 'Trade was obstructed' by the local ruler, who would only allow commerce to resume after they entered into an alliance against an invading neighbour.[1] The attacking army was repulsed, leaving Fergusson so unimpressed with the martial abilities of their Indian foes that he thought 'Ten Thousand Europeans of the regular standing forces', could 'Conquer the greatest part of the Moguls Dominions'.[2] While this scenario was unlikely, European military technology, like its science, was undergoing rapid development in Fergusson's era. Yet, the effects of the Great Divergence would not be complete for some while, during which time Asian powers remained resolute. So strong were they that no less a figure than Edmund Burke asked Parliament in 1783:

> Could it be believed when I entered into existence, or when you, a younger man, were born, that on this day, [...] we should be employed in discussing the conduct of those British subjects who had disposed of the power and person of the Grand Mogul?[3]

Even more than a decade after Fergusson's death it was astonishing to Britons that the EIC had become a territorial power in India and supplanted local rulers. When Fergusson made his voyages, the 'English Company', as our Scotsman called it, held no territory outside its settlements and was one player amongst many, all vying for influence, control, and profitability in the region's trade. For Burke, his era, which saw the rise of British global power, was marked by what he called 'the stupendous revolutions that have happened in our age of wonders'.[4] Fergusson's lifetime was also one of transition and it seems he sought to record its own wonders in the places, peoples, and religious traditions he experienced and heard about on his voyages in a period before Britain was a world power.

There is some uncertainty as to why Fergusson wrote his journals and manifesto. He states in his diaries that he did so 'to Serve as private memoranda of these occurrenceys [*sic*] that I thought worth being notic'd, & remembered [*sic*]'.[5] However, journals are meant to be read, even if they are private. Were the memories of his travels to be noticed and remembered by him alone, or were they recorded for his children or wider posterity? Did Fergusson ever entertain any notions of publishing his manuscript? The answers to these questions likely died with him or his daughters. The diaries clearly do more than just record memories for an old man's nostalgia. Fergusson regularly returns to the themes of rationality and reason, especially concerning religion. This manifesto aspect of the diaries suggest that Fergusson may have had a wider audience in mind. While we will never know for certain what his intentions were in writing his manuscript, they do illuminate certain traits of Fergusson's personality and character. These will be discussed below, along with the Enlightenment worldview he presents through the polemics of his manifesto.

We know Fergusson was educated and well-read. He was therefore likely to have been familiar with, and perhaps even inspired by, the travelogues of his day. The travel

---

[1] See, pp. 101–2.
[2] See, p. 103.
[3] Burke, *The Complete Works*, II, p. 303.
[4] Loc. cit.
[5] See, p. 141.

narrative was extremely popular in the early eighteenth century and it is not surprising that Fergusson's journals adopt many elements of the genre. On his first visit to a town he offered a description of its layout and buildings, while noting any interesting local architectural or design features. Details of the inhabitants took up a significant portion of the journal and Fergusson seemed genuinely fascinated with non-European ways of living. He always mentioned the manners, dress, and customs of the societies he met, and usually offered a few anecdotes. As we will see later below, he was particularly taken with religious practices and always had a lot to say about the ceremonies he witnessed. Following another common feature of the early modern travelogue, he recorded any defensive structures, such as city walls and fortresses, as well as their garrison sizes. As Fergusson's diary attests, conflict and competition were rife across the Indian Ocean, and in an age when information moved slowly, it was common for authors to report on the military forces of potential rivals. Sometimes Fergusson is a frustrating narrator and omits details even when he has the language abilities to inquire into or knowledge to describe accurately what he sees. On his last visit to Madras in late 1738, all he writes of his month-long stay was that he 'mett with that hospitality & friendship I had allways experienc'd at Fort St George'.[1] In China, Fergusson almost taunts the modern reader with what he sees but refuses to describe when he informs us that if he had 'more time & leisure' he could continue to tell of the 'many other things' than the silk, tea, and porcelain available for purchase at Canton.[2] Stylistically, perhaps it is better that Fergusson ends his explanation there. China occupies a disproportionate amount of the manuscript, which makes it uneven in its narrative style. Readers will immediately note that Fergusson's accounts grow lengthier with each voyage. His passage from Ayr to London, while a relatively short trip, is only documented in one fascicle. His second voyage to the Bay of Bengal is lengthier but still fits within two. Fergusson seems to have developed his writing style as he progressed with his project. The third and fourth voyages, which did not last any longer than his previous one, occupy four-fifths of the manuscript and more than half of his final voyage aboard the *Godolphin* relates to China, a place he visited only once.

Fergusson is clearly more impressed with China than any other location he travelled to and his enthusiasm for the country cannot be overstated. As his ship made its way up the Pearl River toward Canton, he recalled how the landscape 'ravishes the Eye with the most Exquisitely beautifull rural view that the Earth is capable to afford'.[3] All around him he saw a countryside that was 'exceeding fruitfull and Populous'.[4] His admiration extended beyond the beautiful vistas and bountiful fields to also include the people, extolling 'the Indefatigable Diligence & Industry of the Chinese'.[5] In his strongest line of praise Fergusson concludes:

> there is not a Country in the world, (as it is generally believ'd) that has Such a variety and Such Plenty of all the necessary, conveniences & Delights of Life within itself, as China hath.[6]

[1] See, p. 169.
[2] See, p. 141.
[3] See, p. 139.
[4] See, p. 138.
[5] See, p. 139.
[6] See, p. 140.

The esteem with which Fergusson describes China reflects the country's position as the world's leading economy before the Great Divergence. Fergusson both offers this as his own conclusion and claims it to be the commonly held opinion at the time. He was certainly not alone in his admiration for China. His contemporaries, including the EIC ship captain and fellow narrator Alexander Hamilton, considered China as 'the richest and best governed Empire in the World' and, perhaps most famously, Voltaire was well known for praising 'China as the model of a secular and humane civilisation' against the deficiencies that he saw his own society.[1] Fergusson was so genuinely impressed with what he saw on his voyage to Canton that he wrote more on China than any other place he visited. By drawing extensively on Du Halde's *The General History of China*, Fergusson offers details on Chinese history, governance, and philosophy, as they were interpreted through his own Enlightenment worldview.

Fergusson viewed his experience in and knowledge of China through the universalist tenets of European Enlightenment thought.[2] China's politics, meritocratic bureaucracy, and approach to religion all offered Fergusson confirmation of his own ideals of rationality and human reason. For him, China's prosperity was due to its ability to apply the principles of rational governance backed by a socio-political moral philosophy that ensured the governed certain rights. As he asserted:

> it is universally acknowledg'd, that there never was in the world an absolute Government, where the People Suffer So litle by it in all their Natural Rights & Liberties, as this of China. And this Happiness is chiefly owing to these admirable Principles, that are as it were the Foundamentals [*sic*] of their government, which intirely turn upon this, that The Emperor is considered, and must consider himself as the Father of his People[.][3]

Fergusson continues by outlining the duties of the mandarins, or scholar-bureaucrats who governed the country, to both the Chinese emperor and the population. Fergusson references the key Enlightenment ideals of natural rights, liberty, happiness, and the responsibility of rulers to their subjects. For modern readers, and perhaps Fergusson too, this framing of Chinese governance through natural principles that legitimized its right to rule, and preserved the freedoms of its people, invokes the idea of the social contract from Hobbes' *Leviathan* and later works by Rousseau. However, in China Fergusson found that these ideas were already centuries old. Modern specialist scholars may find many points on which to disagree with Du Halde's and Fergusson's understandings of China and its intellectual history and political philosophy. While interesting in and of itself, what is important here is what Fergusson inferred from these ideas and where he found congruence with similar positions then being put forward in Europe, not whether he or Du Halde was correct. From *The General History of China*, Fergusson understood that what he referred to in his diaries as the 'Great Maxim' of Chinese governance was *taiji*, which developed its principles independently of Europe, and had its basis in

[1] Hamilton, *A New Account of the East-Indies,* II, p. 291; Bailey, 'Voltaire and Confucius', p. 817.
[2] There is significant scholarship on the influence that China had on European thinkers of the Enlightenment. The introduction here focuses exclusively on how Fergusson's Enlightenment ideals were expressed in his manifesto. Those interested in the wider historical discussion should consult: Jacobsen, 'Chinese Influences or Images?', pp. 623–60; Statman, 'The First Global Turn in Enlightenment World History', pp. 363–92.
[3] See, p. 152.

Confucian thought. This is Du Halde's description of *taiji* as Fergusson would have read it:

> *Tai ki*: They say its Extension is infinite, its Nature pure and perfect, Duration without Beginning and without End: It is the Idea, the Model, and Source of all things, and the Essence of all other Beings: In short in some places they speak of it as an animated Being, and give it the Name of Soul and Spirit, and look upon it as the Supreme Understanding[.][1]

The concept of *taiji* developed out of what is now known as the neo-Confucian movement as a philosophical and spiritual belief system, introduced first in the classic eponymous Daoist work *Zhuangzi*, sometime in the late fourth century BC.[2] It seeks to explain the oneness of the nature of the universe, out of which all things come and stand in relation to one another, and are governed naturally by certain rational unchanging principles, known as *li*.[3] Du Halde explained that it was this that 'establishes the reciprocal Duty between the Prince and the Subject' in China, which Fergusson also described above.[4] As Fergusson understood it, Chinese governance operated on a rational political model informed by spiritual moral principles.

Du Halde also referred to *taiji* as the 'the Sect of Some of the Learned', meaning that it was primarily the educated classes of mandarins, that made up the government of imperial China, who applied these ancient principles most seriously. Reading it described as a religion of the learned may have confirmed for Fergusson the auspicious results of having a rational government guided by a universal natural religion. This is a central issue that he returns to again and again in the pages of his diaries. For Fergusson, China's prosperity was directly linked to how its social contract upheld the natural laws of mankind. In summarizing these views, he offered a lengthy definition of natural religion as he understood the concept that is worth quoting in full:

> Hence it appears, how prevalent the Principles of that first & most excellent Religion are with the wise in all nations. I mean the Religion of Nature; A Religion arising from the nature of things and discoverable of its Self by all reasonable Beings; A Religion previous to & us'd as the foundation of all others, whose worth or merit is only estimated in proportion as they are consonant to or recede from this the only Rule of Good & Bad, of Right & Wrong; A Religion obvious to and embrac'd by all, whose minds have not been perverted & poisoned by Ear[th]ly Prejudices, & untimely prepossessions in favour of Some other absurd & Inconsistent Systems. This is that Great Law of God & Nature, not improperly Said to be engraven on every Rational Soul, to whose Dictates if we firmly adhere, we Shall be preserv'd from these Enthusiastical Delusions & extravagant Superstitious Fancys, that have made Such Distraction in the Universe, tyrannizing over & enslaving the Free Minds of Intelligent Beings[.][5]

At the time natural religion was one of the most popular ideas of the Enlightenment and it is not surprising to see it feature so prominently in Fergusson's diary. Many of his leading European contemporaries concerned themselves with the concept of natural

---

[1] Italics in original. Du Halde, *The General History of China*, III, pp. 55–6.

[2] Du Halde uses an archaic version of the older European spelling Chuang Tzu, calling him and his work 'Tching tse', ibid., pp. 54, 56.

[3] Yu-Lan, *The Spirit of Chinese Philosophy*, pp. 185–6; Cheng, *New Dimensions*, pp. 15–16.

[4] Du Halde, *The General History of China*, III, p. 53.

[5] See, p. 165.

religion and wrote extensively on the subject. As Fergusson suggested in his impassioned version above, natural religion proffered that mankind could use the natural faculties of reason, rational deduction, and observation to investigate religious matters, and even confirm the existence of God. Fergusson believed that there was universal moral principle that had been corrupted by earthly desires resulting in this spiritual essence being hidden beneath the profane institutions and practices of the religions humanity established. Furthermore, he thought that a rational approach to God's original moral precepts and their application in society and governance could lead humanity toward the happiness and wealth he saw in China. Natural religion developed out of the era's universalist assumptions that held that there was a natural condition of humankind, most famously articulated by John Locke as the state of nature. As he explained:

> The state of nature has a law of nature to govern it, which obliges every one: and reason, which is that law, teaches all mankind, who will but consult it, that being all equal and independent, no one ought to harm another in his life, health, liberty, or possessions[.][1]

The problem was that the earthly temptations of power, wealth, and greed meant that people did harm one another. It is obvious that reason and rationality had not kept oppression at bay, in fact quite the opposite. For Fergusson it was clear that the 'Base Impostures & Cunning Machinations of a few [...] propagated from Sordid Selfish views' kept the majority of people ignorant and subservient.[2] In *The Reasonableness of Christianity*, Locke argued that this was because the human-made laws that governed societies were:

> made by such, who had no other aims but their own power, reached no farther than those things that would serve to tie men together in subjection; or at most were directly to conduce to the prosperity and temporal happiness of any people. But natural religion, in its full extent, was no-where, that I know, taken care of, by the force of natural reason.[3]

Natural religion was therefore presented as an ideal of living according to the fundamental truths and laws established by God in the universe. This rational approach to religion was seen as a way to return to the natural moral order that governed all of humankind. Samuel Clarke was the Enlightenment's leading thinker on natural religion and was highly influential in his day. He built upon the positions put forward by Locke, asserting that the state of nature:

> is nothing else but the will of God producing certain effects in a continued, regular, constant and uniform manner which [...] being in every moment perfectly arbitrary, is as easy to be altered at any time, as to be preserved.[4]

It was the free-will and actions of humans which altered God's 'perfectly arbitrary' natural plan. However, as Clarke reminded his readers, it was also the free-will and actions of men that could 'preserve or continue it'.[5] For both Locke and Clarke it was this

---

[1] Locke, *Two Treatises of Government*, p. 197.

[2] See, p. 165.

[3] Locke, *The Works of John Locke*, VI, p. 139.

[4] Clarke, *A Discourse Concerning the Being and Attributes of God*, p. 341 (mis-numbered as 143 in volume).

[5] Ibid., p. 342.

freedom of choice that demonstrated the rational existence of God. A divine arbitrator was necessary to weigh the moral decisions of humanity in the afterlife by rewarding virtue and punishing vice.[1] If Fergusson had not read either Locke or Clarke, he was certainly aware of their ideas, and he saw their understanding of the law of nature reflected in Du Halde's description of *taiji*. 'This is no other than the Religion of Nature', Fergusson wrote, 'first illustrated & taught in the greatest perfection by their most celebrated antient Philosopher [...] Confucius'.[2] Fergusson viewed the universalist moral ethos of Chinese *taiji* and European natural religion as one and the same, and he credited China's most famous philosopher with first articulating the concept. For Fergusson, the prosperity he saw in China that so impressed him was the result of the social contract upheld by a rational government following the moral precepts of a natural religion.

Even though the Jesuit Du Halde offered a parallel between the Christian concepts of God, heaven, and the universe, with the Chinese *taiji* and *li*, he still considered religious beliefs in China a 'monstrous heap of Superstitions, Magick, Idolatry and Atheism'.[3] Fergusson too had little time for what he considered the 'enthusiasms' of idolatrous belief systems. However, unlike Du Halde, he also considered Catholicism as firmly within this category. Like his contemporary Voltaire, Fergusson was an intense critic of the Church. He blamed Catholicism for keeping its adherents bound in a position of 'Slavery in which Poverty & want, are but the least of its evils; where the Free minds of men are bound fast in the inextricable Fetters of absurdities & Ignorance'.[4] Fergusson certainly adhered to a Christian system of belief.[5] Like many others in his day he thought that a rational approach to the Bible had allowed for an accurate dating of Genesis, which meant he 'therefore deem'd impossible' the Chinese historical accounts that pre-dated Creation.[6] His frequent laments to a Supreme Being and his belief in the Bible as an accurate historical record, are evidence of his Christian faith. Throughout his travels he was fascinated by the diverse forms of religious expression he witnessed, even though he considered most of them to be corrupted practices contrary to the spirit of natural religion, none more so than the Catholic rituals he saw in Ireland. While the *Adventure* was lading at Portaferry, Fergusson took a ferry and walked to Struell Wells, an ancient pilgrimage site outside Downpatrick, famed for the miraculous waters of its healing springs. There he witnessed devoted pilgrims crawling and prostrating themselves up a rocky hill as penance, bloodying themselves in the process, all while a priest whipped them into a devoted frenzy. He was appalled at how 'Superstition & false Religion forces Men to committ Actions full of Cruelty & Inhumanity, thinking it is their Duty So to do'.[7] On his last stop at the Cape of Good Hope Fergusson offered his most scathing attack on what he called, 'that hellish Religion'.[8] There he found a Catholic missionary

---

[1] Bristow, 'Enlightenment', *SEP*, sect. 2.3.

[2] See, p. 161.

[3] Du Halde, *The General History of China*, III, p. 52.

[4] See, p. 158.

[5] Nothing in the historical record has yet confirmed Fergusson's membership of a church or denomination, however, he was probably Protestant.

[6] See, p. 154. For an excellent discussion of how Chinese historiography challenged early modern European universal histories, see Van Kley, 'Europe's "Discovery" of China', pp. 358–85.

[7] See, p. 39.

[8] See, p. 123.

proselytizing amongst the indigenous Khoikhoi populations. Fergusson hoped that his efforts would be 'fruitless' and doubted whether the Khoikhoi had anything to gain from hearing the 'Absurd jargon of the Romish Religion'.[1] Though the Khoikhoi existed in an innocent state of nature absent of 'arts or learning', according to Fergusson, they certainly had enough,

> knowledge [...] and Religion Sufficient to dispose them to the practise of [...] Virtues towards all Mankind; but not enough, it seems, to teach them to be treacherous, Cruel and inhuman to those of a different profession from themselves. Happy Ignorance! when Such are its amiable effects.[2]

The Khoikhoi genuinely interested Fergusson and he spent much time describing them in his diaries. They invoked for him perhaps Rousseau's notion of 'native man' who lived in a primitive state of compassion within the laws of nature.[3] He certainly saw in them a 'Native humanity & innocence', who lived 'far Superior to Most in Native fidelity and Integrity of Life'.[4] For Fergusson, Catholicism would only serve to disrupt the natural state of the Khoikhoi who led a far purer existence closer to the teachings of a universal God rather than the dictates of a religion he saw as corrupted.

While Fergusson reserved particular vitriol for Catholicism, he disliked organized religion of any faith, viewing them all as adulterations of natural religion. He is less disparaging towards Islam, though he still considered it as responsible in Arabia for corrupting,

> the Minds of Men in Many Cases, by banishing from them the Most Sociable and amiable Virtues of Humanity & Hospitality, and filling them with Enmity and Cruel Hatred against all those Who happen to be of a Different persuasion from theirs![5]

In this passage we also have another instance of Fergusson's dislike of any form of bigotry and prejudice. Considering his sentiments towards universalist natural religion, he likely believed that humanity should not be divided by human-made religious institutions, unlike some of the Muslims he met in Yemen. Nonetheless, he is quite disparaging of Hinduism, or what he called the 'Gentou' religion, considering it as another of the 'ridiculous Systems that are profess'd in many parts of India'.[6] Fergusson witnessed many Hindu ceremonies across South Asia. He saw a child-wedding in Madras and was particularly amazed with body-modifying ascetics and the hook-swingers who pierced the flesh of their backs with iron hooks and were then hoisted up into the air to swing around suspended from a pole. He also described *sati*s, or widow-immolations, but confessed that he had never seen one as the authorities in Madras did not allow them within their jurisdiction.[7] While impressed with the wedding, he considered all these other rituals as nothing more than the 'Stupendous Instances of the force of Enthusiasm

---

[1] See, p. 123.
[2] See, p. 75.
[3] Rousseau, *A Discourse Upon the Origin*, pp. 76–7.
[4] See, pp. 123, 75.
[5] See, p. 87.
[6] See, p. 166.
[7] See, p. 51.

in many of this Religion'.[1] European travellers to India were often both horrified and fascinated by the violent rituals of hook-swinging and *sati*. Both became key issues in legal debates over 'native' customary practices under the Company-Raj government and stood as examples of Indian barbarity, which were used to justify the British presence in India and evangelical missionary activity.[2]

It would be amiss not to comment on how Fergusson concluded his journals. In a *nota bene* he said that Cicero 'takes notice of the custom of Wives burning themselves with their deceas'd Husbands in the following beautifull passage', and then includes a selection from the *Tusculan Disputations*.[3] In the passage, Cicero begins with the statement, 'pain seems to be the sharpest adversary of virtue [...] which threatens to crush our fortitude, and greatness of mind and patience'. Pain therefore has the power to obstruct rational thought and reason, obstructing 'the happy life of a wise and consistent man'. Cicero then asks the question: 'Is any country of barbarians more uncivilized or desolate than India?', and then goes on to discuss *sati*.[4] Fergusson seemed to be offering evidence from European antiquity to further buttress his own views on natural religion and the folly of religious enthusiasm. It also served to confirm the objective of Fergusson's manifesto. As we have seen, Fergusson used the language of the Enlightenment throughout his manuscript. However, the unifying thread of his polemics is the issue of rational approach to belief in God absent of the devotional practices that keep one bound within false truth, contrary to the universal morality that is the natural condition, and therefore religion, of humankind. His manifesto of the Enlightenment is really a treatise against what he called, the 'fantastical things, [which are] the effects of Ignorance and Imposture'.[5] Into this we can again read the ideas of Locke and Clarke, who both argued that the power of organized religious institutions, especially the Catholic Church, had corrupted the true teachings of God, resulting in horrific practices that ran counter to the original moral principles of the faith revealed for all humanity at the moment of Creation. Clarke warned against those 'pretending to be a prophet' who performed miracles 'in order to draw men from the worship of the true God, and tempt them to idolatry, and to the practice of such vices as in all heathen nations'.[6] For Fergusson, the rites and rituals he saw across India, the attitudes of Muslims in Arabia, and the Catholic pilgrims seeking miracles at Struell Wells, were all examples of false religion that kept humanity living in darkness, away from the morality prescribed by God's original law. Locke offers the following example of how this affected Christians in Europe:

> Though, at the same time, whilst he is exercising the utmost barbarities against others, to prove himself a true christian, he professes himself so ignorant, that he cannot tell, or so uncharitable, that he will not tell, what articles are absolutely necessary and sufficient to make a man a christian.[7]

---

[1] See, p. 98.

[2] Mani, *Contentious Traditions*, p. 178; Oddie, *Popular Religion, Elites and Reform*, p. 109.

[3] See, p. 172.

[4] See, p. 172, n. 3. For the original in translation, see section XXVII of Book 5 in Cicero, *The Tusculan Disputations*, trans. Yonge.

[5] See, p. 53.

[6] Clarke, *A Discourse Concerning the Being and Attributes of God*, p. 345.

[7] Christian is uncapitalized in the original. Locke, *The Works of John Locke*, VI, p. 231.

Our surgeon agreed, writing, 'Christians, tho' pretending to a More rational Religion than these blind Pagans, have I'm afraid, been as much Subject to this Irrational Passion'.[1] It is clear in the manuscript that Fergusson thought Islam, Hinduism, and Christianity had all suffered from this problem of conflating devotional frenzy with truth, keeping their adherents from experiencing true happiness and prosperity. '[T]here is No Country in the world where Religion has done So litle harm', Fergusson wrote of China. For him, the country's bounty was a direct result of the priests having 'no power or authority', which allowed the principles of natural religion to guide governance and society.[2] He extolled the virtues of their 'Moral Philosophy':

> As an effectual Demonstration of the esteem that the Chinese have allwise had for Arts & Sciences, we Need only consider what has been taken notice of before, Viz. That the only means of advancement to Dignity or Power, were Knowledge in these Particulars, which is the Source of all Nobleness, Grandeur & Preferments.[3]

In ending his discussion of China, Fergusson hailed the example that the country offered to the rest of the world in following the precepts of God's universal morality:

> Whereas it must afford uncommon Satisfaction to all those who have learn'd to think & judge for themselves, to observe that amicable System of Natural Religion embrac'd by the few & wise of all nations however Distant, and differing in other things, Yet in this uniformly agreeing in all its Essential Precepts. A Sure demonstration of its fix'd invariable nature and of its Intrinsick Excellence![4]

It is clear religion was at the forefront of Fergusson's mind when composing his narrative. His descriptions of the places he visits and cultures he interacts with all conform to the standard practices of the contemporary travelogue. However, Fergusson's manuscript differs in its continual return to the issues of natural religion and moral philosophy. Because Fergusson recorded his memories in 1767, there is no way to know with any certainty when he came into contact with the ideas of thinkers like Clarke, Locke, Rousseau, and others. It is impossible to know whether he already had their ideas in mind when he sailed the world, or whether he reframed what he saw according to notions he learned about only later in life, as this is the only piece of Fergusson's writing known to survive. However, it is clear that the spectacles and ceremonies he witnessed in the diverse places he travelled, all informed how he viewed the world, and confirmed for him many of the Enlightenment's leading ideas concerning faith and reason.

Just because Fergusson did not agree with the belief systems and practices of the people he met does not mean he did not strive to understand their ways. Indeed, Fergusson comes across as an empathetic observer who makes an effort to try to better know the world around him. He converses with people on matters of faith and records their answers on how they understand their own religion, or indeed, how they understand his, such as how Muslims in Mocha viewed certain Christian tenets. Despite what else he may have written about Hinduism he did admire some of its attributes. He believed that it taught 'its Followers Charity of a More Extensive and disinterested kind,

---

[1] See, p. 100.
[2] See, p. 158.
[3] See, p. 167.
[4] See, p. 166.

than is commonly observ'd by the greatest part of Mankind of a Different Religion'.[1]
He also admired the vegetarianism practised by many Hindus, admitting that he can
offer no good reason 'for butchering So many of our fellow Creatures', when so much
sustenance may be had from other sources.[2] Fergusson may never have given up eating
meat but we do know that when confronted with foreign cultural practices he was
willing to be open to different ways of living. He is frustrated when his own ignorance
keeps him from fully understanding what he witnesses. In China he offers a mild
lamentation:

> The not knowing the Language [...] is a great obstruction to one's being able to form just
> notions [...] from their own observations; for altho' one has the opportunity of Seeing many
> of their Religious Ceremonys, the not understanding what they Say keeps one a Stranger, to
> their Nature & Intent.[3]

Throughout his travels Fergusson is honest about what he understands and from where
he received his information, making him a fairly reliable narrator. Of course, this does
not always mean he is accurate. In describing Hindu belief systems he asserts: 'Some I'm
told worship the Cow, Some other animals, Some a particular kind of Nutt some a kind
of Image of a peculiar frame, and other fantastical things'.[4] Fergusson claims they did so
out of 'the effects of Ignorance and Imposture', however, clearly the ignorance is his. Most
of the time he admits when he does not know something or if he got his information
from someone else. Several of the anecdotes and stories Fergusson tells have been verified
in the historical record, others remain instances of local lore that did not make it into
the archives, and therefore, true or not, may only be recorded within the pages here.

Fergusson was also a curious interlocuter who seemed to use any opportunity he could
to get off the ships and explore or interact with the local people. One such chance took
place while anchoring in the Hooghly River when he joined a provisioning party 'on
purpose to divert myself and See the Country'.[5] From that small adventure Fergusson
witnessed a local Hindu ceremony, complete with dancers and musicians. He certainly
enjoyed travelling and the diverse situations it brought him into contact with. On an
earlier visit to Madras, Fergusson wrote that in the evenings he went 'walking out into
the fields' just to explore and report on whatever he observes. Even in the British Isles he
finds opportunities for diversion and is able to see customs he finds strange. During his
first voyage Fergusson joins the shipmaster and some crew of the *Adventure* to enjoy a
bird-hunting and egg-collecting expedition in Luce Bay. A few days later, as we saw above,
he makes his way to Struell Wells just in time for an annual religious gathering. Fergusson
found enjoyment in meeting and observing local people and their customs, even if he did
not always agree with their practices.

Fergusson also enjoyed observing many other things, including women's bodies. In
the pages of his diaries he reveals himself to be quite a man of desire. He comments
frequently on particular female physical attributes and is sometimes concerned with their
sexual practices and reputations. Within the first few pages of his manuscript, Fergusson

[1] See, p. 101.
[2] See, p. 100.
[3] See, p. 157.
[4] See, p. 53.
[5] See, p. 59.

recalls how the position of pilgrims crawling up a hillside in Ireland offered him the 'favourable Situation' of almost seeing up the women's skirts.[1] In southern Malabar, where until the mid-nineteenth century low-caste women were not allowed to cover their upper bodies, Fergusson comments on how with 'girls or Young Women' this was 'not So disagreable' a view, while older women offered him 'No pleasant Sight'.[2] These serve as early modern examples of what is now referred to as the 'male gaze', which are passive representations of women wherein they are 'displayed as sexual object[s]' of male desire.[3] In a final example while in China, Fergusson regrets that the clothes women wear hide the shape of their waist and breasts so as 'to Spoil in a great measure that agreable prominency of the chest, which we in Europe Consider as a very essential part of the Beauty of the fair Sex'.[4] Throughout his diaries, Fergusson regularly presents women as objects of his own desire and visual pleasure. Despite how these observations come across today, it is unfair to judge Fergusson outside the context of his times. After all, Enlightenment thought, for all its claims to universal rights, gave little consideration to the role of women and people of colour in European society. We saw above that Fergusson held both progressive and racialized attitudes towards non-European peoples. His attitudes towards women of the societies he encounters is also mixed. To his credit, he blames the 'Jealousy of the men' for the painful patriarchal practice of binding the feet of upper-class Chinese women.[5] This left these women unable to walk unhindered and therefore bound them to their homes. Whatever his critique of certain patriarchal traditions, Fergusson was very much a man of his times who approached the world through the prevailing ideas and opinions of the Enlightenment.

The world that Fergusson recorded on his voyages in the 1730s was one in transition. Europe was not yet the leading global power, though it soon would be. Fergusson's diaries provide unique insights into this period of global reconfiguration. Crucially, they show that, while Europe was beginning to jump ahead in medicine, science, political philosophy, and other areas, Europeans continued to draw inspiration from other parts of the world. The effects of people like Fergusson on the intellectual development of Europe during the Enlightenment is not yet understood. Once thought of as a phenomenon with uniquely European origins, scholars are beginning to understand it as the result of European engagement with the wider world. In a recent joint paper, a group of leading historians, asserted: 'The Enlightenment of the eighteenth century, we increasingly acknowledge, borrowed aesthetic and political models from China, India, Japan and relied on contacts with remoter cultures.'[6]

Fergusson's journals and manifesto are one piece of evidence in this emerging re-evaluation of global intellectual history. In the pages here presented, one can see how the popular ideas of the Enlightenment held by Fergusson, were challenged, reconfigured, and confirmed by his interactions with foreign cultures. Readers will surely discover many other insights within the pages of this volume than those mentioned here. This journal is Fergusson's unintentional legacy to the world. In the absence of any of his other

[1] See, p. 39.
[2] See, p. 104.
[3] Mulvey, 'Visual Pleasure and Narrative Cinema', p. 62.
[4] See, pp. 149–50.
[5] See, p. 150.
[6] Burke, Classy, and Fernández-Armesto, 'The Global Renaissance', p. 11.

writings or information about his life, it stands as the only representation of the person who was William Fergusson. Since this is the only piece of his thoughts known to have survived, the narrative has thus become the subject. It is my sincere hope that the individual revealed through the pages of this volume is an accurate representation of his life and character. I hope too that William Fergusson would be pleased that over two hundred years later, his words would appear in print and he and his ideas would be brought to a wider audience.

5. The Text

The text presented here is as near to Fergusson's original manuscript as possible. It preserves any eighteenth-century conventions in language, inconsistencies in spelling, and mistakes made by its author. Crossed-out words are kept in place in an effort to shed any additional possible light on Fergusson's thought process while he wrote. To aid the reader, the archaic letters long s and thorn have been replaced by their modern equivalents. Also, any abbreviated words have been expanded or completed with letters in italics, such as with Fergusson's title 'Journals of my Voy*ages* & Manifesto', except for commonly used abbreviations such as 'St' for 'Saint'. Only when absolutely necessary to provide clarity to the narration has punctuation been added. In a couple of instances in the second voyage, Fergusson uses a floating letter 'e' in what likely is contemporary shorthand for 'is', 'es', 'ys' to denote, or in these cases to emphasize, the plural form of the preceding word. Like many of his contemporaries, Fergusson was inconsistent in his capitalization and he frequently writes the letters C, K, M, N, S, and V as capitals when at the start of a word. He also uses a double dash (=) as a hyphen, including one both on the page where the word was broken, and on the page where it continued. These and other stylistic choices made by Fergusson, such as his use of ampersands, and his contemporary shorthand for *et cetera*, (&.C.) and *videlicet* (namely) (Viz, with or without a full stop), have also been maintained. In all cases ships' names have been italicized for clarity.

When referring to locations in their historical context the contemporary place name is used (e.g. Madras). In all other cases places are referred to by their current toponyms (e.g. Chennai). Annotations accompany the first instance of any place name, offering both their various historical and current variations. Fergusson's name was spelled inconsistently in the various records where it appears, either with one or two s's. As seen in this volume's frontispiece, Fergusson himself signed his name with two, and this is the spelling adopted here.

The division of the narratives comprising Fergusson's voyages is somewhat erratic. His paragraphs sometimes begin and end abruptly. He usually separates his sections with a header giving the day, month, and year followed by the announcement of arriving or weighing anchor at a port. These begin in a new paragraph break and are presented in boldface, along with any missing information in square brackets for consistency. As with all other Hakluyt Society volumes, annotations guide the reader through the text to explain contemporary nomenclatures and contextualize the narrative. Where necessary, clarifications in square brackets have also been embedded within the manuscript to facilitate understanding and not interrupt the reading process. Fergusson also experimented with different formatting as the narrative progressed. He sometimes drew a line across the page to denote a new section, and these too have been reproduced in the present volume.

Readers will surely find Fergusson's narration entertaining and insightful. His deviations from the standard travelogue format by launching into impassioned polemics offer interesting diversions into the mind of a man representing the attitudes and ideas of his era.

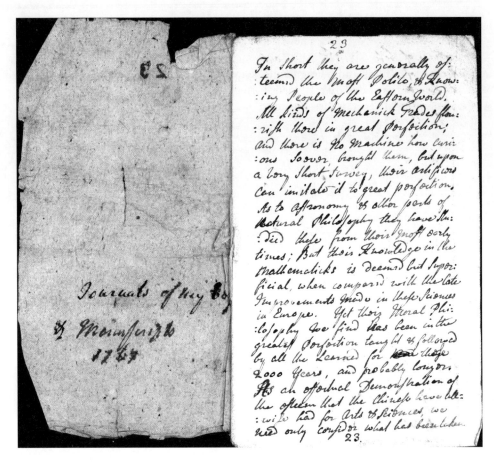

Figure 3.   Sample page of the manuscript showing Fergusson's intended title 'Journals of my Voy*ages* & Manifesto 1767', written on the inside cover (fasc. 23, f. 1r). The page shown here is transcribed at pp. 166–7. Reproduced with kind permission from Andrew Gladstone and The Centre of South Asian Studies, University of Cambridge.

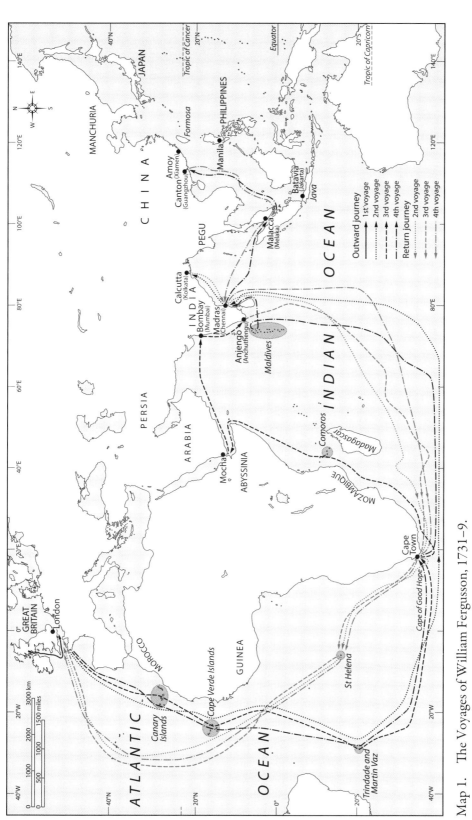

Map 1.   The Voyages of William Fergusson, 1731–9.

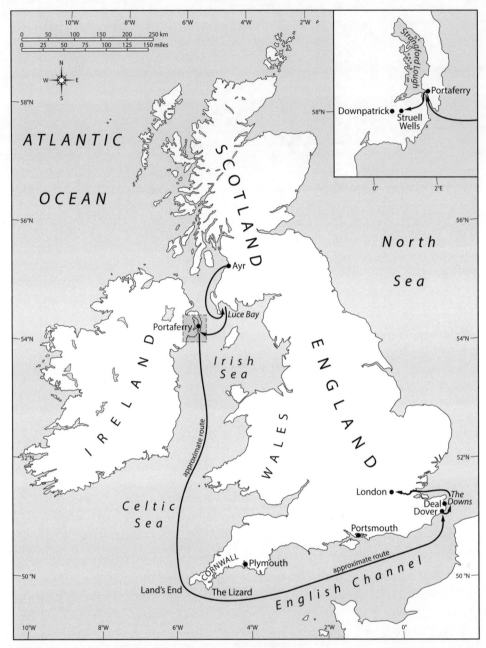

Map 2. Voyage 1: Passage from Ayr to London, 7 June–16 July 1731 (approximate route shown).

VOYAGE 1: PASSAGE FROM AYR TO LONDON VIA IRELAND 7 JUNE–JULY 1731[1]

[fasc. 1, f. 1r][2] **Monday, June 7th 1731.** in the afternoon, I Sailed[3] from Ayr on board the *Adventure*, and next Day in the afternoon came to anchor in the Bay of Glenluce in Galloway, where we continu'd till the 22d.[4]

Having little to do, the Master and I with Some of the men Sail'd in the Longboat to a Large Rock of about a Mile in Circumference, which stands in the Mouth of the Bay.[5] Our Design was (knowing it a proper time of the Year) to divert ourselves by catching of young fowls, and getting of Eggs, with which we were inform'd that place was well Stor'd. Nor were we frustrated in our Design, for approaching the Rock, we beheld the Top of it Covered with an incredible multitude of Fowle, besides Vast [fasc. 1, f. 1v] Numbers Sweeming[6] on the Water all around it, most of which were what our people Call'd Ilsa-Cocks,[7] with some few call'd Scarts.[8] The most of them seem'd not to be much afraid of us, untill we had frighted them by firing among them. When I came to the Top of the Rock, I was still more surpris'd to see it overspread with an infinite Number of Eggs, so that we could scarcely putt down our foot without Crushing some of them. They lay in Such multitudes, and seemingly in such disorder, that it made me believe the Dames could not possibly know their proper Eggs, so as they might nourish them by incubation 'till the young was ripe for coming out. And indeed it is not unlikely that Many of them never do come to Maturity, for want of a Due incubation, through the inevitable Mistake, and Neglect [fasc. 1, f. 2r] of some of the Dames. And of those that do, it is More than probable, that many of them are brought forth by those that are not their own Dames. Besides I believe the Heat of the Sun which is much encreas'd by the reflexion from the Hard rugged Rocks, does not alitle contribute to the bringing of the Chick to Maturity.

---

[1] Chapters and their headings have been organized and chosen by the editor and correspond to the four voyages Fergusson made between 1731 and 1739.

[2] Fergusson's notes were written in a series of booklets, or fascicles, of varying numbers of folios. Pagination throughout this volume thus accounts for both fascicle and folio in square brackets. Thus fascicle 1, front face of folio 1 becomes [fasc. 1, f. 1r], followed by [fasc. 1, f. 1v] and so on through to fascicle 23.

[3] Fergusson is rather inconsistent in his spelling, particularly concerning words ending in -ed. He frequently contracts such words replacing the 'e' with an apostrophe. Thus 'sailed' often becomes 'sail'd'. This text replicates Fergusson's usage as it appears in the manuscript.

[4] Now Luce Bay. Fergusson was only a passenger on this voyage.

[5] This is Big Scare, the largest islet of The Scares, a cluster of rock outcroppings at the mouth of Luce Bay, though it is much smaller than Fergusson describes.

[6] Meaning swimming.

[7] More commonly Ailsa cock or Ailsa parrot, a Scottish name for the puffin named after Ailsa Craig, a well-known breeding ground for the birds in the Firth of Clyde.

[8] Archaic common Scottish name for the cormorant.

For I observ'd that the Eggs were all deposited either on the Top of the Rock, or on that Side that fac'd the sun at Noon.

After having sufficiently amus'd ourselves, and gott plenty of fowls and Eggs, in the Evening we Sail'd back to the Ship which lay about 15 Miles from that Rock, which by the Inhabitants of the Neighbouring parts is call'd BrigScars.[1]

Tuesday June 22d. We sail'd from that Bay, and next Day in the Evening we arriv'd at [fasc. 1, f. 2v] Portéferré[2] in Ireland. This is a Small Town in the North part of Ireland, which lies at the Side of a Sinus or Neck of the Sea, which at its parting from the Sea is Very Narrow, but turns wider and wider as it advances into the Land, into which it reaches in 10 or 12 Miles.[3] The Current at the Entry is Very quick, occasioned by the Narrowness thereof.

The Morning after we arriv'd, other two Passengers and I cross'd over the Water,[4] and in order to divert ourselves and See the Country, went towards Dun Patrick,[5] which is a pretty large and well built Town, about Six Miles from Portéferré. About a Mile from Dun Patrick, there is a large well or rather several fountains of Water, famous in that Country for curing many Diseases.[6] At this place the Roman Catholicks from the Country all around had mett together (it [fasc. 1, f. 3r] seems according to custom, it being St Johns Day the 24th of June) in order to perform their Devotion and Ceremonies according to Custom on that Day.

The Congregation Consisted of Several Thousands, all in the open field hearing Sermon which was delivered by a Priest in his Papistical habit. It being in Irish I did not understand it, but could discern by his manner of delivery, which was with a loud Voice, & a Violently Pathotick[7] gesture, that it was on Some extraordinary Subject, and with a Design, Very much to affect his hearers, as indeed appeared by the Effect: for after almost every Sentence express'd in that Elevated Tone, & Pathotick Gesture, the Multitude sent forth Dolefull Groans, muttering some Words, and sometimes beating their breasts with Violence. [fasc. 1, f. 3v] In short he seem'd to be entirely Master of their Passions, and to be able to persuade the Whole Ignorant Crowd to any thing he enclin'd. But what of all appear'd to me most remarkable, was to behold a great Number of People with their heads and Legs uncovered, creeping up and Down some high Steep and rugged Rocks[8]

---

[1] Fergusson runs these words together with capital letters. Now the island is known as Big Scare.

[2] Portaferry on the Ards peninsula in North Ireland.

[3] This is Strangford Lough, the largest inlet in the British Isles, covering some 58 square miles.

[4] The channel leading into Strangford Lough.

[5] Downpatrick.

[6] Struell Wells is a site consisting of four holy springs associated with St Patrick, which were an important site of pilgrimage from the medieval era to the end of the 19th century. As Fergusson notes, the waters were held to have curative properties, and the most popular time to visit Struell was Midsummer's Eve, which happened to coincide with his visit. Philip Dixon's mid-19th-century book on Ireland's holy wells had this to say about Struell: 'One of the wells is appropriated to the curing of the blind, one to select company, one to general and promiscuous use, and one, we believe, reserved for drinking [...] Wonderful are the cures which are performed, it is said, at these wells – the blind are enabled to see, and the lame to dance. Those who are not cured, eagerly inquire "who has got the blessing?"' Quoted in Hardy, *The Holy Wells of Ireland*, pp. 67–8.

[7] An archaic adjective derived from pathos, meaning to elicit sympathy or stir emotion.

[8] This natural rock formation is known as St Patrick's Chair, and formed an important part of the ritual associated with the visit to Struell Wells. Pilgrims would climb onto the 'chair' and be turned three times by an attendant. See Hardy, *The Holy Wells of Ireland*, pp. 67–8.

that were near the place, upon their bare knees and hands, which could not but be Very painfull to them; Besides some Danger I thought they underwent in coming down those high precipices with their head and hands foremost. This piece of Pennance was undergone by great Numbers of both Sexes and all ages, except Children. The Women I mostly pitied, they being Naturally less able to endure hardships of this kind, especially those of the Younger Sort. Some of which (I suppose out of a great deal [fasc. 1, f. 4r] of Devotion) had their Legs very far uncovered, and being in a high and favourable Situation, might have afforded a View farther than could consist with the Modesty of their Sex. They had Certain formalities with regard to the Manner they began and Carried on their Pennance, & as to the Number of times &.C. they Were to go up and down Such a place, in all which, I observed, they were much influenc'd by this Priest, who during the Sermon frequently turn'd his Eyes and hands toward the Sufferers, using Some Moving Expressions, at which great Numbers of the Hearers, remov'd from the Crowd and underwent that unreasonable Torment.

I was much affected to See a Number of reasonable Creatures doing Such Violence to their own bodies, from a false persuasion, that they would thereby recom= [fasc. 1, f. 4v] =mend[1] theirselves to the Deity, as if their Pain and torment could be well pleasing to him, who is good & Mercifull in the most perfect Manner. – How much better is it to have no Notions of God at all than Such as are unworthy of him! Pure & untainted Nature would teach us to be Carefull of ourselves & compassionate to our Fellow=Creatures; And a Suitable persuasion of the Existence and Nature of the Supreme Being, would confirm and encrease these good Inclinations. But Superstition & false Religion forces Men to committ Actions full of Cruelty & Inhumanity, thinking it is their Duty So to do.

These were the Reflections that occurr'd after seeing that Melancholy Cruel Scene.

Monday July 5th. We Sail'd from Portéferré for London. The Night after we had made the [fasc. 1, f. 5r] Lands-End of England, as we were becalm'd off Plymouth, we were boarded by A Longboat belonging to one of the Kings Ships, who press'd from us all our hands, and among the rest two other passengers with me. But after we came aboard of the Ship, the Captain finding us not Sailors, after chiding the Pressmaster for disturbing us, it being Midnight, he ordered us to be presently putt aboard of our own Ship.[2] On the 13th we came to the Bay of Dover, where the Pilot boat coming aboard of Us, I went ashore to see the Town, which is a fine Large Place Standing closs[3] by the Sea Shore. It has a Large Harbour which is Curiously built, running up into the Middle of the Town, so as it is divided into several Basons or Partitions Capable of Containing a [fasc. 1, f. 5v] great Many Ships. This Harbour in Short Seems to be entirely the effect of Art, their being no River that assists in the formation thereof. Only a Very Small Rivulett or two that empties themselves into it. And it must have cost a great Deal of Labour and Expence

---

[1] Normally, Fergusson uses a double hyphen when splitting words. I have retained his usage throughout when a word is split between pages.

[2] From the mid-17th century into the early 19th, impressment was used by the British government to counter the perennial shortfall in manning the ships of the Royal Navy, particularly during wartime. Press gangs would roam streets and commonly embarked inward-bound merchant ships, as Fergusson experienced, looking to forcibly recruit able-bodied seamen to serve in the navy for periods up to a year.

[3] Fergusson spells close as 'closs' throughout his text.

to have built it at first; besides I was told that it still required a good deal of Care and trouble to Support it and keep it Clear, which was a great Charge to the Inhabitants. Tho there are Several Curious Contrivances, which make the charge the Easier. Particularly I observed at the entry of their Basons (So I call the Different appartments of the Harbour) there were Large Wooden Sluices, which by Shutting upon occasion, confin'd the Water till being full, they then give it a Large passage, so that by bursting out [fasc. 1, f. 6r] with Violence it carries all the loose rubbish that lies in the Passage, before it into the Sea, and So makes Clear the Entry into the Harbour.[1] Hard by Dover upon the Side of a Steep Hill by the Sea Shore, there is an old fortification with a Castle which however Seems to be much in a Ruinous Condition.[2]

The Same Day being provided with a Pilot, we Sailed from Dover, and that afternoon we Sailed through the Downs[3] where there lay at anchor Several Ships of War with a great many Merchant Ships, that being the usual Road for Ships, who wait for a Wind either to or from London. There close to the Sea Shore we saw the Town of Dale,[4] which did not look by Much So Large as Dover, neither has it any harbour. Nigh by it is a Small Castle [fasc. 1, f. 6v] with a garrison in it.[5] Our Pilot Carried us safe up the River,[6] and the 16th of July 1731 we arriv'd nigh London Bridge, late at Night, And I with the Merchantt Mr. Ross went and lay ashore. In my passage up the River, I had some Very agreeable Prospects of fine fruitfull plotts of ground. As We came Nigher London, I observed by the RiverSide Several Small Towns. Att some of which particulary Woolage, Blackhall, & Deptford, were Large Yards with Several Big Ships a building.[7] But the Most agreeable View of any was that of Greenwich hospital which Stands hard by the Waterside about four Miles from London bridge. It is the Largest the finest and most Beautiful Building I had ever seen, tho then it is yet far from being finished & compleat.[8]

---

[1] Dover's harbour entrance was subject to regular silting up due to its proximity to mineral deposits brought and left through a phenomenon known as the Eastern Drift. Plans were drawn up in 1689 to solve the issue by dividing the harbour with barriers, each with a sluice gate, into three separate pools, known as the Harbour, the Bason [sic], and the Pent. This plan was finally executed under the reign of Queen Anne (r. 1702–14), which explains why Fergusson is aware of the high costs to the townspeople as they were taxed a toll to pay for its construction and maintenance. Fergusson is correct that water was pooled in the Pent to release at low tide, but this was to attempt to wash away the silt at the mouth of the harbour, not simply to get rid of rubbish, though it was apparently more effective at the latter than the former.

[2] Dover Castle was established in the 12th century and commands a view over the English Channel. Extensive renovations and rebuilding began in the later 18th century, giving the fortification its current look. Fergusson would have seen the castle in one of its more decrepit states.

[3] The Downs was a major roadstead, or sheltered ship anchorage, off the coast from the town of Deal. It was used as a base for the Royal Navy patrolling the North Sea and was a popular staging area for merchant ships awaiting favourable conditions to take them into the Thames or the English Channel.

[4] Meaning the town of Deal, Kent.

[5] Deal Castle remains one of the finest examples of a Tudor coastal artillery fortress. It was built in 1539–40 by Henry VIII.

[6] Meaning the Thames.

[7] Woolwich, Blackwall, and Deptford were all major centres of shipbuilding for over three hundred years beginning in the 1500s. The EIC initially used Deptford but soon outgrew the facilities there and moved to Blackwall. Deptford and Woolwich were important dockyards for the Royal Navy from the 16th to 19th centuries.

[8] The Royal Hospital for Seamen at Greenwich was founded by Queen Mary II (r. 1689–94), who was inspired by seeing injured sailors returning from the Battle of La Hougue during the Nine Years' War in 1692. The principal buildings were completed 1705–42.

[fasc. 1, f. 7r] As We came within two or three Miles of London Bridge, I observed all along the River, crowded with the Most amazing Number of Ships I could have possibly conceived. It was a Sight to me Very astonishing, as not thinking ever to see Nigh Such a Number; Besides all the Vacant places of the River Seem'd to be covered with Small boats Lighters[1] and others; So that it made it a hard task for us to gett through clear of them.

A Day or two after I came to London I took a Private Room with one Mr. Wood on Litle Towr Hill,[2] Where I Liv'd till the 9th of August, When I went to Mr. Gilletts apothecary in Grosvenor Street,[3] with whom I liv'd till the 4th of January 1732,3,[4] when I remov'd to My old Quarters in order to prepare for My Voyage [fasc. 1, f. 7v] to the East Indies, whether [*sic*] to I was engag'd to go as Surgeons Mate on board the *Britannia* Caleb Grantham Commander.

---

[1] A type of flat-bottomed barge typically used to transport goods and people to and from moored vessels.

[2] An area directly to the north-east of the Tower of London, later occupied by the Royal Mint before they moved operations to Wales in 1967.

[3] There is a record of a William Gillet who rented house number 4 Grosvenor Street 1731–55. See Sheppard, ed., 'Appendix 1', pp. 172–95, and the introduction to this volume, pp. 6–8, 10.

[4] The British Isles adopted the Gregorian calendar in 1752, well after many continental European countries. Until then the legal new year in England was not 1 January but rather 25 March. To add to the complication, Scotland had adopted 1 January as the beginning of the new year in 1600, but otherwise kept the old calendar until 1752. To specify the actual year and avoid confusion, Fergusson followed the convention of the day by giving both years when the calendars overlapped.

Figure 4. 'An Outward bound East Indiaman Sailing from the Downs', print by Robert Dodd, 29 May 1788. Courtesy of NMM, Greenwich, London. No known images exist of any of the three vessels that Fergusson sailed in, however, the ships *Britannia* and *Godolphin* would have looked similar to the vessel shown here.

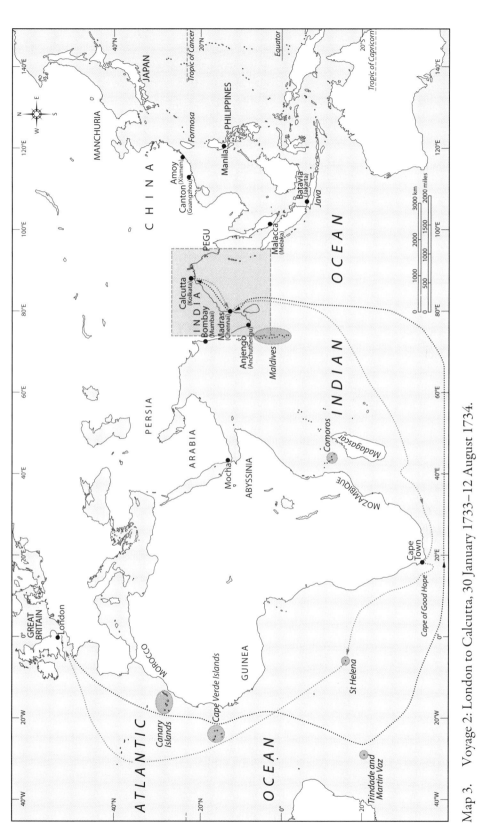

Map 3.   Voyage 2: London to Calcutta, 30 January 1733–12 August 1734.

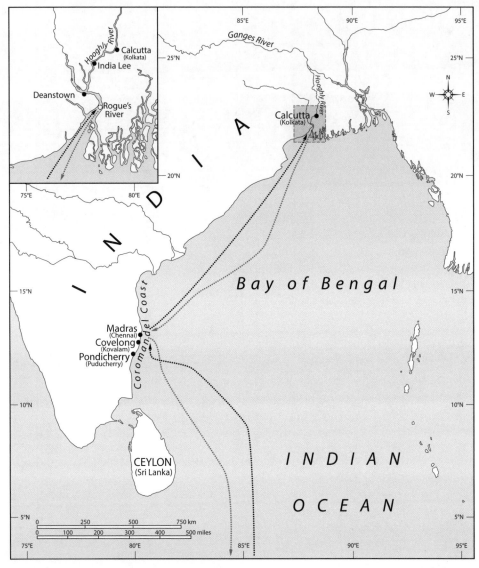

Map 4.   Voyage 2: Detail of the Bay of Bengal.

VOYAGE 2: FROM LONDON TO CALCUTTA
30 JANUARY 1733–12 AUGUST 1734

[fasc. 2, f. 1r] **January 30, 1732,3.** I Sett out from London in a Small Boat, and a few hours after gott on board of the ship[1] lying then at Gravesend.[2]

Thursday February 2. Our Captain having come on board the Night before,[3] this Day we Sailed from Gravesend, and having a favourable Gale we gott Safely out of the River; But on Saturday following going over the flatts, through the inadvertency or ignorance of our Pilote (who notwithstanding was reckoned one of the best) we were run aground upon one of the Banks, where the Ship beat for an hour or two, While every body on board were under no Small apprehensions, of the Ships losing her bottom; Our Captain having ordered a Gun to be fired and a Wiff[4] hung up as Signals of Distresse, but [fasc. 2, f. 1v] there being yet flowing Water, we gott happily off without any considerable damage, and on Monday following we came to an anchor in the Downs.

Wednesday: February 28. I was Seized with a Very acute fever, but happily recovered, after lying confin'd to my Bed about 18 or 20 Days.

Saturday: March 3. We Weighed anchor and Sett Sail from the Downs in company with the *Decker*, Captain Williamson our Commander.[5] Having fair Winds we came within Sight of the Cape De Verd Islands on the 22d of March.[6] The 26 of this Month we gott in about 7 Degrees: North Latitude, when it began to be calm & exceeding hott. And 3 or 4 Days afterwards betwixt the Latitude: 5 or 6 we had Very frequent thunder & lightning with Very heavy rains; These continued by intervals for about 8 or 10 Days till we had gott 2 or 3 Degrees: over the Line.[7]

---

[1] The *Britannia* was a 30-gun ship of 560 tons that made four East Indian voyages between 1733 and 1743.

[2] As surgeon's mate Fergusson was an inferior officer responsible for acting as a nurse, and preparing medical instruments and pharmaceutical applications used by the ship's surgeon. He earned £23 17s 10d for this voyage (BL: IOR L/MAR/B285A, *Britannia* Pay Book).

[3] Caleb Grantham (1691–1762) was born into a well-known maritime family in service with the Royal Navy and EIC and associated with the Corporation of Trinity House. This voyage was his third time commanding a ship to India (NMM: TRN/37, 'Grantham Family of West Thurrock, Essex', pp. 6–9).

[4] A 'wiff', or 'whiff', was a common makeshift distress signal of the age, usually consisting of a hoisted flag that was rolled or knotted.

[5] Captain Edward Williamson. The *Decker* was lost after running aground in the Hooghly River in India in September 1737.

[6] According to the ship's log, land was spotted at 10 in the morning and at noon the westernmost part of the island of 'Sol', meaning Sal, was identified. The following afternoon the island of 'Bonavista', properly Boa Vista, was sighted (BL: IOR L/MAR/B/285AA, entries for 22–23 March 1733).

[7] The equator.

April: 5[.] We pass'd the Line and the Same Night Los'd Sight of our Com*man*der, But discovered him again on Tuesday Morning.[1]

[fasc. 2, f. 2r] After we had gott 3 or 4 Degrees over the Line we gott in to the *South East* Trade, which is a constant wind which continued to blow from betwixt the South and the East, till we had gott into the Lat*itude* of 25 or 26 South, during which time we stood away much to Westward, in Expectation of the Westwardly Winds, which commonly blow fresh near the Cape;[2] As we approach'd the Cape we had Sometimes Very hard Gales of Winds with prodigious Large Seas.

On the 14th of May, We came in to soundings off the Cape in about 85 Fathom Water; After which we stood away almost Due East for above a forthnight[3] having favourable winds, this we Did while we had gott almost into the Merid*ian* of Ceylon, which is the first Land we propos'd to make upon the Coast of India. I should have observed that after we had gott Some Degrees over the Line, the Weather began [fasc. 2, f. 2v] every Day to be cooler. And about the Cape, it was Sensibly cold, much Such as it is in Britain in the Month of Oct*ober*.[4]

Our Sailing So far to the Eastward, was on purpose to have the *South East* Trade full ~~and Hot~~,[5] which Wind we mett with, almost in the same Lat*itude* that before 6° It kept us in, And continued untill we had gott within three or 4 Deg*rees* of the Line, which as we approach'd, the Coolness of the Weather gradually diminish'd, and after we had gott over the Line it turn'd extremely hott, the Sun being then on the N*orth* Tropick, being about the Middle of June.

Our Men hitherto had been pretty healthy, neither did I observe any particular or Violent disorders reigning amongst them; only as the Weather began to grow Warmer there were Several Complaints of Pains in the Head, Back, & Breast, attended with a Small Fever; which however by bleeding and Vomiting with a cool Regimen were Soon [fasc. 2, f. 3r] remov'd.[6] Likewise, we had Some troubled with Coughs, and in Particular, when the weather was now turn'd Very hott, there were two or three Boys affected with the most Violent Coughing I almost ever have known; the Coughing was almost incessant, attended with a Pain of the Head & Breast (but not very Violent), a Dyspnea,[7] and Feverishness, yet none of them were confin'd to their Beds. These Disorders after Sometime were remov'd by Phlebotomy repeated as the Fever and constitution requir'd, with the Use of a Pectoral Linctus and Apozeme.[8] And Now the Scorbutick habit

---

[1] 10 April 1733. The *Britannia* was able to join company with the *Decker* around noon the same day (BL: IOR L/MAR/B/285AA, entry for 10 April 1733).

[2] The Cape of Good Hope, see Plate 1.

[3] Fergusson probably means fortnight.

[4] The ship's journal records that they were 2 degrees east of the Cape of Good Hope (BL: IOR L/MAR/B/285AA, entry for 14 May 1733).

[5] This is crossed out in the original.

[6] Humoralist medical science of the time believed illness was due to imbalance in the body's four humours: black bile, yellow bile, blood, and phlegm, each of which corresponded to one of the elements. Thus, Fergusson believed that by draining a little of a patient's blood or inducing vomiting that balance, and thus health, would be restored. See above, pp. 3–4.

[7] Shortness of breath.

[8] Phlebotomy refers to the drawing of blood, in this case again to heal by restoring balance to the humours. A linctus is a syrup or sticky liquid of medications applied topically, in this case to the chest as indicated. An apozeme is a herbal extract prepared through boiling plant parts.

discover'd it Self in Severals of the Men, by hard Livid or Redish Swellings about the Joints especially the knees, and sometimes Livid Spots upon other Parts of the Body.[1] Those who were affected with those Swellings, I observ'd, allwise imputed it to Some Previous hurt or Bruise, which at first they took no notice of, [fasc. 2, f. 3v] which, whether it was really So, or affirm'd from Some other Motive, I cannot well determine. The Colour of the Skin all around those Livid Swellings, was of a Dusky yellow, which colour was likewise intermix'd with the Livid, so that the parts affected in some appear'd Speckled. We had no hopes of being able to cŭre[2] those patients, as long as we continu'd at Sea; For it being occasion'd by a Long Diet upon Sett Victuals, the only Cure could be expected was a Diet of Fresh Victuals with greens and acid Fruits. However in Some Measure to palliate the Symptoms, and relax the Hard Stiff Swellings we fomented them Night & Morning, afterwards anointing the parts with a Liniment of Ung*uentum* Dialth*ea* & ol*eum* Ros*arum*.[3]

We miss'd seeing of Ceylon, being alitle too far to the Eastward, and having the Wind Scrimp.

[fasc. 2, f. 4r] **Thursday June 28.** As Soon as it was Day, we found ourselves within 2 or three Leagues of the Shore, betwixt 20 and 30 Miles below Madarass;[4] Where there was a Factory belonging to the French.[5] And a few Miles nearer Madarass, we Saw a Fortification which they Said belong'd to the Ostend Company, where the Emperor of Germany's Flag was hoisted; This Fort I think they called Carbelons.[6] About Eleven in the forenoon we discovered Madarass Fort[7] and the Ships in the Road, Where we came to an anchor about three o'Clock, Our Com*mand*er getting in about ¼ hour before us.

[1] The 'Scorbutick habit' relates to scurvy, the bane of long-distance voyaging in the early modern era. Caused by vitamin C deficiency, symptoms include fever, lethargy, joint aches, bleeding from the gums, teeth loosening, jaundice, and death if left long enough. It was not until the following decade, in 1747, that Scottish physician James Lind proved that citrus fruit cured scurvy. Though, as Fergusson makes clear, cures for scurvy were already thought to be associated with fresh food, particularly 'greens and acid fruits'. Even by the early 17th century the link was well enough established that the standard EIC surgeon's manual declared: 'The use of the juice of Lemons is a precious medicine and wel [*sic*] tried, being found & good.' See Woodall, *The Surgions Mate*, p. 185.

[2] In his diary, Fergusson added the breve diacritic mark above the 'u' in cure to indicate the short vowel sound. This has been replicated in the text wherever he did so, though Fergusson is far from consistent in its usage.

[3] In archaic usage, foment referred to bathing an afflicted area of the body in a warm or medicated lotion. In this instance he is applying an ointment of marshmallow plant and rose oil twice a day.

[4] Fergusson spells Madras (now Chennai) several different ways.

[5] Pondicherry (now Puducherry) is roughly 100 miles south of Chennai. It was the base of French operations in India from 1674 until the mid-20th century when it became part of the modern Indian state.

[6] By the 'Emperor of Germany' Fergusson means the Hapsburg Holy Roman Emperor, Charles VI (r. 1711–40). Along with Austro-Flemish private interests based out of Antwerp he established the *Kaiserliche Ostender Kompanie*, or Imperial Ostend Company, in late 1722, as an attempt to enter the East Indian trade markets. They founded two factories in India. One, which Fergusson refers to here as 'Carbelons', and later as 'Cabalong', is his interpretation of the Tamil toponym Kovalam, which the British called Covelong, now a small fishing village about 30 miles south of Chennai. The other factory they established in Bengal at Banquibazar (now Ichapore). It was one of the shortest-lived European East India companies as its operations were suspended after only 5 years and it was finally dissolved in 1731, as part of Britain's terms in the Treaty of Vienna.

[7] Founded in 1640, Fort St George was the focal point of Madras and was where EIC officials resided and conducted business. The so-called 'Black Town' (now Georgetown) was located immediately to the north of the fort (see Plate 2).

At our coming in to the Road we Saluted the Governour of the Fort with 9 Guns, which was answered by him with as Many.[1] After which we Saluted the Com*mander* with 9 Gunns which likewise was return'd.[2]

[fasc. 2, f. 4v] Immediatly [*sic*] after, our Capt*ain* Went ashore in one of the Indian Boats, and at his Landing was Saluted from the Fort, which was returned by us. We had Scarcely dropp'd anchor, when there came aboard 6 or 7 Boats,[3] carrying Servants in them, or De Bash's as they are call'd in that Country.[4] These are a kind of Trading Natives, who come to offer theirselves as Servants to those who have any goods or Money to dispose of. They go about and endeavour to find Merch*an*tts for Your goods, of which they take an acc*oun*tt or carry a Muster with them, afterwards they bring you an acc*oun*tt of what they are offered; that they may know if you are willing to part with them at that Rate; If not they enquire further, allwise giving you their advice. They appear a cunning artfull kind of People, and have a great deal of address, with them; of Every [fasc. 2, f. 5r] thing they Sell for you, they are allwise Sure to have a certain quota for themselves. Upon which acc*oun*tt they insist upon litle Wedges[5] for their service, leaving that to your own Discretion. What they Sell to Blackmen or Natives; they have a Finam for every Pigoud, which is a 36th part;[6] But from the English Inhabitants there, to whom they sell any goods, they dare not demand their Batti, which is the Name they give to that perquisite.[7] And therefore it is, that if your goods be principally Sold to White men, they expect to be rewarded from you more largely; whereas if the Natives buy them, then they look for litle other reward.

The Manners and Religion of the Natives, are Very difficult to be understood by Strangers, upon account of the Vast Variety of Different Sects or Casts, each of which have particular Manners and ~~different~~ Ceremonies in Religious Matters differing from one another; as also [fasc. 2, f. 5v] by reason of their Shyness in admitting any of a Different persuasion into the Knowledge of them. All of them however seem to admitt of one Supreme Being, tho' their Notions concerning him seem to be Very Mean & imperfect, as they indeed are with the Common people of all Country's and Religions.[8]

[1] The governor of Fort St George at the time was George Morton Pitt (1693–1756), who was born in Madras and educated in England before returning to India in 1724 in the Company's service.

[2] There is a discrepancy between Fergusson's account and the ship's journal, which has the *Britannia* anchoring in Madras at 3 o'clock, the day after (BL: IOR L/MAR/B/285AA, entry for 29 June 1733).

[3] These were probably *masula* boats which were designed to break through the surf in order to reach ships at anchor. They were flat-bottomed and made of planks of wood tied together so as to flex when beating through rough waves.

[4] Fergusson means *dubashis*, from the Hindustani *dho*, or two, and *bash*, meaning language. *Dubashis* acted as interpreters, cultural liaisons and middlemen for Europeans, negotiating almost every transaction on their behalf, from lodging, to procuring goods and services, to conducting private trade.

[5] Meaning wages.

[6] South Indian currency was gold-based. The British referred to the coins as pagoda, fanam, and cash. 80 cash = 1 fanam, 36 fanams = 1 pagoda. This system prevailed in Madras until the 1750s. Around the time of Fergusson's visits the pagoda was worth about 8 shillings. See Mukund, *The Trading World*, p. 80, n. 12.

[7] An Anglo-Indianism meaning allowance, also spelled 'batta'.

[8] Fergusson is referring to Hinduism here in monotheistic terms, which may seem odd for those more accustomed to classifying the religion as polytheistic. However, there is actually significant debate as to the exact nature of God within Hinduism, leaving many to consider the religion as both. See Doniger, *On Hinduism*, pp. 10–20.

The Sects or Casts are Very Numerous, Such as Moremen~e~[1] or Mahometans, Gentou,[2] Bramminy Cast, Right Hand Cast; Left hand Cast, Parriar Cast, & Many others, all of which so far as I could understand do likewise differ among themselves, as they do from one another.[3] The Moremen are Believers in Mahomet, which is the prevailing Religion through the Dominions of the great Mogul.[4]

The Gentou Seem to be the Most Numerous of any about Madarass, Besides they are the Most Genteel & Neat in their Dress, and with all the most Superstitiously Nice and [fasc. 2, f. 6r] reserv'd in their Religious Ceremonies, of which they have a Vast Number, that are Very troublesome, and in some Cases Scarcely possible to be observ'd. Such as their not being allow'd to eat or drink any Victuals, that has been dress'd or almost even handled by those of another Cast, Neither do they eat with those of their own Cast, except they be perfectly well known to them. They wash themselves all over every Morning, and after their Victuals. After which, Upon the Midle of their foreheads they Mark themselves with Paint, which is generally red or White, or sometimes both, this and the figure of the Mark I suppose being left to Discretion.[5] They care not to admitt any Strangers into their houses; probably upon acc~oun~tt of their Wives, of which they are Jealously carefull, especially those of the better sort, whom they keep closs withing doors Shutt up from the [fasc. 2, f. 6v] Sight of Strangers;[6] These they generally Marry when children, tho they dont lye with them till they come to the years of puberty; They are allow'd to have mo[r]e than one Wife if they please.[7] And even some of them keep Whores or Concubines, which however I believe is not allow'd of by their Religion.

Instead of having any Dowry with their Wives, they are oblig'd to pay So much money for them to the Parents;[8] which makes the Wife intirely Subject to the command of the

---

[1] Uniquely in this voyage, Fergusson uses the contemporary 'e' as shorthand to denote plural. There seems to be no reason for him to have done so since 'Moremen' is already plural, except perhaps to emphasize the fact for himself and readers.

[2] 'Gentou', more commonly written as 'gentoo', was used throughout the early modern period to describe the non-Muslim indigenous inhabitants of India. It derived from the Portuguese *gentio*, 'a gentile' or heathen, and was used to distinguish Hindus from 'moors' or Muslim Indians.

[3] Fergusson groups together adherents of the Islamic and Hindu faiths as members of the various 'sects or casts' of India, which is perhaps not altogether unfitting considering that Indian society comprised both. However, Muslims, like Christians, are considered to be outside the caste system. Hindu caste groupings and relations are incredibly complex and constantly in flux. His list begins with 'Gentou' described in the previous note, and then lists 'Bramminy', or Brahmin, the priestly Hindu caste, followed by right- and left-hand castes, which were specifically southern Indian distinctions more properly known as the Valangai and Idangai, respectively. Members of right-hand castes were engaged in agricultural occupations while the left-hand castes were manufacturers. 'Parriar', or Paraiyar, was originally anglicized as 'pariah', and is one of the Dalit caste groups commonly referred to as 'untouchables', due to their traditional occupations generally being considered unclean.

[4] By the 1730s Mughal power was on the wane, replaced in south India by the rise of the local successor states ruled by nominally Mughal-aligned Nawabs. While accurate census data does not exist, it is understood that throughout India Muslims were a minority, albeit a large one, even in the Mughal heartland of north India.

[5] Known as the *tilaka*, the markings are patterned according to sect.

[6] This may be a description of *purdah*, the practice of secluding women by some communities of both Hindus and Muslims in South Asia. Ritual pollution was likely another reason that strangers were not invited into households.

[7] Polygamy is allowed in Islam and was practised historically by some Hindu communities.

[8] The payment of a bride price in India is still practised, though dowries are now more common despite their being made illegal in 1961.

Husband; who frequently beats her upon any Misdemeanour, looking upon her intirely as his Property.

Their Manner of Religious Worship is not to be known, because they neither will acquaint Strangers of it, nor upon any account admitt them into their Pigod's,[1] after so they call the Publick place of their Religious Worship.

All I could understand was, that in those Pigouds, (which without[2] [fasc. 2, f. 7r] I saw finely built and adorn'd with carv'd StoneWork) they had Several Images of Different kinds to whom they pay'd their adoration. They have Brachmans, or as they are commonly call'd Bramminys, which are their religious Priests, some or all of whom, I was told, do pretend to foretell events, and do several other things in a Magical Way. These keep themselves reserv'd, and dont converse with Strangers.

The Gentou do forfeit their Cast, upon breach of any of the Ceremonies that are enjoyn'd them, such as Eating or drinking with Strangers, or of Meats forbidden them. Yet when Hunger pinches, or upon other occasions, providing, they think they will not be discovered, Some of them are So bold or free as to transgress, of which I have known Instances.

Their Cast if forfeited is not to be redeem'd but with a great deal of trouble, and at great Expence, [fasc. 2, f. 7v] which makes them afraid of transgressing; And because they live in the greatest Shame and contempt untill once they have aton'd for their transgression. The Particular Tenets belonging to other Casts, of any considerable Difference from those Mentioned, I could not discover. And indeed it is Somewhat a Wonder that even those who have liv'd in the Country many years, and Sometimes been inquisitive about these Matters, yet were not able to Satisfy themselves any way tolerably concerning the Tenets or Ceremonies of any of these Casts.

The People dont appear any ways rude or barbarous in themselves, Seeing a Stranger may safely enough travel any where unmolested. Only they seem somewhat inhospitable because they dont Care that Strangers should enter their houses. And it is a Difficult Matter for one unac= [fasc. 2, f. 8r] =quainted to gett any provisions from the Natives in the Country, which makes it necessary for a Traveller to carry Victuals along with him. Yet this inconveniency is in a good Measure remedied by a Very ~~good~~ commendable Institution of their Brachmans; Who have gott erected in different parts of the Country upon the highroads, Places of Entertainment, where Strangers are lodg'd and Victualed gratis. These Publick places are Maintain'd by a kind of Collection or Fines arising from certain delinquencys, which by the Brachmans are appropriated to this Use. And over each of these places a Brachman presides and takes care of the entertainment of Strangers.[3]

The Natives here use that Custom of burning the Dead, which the Vulgar do by laying them on a pile of Sticks, and the Excrements of Cows dry'd and harden'd by the Sun,

---

[1] Meaning 'pagodas', or more accurately, Hindu temples.

[2] Here Fergusson means outside, not without in the sense of lacking something.

[3] European travellers frequently complained of the difficulty of procuring provisions and the lack of guesthouses in India. In the north, most towns and certainly all cities along central trade routes had *serai*. In south India, more common were *choultries*, resting places where rooms and food were provided to travellers for small rates, or free, by charitable institutions. Additionally, *dharamshala*s, or religious guesthouses for pilgrims were also common. Fergusson had no first-hand knowledge of these inns and therefore may be conflating different types available to travellers.

[fasc. 2, f. 8v] which they gather, to Save the expence of Wood. The better Sort are Sometimes at a great charge by burning them with Valuable odorous Wood, intermix'd with other perfumes.[1]

And what of all is Most remarkable, In Some Casts particularly the Bramminy, some say also the Gentou, It frequently happens that the Wifes Voluntarily committs herself to the Pile in order to be burnt with the Corps [sic] of her deceas'd husband, providing she lov'd and respected him much;[2] chusing rather to accompany him than live forlorn'd in a World where She has no more a chance of having another husband, because no one will Marry a Widow, which makes many of those who are not So devout as to accompany their husbands, turn whores. This custom is Seldom or never practis'd at Madarass, the English hindering them, But in the country I'm told it is Very frequent. And even Some of the Very pious Wifes at Madarass, carry the Corps of their husbands into the Country that, [fasc. 3, f. 1r] there they may with liberty perform their pious Design.

The Husbands are never So complaisant to their Wifes, but if they please take another after one is Dead.

3

They pay a great respect to the Cow, which by Some Casts is carried even to Devout Veneration; Upon which accountt they look with abhorrence when you ask them to Eat any of their flesh. The Diet of the Common people so far as I could understand is chiefly upon boil'd Rice and fish, which is Mostly Salt; Tho those of the Better Sort eat Fowl and other Animals.

They have a Liquor which they call Toddy which is drank either fresh or Fermented. It is Procured from the Coco Tree by cutting the end of one of the top branches, and bending it Down they hold a Vessel under it into which the Liquor distills sometimes in great plenty. [fasc. 3, f. 1v] When fresh drawn it is lusciously Sweet, but by fermentation it acquires a more pungent beer-like taste.[4] Those whose bussiness it is to gather or draw this Liquor have a Very Curious Way of Climbing the Trees, which are Straight and without branches except at the Top, from whence they draw this Liquor; for having a kind of Sling which is hook'd round themselves and the Tree, and likewise their feet being join'd together by another Smaller kind of Sling, they gett up Very quickly, and Stay at the top Securely untill they extract their liquor. Sometimes they fasten earthen Potts to the amputated branches, and letting them remain there all Night, they are fill'd by Next Morning. Those Trees are the Most Numerous of any I could See, and from what has been Said, it is plain they are Very Succulent, which is somewhat a wonder in such a climate, and likewise Considering all those I Saw grew upon a Sandy ground. The Nuts [fasc. 3, f. 2r] which grow at the Top, have their Cavity fill'd with a liquor resembling

[1] Such as sandalwood.

[2] *Sati*, or widow-burning, was an object of perennial amazement and horror for European observers. There is considerable debate as to how widespread *sati* actually was relative to the amount of attention it received from foreigners. The practice was eventually banned under EIC rule in 1829, after a campaign led by influential Bengali intellectual and reformer Rammohan Roy. See Mani, *Contentious Traditions*, pp. 42–65.

[3] Fergusson begins inconsistently demarcating sections in this fascicle with a horizontal line to separate paragraphs or sections.

[4] Palm wine, also known as toddy, was one of the more popular alcoholic beverages in India during the early modern period, especially with European sailors. It is brewed, as Fergusson describes, from both the coconut and palmyra trees.

Whey, but of a Sweeter Taste, and is reckon'd Very Wholesome. The largest of them Contain above a Pint. The Inside Next to the Shell is lin'd with a Very White Substance resembling a Nut kernel, and about ¼ inch thick. It is very Sweet to Eat; but is reckoned burthensome to the Stomach, as containing a great deal of oil.

Their Dress is somewhat Different according to their Different Casts and Abilities.[1] The Common people & those of the Inferior Casts (I speak now only of the Men) have for the Most part No other clothing but a kind of Cape upon their heads, & as Much as covers their Nakedness, which is done by having a kind of girdle or String round their Waste[2], to which is fastened a cloth or clout[3] which passing betwixt their feet is fix'd again to the same girdle behind.[4]

The better Sort have a Very Neat dress, which consists of a pair of Long Loose breeches somewhat like Trousers, with a Long White Bannyan Somewhat re= [fasc. 3, f. 2v] =sembling a Womans Night gown;[5] round their Waste they have a large girdle, which is made of a Large broad piece of White Cloth wrapp'd together, and so putt round them. This Serves likewise to wrap up any things in that they have occasion to carry about with them. Upon their heads, they have a kind of Cape made of the same kind of roller Nicely wrapt round it.

The Women have all a kind of Petticoat, which covers them intirely from the Waste downwards. And they have their breasts covered with a broad cloth which like a Sash goes over one of their shoulders.[6]

Both men and women of the Gentou have large Ringlets through their Ears, made of Gold, and Sett with other precious Stones. They likewise wear Plenty of Rings upon their fingers. And Some of the Women have ringlets through the pinna or Sides of their Nose.

The Women Never cutt their hair, [fasc. 3, f. 3r] which is long and perfectly black, but have it platt or ty'd up in a particular Manner.[7] The Dress of their Women I cannot think Setts them out to such advantage, as our Europeans, who surely are much more obig'd[8] to their Dress than the Indians, Who have a Custom of painting their faces &

---

[1] Referring to South Indians.

[2] Fergusson consistently spells 'waist' as 'waste'.

[3] Meaning a fragment of cloth.

[4] Fergusson is most likely describing a *langota*, a traditional loincloth worn by men. It is still worn, particularly whilst undertaking hard physical exercise, or certain Vedic practices.

[5] The banyan was an article of clothing popular among European men in the early and mid-18th century, influenced by Persian and South Asian clothing. The garment was also called a morning gown, and contradictorily also nightgown, it could be a loose or fitted gown that was worn over breeches and the shirt. Fergusson, however, is likely referencing the *kurta pajama*, from whence the latter word entered into the English lexicon. Common across India, long billowy trousers (*pajama*) were worn under a long loose shirt (*kurta*), and traditionally finished with a sash around the waist. This resembled the European version of the garment with which he was familiar.

[6] The *sari* is the most common and well-known item of dress for South Asian women. Traditionally it was worn according to regional styles, differing in how it was tied and draped over the body. In South India a petticoat, or *pavadai*, was usually also worn.

[7] This is still common in many parts of India, particularly among the rural and more conservative population, and has to do with traditional conceptions of femininity and beauty.

[8] This is an archaic form of 'obliged'.

Necks with a kind of yellowish paint, which to me makes them appear Very disagreeable.[1]

The Children that are Very young, or below 4 or 5 years of age, go quite Naked.

They have publick Schools where their children are taught to read and write, of which I saw Severals.[2] They Write upon the Leave of a Tree call'd the Palmar or Palm tree,[3] Which resemble somewhat the leaves of our Common orrice,[4] being long about 2 foot, and of 1 & ½ or 2 Inches broad at Most. They dont use Ink but make an impression or Scratch upon the leaves with a particular kind [fasc. 3, f. 3v] of Stilet made of Iron.

Their characters appear pretty Neat, and look very well upon the leave. Sometimes likewise they Write upon paper as we do.

Their books consist of a Bundle of those leaves fastened together. And those leaves are alwise dry before they Write upon them, because the green wont take or bear the Impression.

I have omitted Mentioning any thing concerning the Ceremonies of the other Casts, not being able to make out any thing Distinct concerning them. Some I'm told worship the Cow, Some other animals, Some a particular kind of Nutt,[5] some a kind of Image of a peculiar frame, and other fantastical things, the effects of Ignorance and Imposture.

One Evening walking out into the fields I had the fortune to [fasc. 3, f. 4r] See a kind of Sacrifice perform'd. For seeing one of their Pigod's_e[6] at a Distance, our Curiosity led us to go Nearer,[7] where we Saw the Doors open, and a Sheep Standing fastened to one of the pillars; Having enquir'd what was the Meaning thereof, the Black Fellows who attended us being our Servantts, told us that that Sheep we observ'd was to be kill'd by and by, by the Bramminy.[8] Upon which we Waited to see the Ceremony, which we were told was to be about Sunsetting; About which time their Bramminy coming, (Who seemed to differ nothing in Dress from the others, He being one of an Inferior Cast)[9] the Inner doors of the Pigod were opened, where there were Lamps lighted, and he and others imploy'd, in some Ceremonies, particularly in adorning a kind of Image we were

---

[1] This 'paint' is actually a paste made from dried turmeric. Known as *kumkum* in Hindi, or *kunkuman* in Tamil, its use is still in practice across India among Hindus as a marker of social, religious, and marital status.

[2] Education was conducted according to caste groups, such as Kanakkans, the scribal caste in Tamil Nadu and Brahmins. Fergusson was able to witness many schools, known as *tinnai*, because they took place in open view on verandas, with several students seated before an instructor. Later these would become known as 'pial' or veranda schools in the Anglo-Indian vernacular of British India.

[3] Palm leaves were the traditional medium of record in India and remained in use through to the early 19th century, when the printing press was introduced widely across South Asia. Palm leaf manuscripts were used for contracts, accounts, official records, titles and religious texts.

[4] The common iris (either the *Iris pallida* or *I. germanica* species). Its root was frequently used in the preparation of early modern medicines. The leaves are broad and flat, similar to a palm frond.

[5] The fruit of the areca palm (*Areca catechu*), known as betel nuts, are considered holy and are frequently used as offerings in religious ceremonies (*pujas*).

[6] Again Fergusson has included the plural shorthand 'e'. Perhaps he did so to make sure the reader understands that he ment 'Pigod' to be plural as well as possessive, even though the latter is a clear grammatical error.

[7] Fergusson tells us below that he is in a group accompanied by local attendants, but never specifies who he was with, whether they were fellow crew members, other foreign merchants or other local inhabitants, such as their *dubashis*.

[8] Brahmin, or in this case the temple priest.

[9] Fergusson clearly is not aware of the function of Brahmins as a caste responsible for priestly duties and the transmission of sacred knowledge.

told they had at the Further end, of the Pigod, which we could not See any way distinctly they not allow= [fasc. 3, f. 4v] =ing us to enter. Besides we Saw them Carry in Water in different Vessels, Some Cold, and some hott, but could not learn for what end. Without[1] before alitle Place resembling a kind of Altar Others were imploy'd in Boyling Rice, which afterwards was took out and laid before the Altar (as I call'd it) upon some leaves Sow'd together. After these Ceremonies were over the Sheep was led before the altar, one holding him with a kind of chord by the head, and another by the tail; And the Bramminy coming out of the Pigod with a Large Sharp kind of Scimmiter, after a Boy had thrown Water upon the Sheeps Neck, he threw A handfull of Flowers upon it, and immediatly after with one blow Sever'd the Head from the Body. It turning late we could not Stay to See the rest of the process; But enquiring into the reason [fasc. 3, f. 5r] of this Sacrifice, we were told, that a certain Woman whom we Saw there imploy'd in Some of the Ceremonies, having a child Sick, had made a Vow, that if the child recovered, she would make an offering of a Sheep and So much Rice to the Pigod. And was accordingly now come to perform her Vow. The Body of the Sheep and Rice they said was to be dress'd and given to the Poor.

After all, as I observ'd before, they seem to acknowledge one Supreme being, I Mean those I convers'd with did. Tho it is hard to tell if the Vulgar have any consistent Notions, concerning him; or even if the More polite have these Notions by their religion or Education, or if they have acquir'd such opinions from the Europeans, that trade with and reside among them.[2]

A Conversation I had with one of the [fasc. 3, f. 5v] Gentou is Worth the remarking. He was one who understood English pretty well, and Seem'd to be a pretty Sensible Man. I ask'd him what he thought God was, or what he understood of God? He answered, What God was he could not tell, because he could not be seen. But that God gave us power to perform all the actions we are Capable of, and that he is in every one. Seeming not well to understand what he[3] meant, he told me the following story. There was one of their people who wanted much to See God; So that he went to and fro every where endeavouring to find what he wanted, but all in vain. Upon which he turns Melancholy, & pensive refusing to eat or Drink. Atlast [sic] one of his Friends knowing the Matter, & coming to him told him, if he would go along with him, he would Show him what he wanted. He leads him into a Room where [fasc. 3, f. 6r] there was provided a Wooden Machine in shape of a Man, such as we See in our Common Puppet Shows. This he observ'd to Have its arms and Legs, and perform Several gestures as if it had been alive. At which being surpris'd as knowing it made of Wood, he approach'd to examine it more Minutly; And lifting the Courtain discovers the Strings by which the Members were Mov'd, and withall the Man conceal'd above who pull'd the Strings to give it the Several Motions. He then cry'd out, I see the God and from thence was convinc'd that that God who gave us the Several powers and faculties dwelt within us and could not be seen.

I ask'd him if he thought he would again live after he had once Dy'd? He answered, after Death My Body is no more, but My Life & my Thinking cannot Die. To show me further

---

[1] Again, this is archaic usage. Fergusson means outside.

[2] It is interesting, though perhaps not surprising, that Fergusson suggests the possibility of Europeans influencing tendencies toward Hindu monotheistic beliefs rather than the centuries-long Muslim or Christian presence in India.

[3] 'I' has been written on top of 'he', so as partly to obscure it. It is not clear exactly which Fergusson meant.

that his Soul or thinking [fasc. 3, f. 6v] was not to die along with his Body, and that it could live separately from it, he made use of the following Simile; Suppose you want much to be in any place, Suppose in Madarass or in England, then your Mind will be much there, you think you see your friends, and that you converse with them, tho you are still aboard of this ship.

Inquiring of him if he thought there would be any difference betwixt the good and the Bad, After Death? He answered yes, but asking further if he knew in what way or where, he Said he could not tell, God alone knowing.

I further ask'd him, Why, if he believ'd in god, did he Worship a Senseless Image that could neither do him good nor hurt? He reply'd, When I close My Hands and approach to Worship that Image, it is not through fear or respect barely to it; but by doing So I [fasc. 3, f. 7r] in My thoughts Worship the great god above whom I cannot See. Pressing him further by asking Why he could not Worship the great god without Such an Image? His answer was, that he could so; but that it was their Custom to do it by the Image.

Madarass is commonly divided into the White and the Black Town, both of which are Separately surrounded with a Strong Wall and Ramparts. The White Town Stands closs by the Sea Shore at the place of Landing, in the Midle whereof is the Fort,[1] with another Distinct Wall round it, Mounted with some small Guns, as are the Walls of the White and Black Towns, at the Gates, and other Convenient Places with Large.[2] The White Town is not Very [fasc. 3, f. 7v] large, nor populous.[3] It is Chiefly inhabited by British, & a few other Europeans, especially Portugueze and French. The Governour and Some others of the Council, dont commonly live within the Town, but about ¼ of a Mile from it.[4] The Houses of the Europeans, are all large, & mostly built with flat roofs; and somewhat ressemble So many litle fortifications. The Walls are of some built with Stone, of others with Brick and Mortar as in England, but mostly plaistered over. They have no glass in their Windows. But instead thereof their Sashes are Woven with a kind of Small Cane, latticelike, as we see some chairs in Britain. This is done for the benefit of the Air; Besides they have Shutters to use upon occasion. Their Rooms are [fasc. 3, f. 8r] all plaister'd over in the inside, which is the only Furniture, I mean of those I saw.

The Black Town is very large and exceedingly populous. I may almost Venture to Say, that it with its suburbs contains as Many Souls as any Town in Britain, London and 1 or 2 others excepted.[5] I was surpris'd to See upon the Roads leading in to the Town, Such Numbers of People going to and fro; and in the Publick Parts of the their Streets, where

---

[1] Fort St George, the administrative headquarters and residential area of the EIC in Madras.

[2] It is assumed that Fergusson meant to finish the sentence with 'Guns'.

[3] Population estimates are notoriously difficult for the period. Figures suggest that there were only a few hundred European residents in the 'White Town', including military personnel, though this number would increase to over a thousand as a result of the mid-century Carnatic Wars. Meanwhile, the Indian 'Black Town' population was certainly much larger, numbering in the tens of thousands.

[4] This was known as the Governor's Garden House and was located on the site where the present Tamil Nadu Government Hospital stands. In 1753, a larger garden house at the far end of Mount Road (now Anna Salai), was purchased from the estate of Antonia de Madeiras, a Portuguese merchant. This became the Government House (now Raj Bhavan), the official residence of the British governors of Madras, and remains the official residence of the governor of Tamil Nadu.

[5] Indeed, the modern city of Chennai developed through the growth and amalgamation of these suburbs, or more appropriately, villages. Many neighbourhoods of the city still retain their original village name, for example, Egmore, Triplicane, Mylapore, Nungambakkam, and others. As reference, the population of London during the second quarter of the 18th century was around 700,000.

their Marketts are held, they are crouded so as to make it troublesome to pass. Besides that in the other Parts of the Streets there are Numbers of People to be seen.

The Houses are Very low, consisting only of one Story; those of the Poorer sort, are so Very Small and low, as Scarcely to [fasc. 3, f. 8v] contain a Dozen of People. The Better Sort have their Habitations more Spacious; Some of them especially those concern'd in Merchandise, have large Courts or Squares, where their Dwelling houses, and shops & storehouses, or Godouns (as they call them) are.[1]

Their Houses are built of Clay with Pieces of Wood to Support it; Some of Stone or Brick, smoothly Plaister'd in the outside, with Lime or Mortar. Those of the Better Sort are covered with Tiles; But the Meaner are with a kind of Thatch.

The Streets are broad, Streight, & regular, but have no kind of Paving, which indeed would be rather hurtfull than usefull, because all the people go barefoot, excepting some few, who now & then Wear a kind of Slippers or Sandals.

[fasc. 4, f. 1r] The Extent of the Town I cannot guess; But this I know, that I travelled, Several times and Several Ways till I was Wearied without being able to compass its Extent.

Besides this Part now describ'd which is only inhabited by the Natives; there is one Corner where other Trading People of Different Countries live, such as Armenians, Jews, Rich Moormen, & others. These have large fine houses built like those in the White Town.[2]

The Country Nigh the Town is Very well inhabited, as I'm told, besides that I Saw the Hutts, dispers'd here and there Very frequent. These Indeed are the Meanest Habitations, that one can well concieve [sic]; Some of them are just large enough to lett one creep into them, and with in to allow two or three people to lye along.

[fasc. 4, f. 1v] Both white & black Town, with some few Miles of the Country round, are in intire subjection to the English Governour, who with his Council is absolute Judge in all Civil Matters.[3] This being founded upon a grant made by their Emperour the Great Mogul, to the English at their first Settlement.[4] The English Company in return I'm told,

---

[1] More commonly, *godown* a kind of warehouse typical in India and East Asia. The principal exports of Madras were textiles, such as cotton broadcloth, longcloth, and calicoes, however, coral, arrack, and precious stones were also traded.

[2] Now considered a part of Georgetown, this neighbourhood was to the north of the fort and used to surround the Armenian Church of Virgin Mary. The church was first constructed in 1712, and rebuilt in 1772, after it was destroyed by the French during their occupation of Madras in 1746.

[3] Fergusson is not entirely correct. While the Company-appointed governor and council were in control of all matters of government pertaining to the territory of Madras, encompassing Fort St George, Black Town and environs, they did not have legal jurisdiction over the Company's subjects residing within Madras – Indian, British, or otherwise. The Mayor's Court of Madraspatnam was first established by the EIC in 1687, making it the oldest British legal institution in India. This court was indeed under the authority of the Company's governor and council. However, in 1727, a British royal charter was issued that brought the Mayor's Court under royal jurisdiction, stipulating that an elected mayor and aldermen were to adjudicate civil and criminal matters. This court remained in place until it was superseded by the creation of the Recorder's Court in 1797, followed by the Supreme Court 3 years later.

[4] Again, Fergusson is mistaken. The Mughals came to power in the Madras region only after Aurangzeb defeated the Qutb Shahi dynasty of Golconda in 1687. The 3-mile stretch of coast and the fishing village of Madraspatnam were granted to the Company much earlier, in 1639. Francis Day, a factor based to the north in Masulipatam, secured the original *jaghire* (land grant) from the Vigayanagara governor of the Coromandel, Damarla Venkatadri Nayaka. This allowed the Company to build a fortified settlement and secured their rights over the territory for a period of two years. Early the next year, construction on Fort St George began. At the time of Fergusson's visits, the Mughal emperor was Muhammad Shah (r. 1719–48), however, his political control over South India was in title only.

pay a certain annual Few[1] to the Mogul or his Deputies (or No Bobs[2] as they are Call'd) as an acknowledgement for this Priviledge. The English on the other hand, lay a kind of assessment upon all those that live with in their bounds, from whence arises a considerable Revenue to the Company. Besides for all goods landed at Madarass for Sale, from Englishmen they have 5 per Cent; and from others, I'm inform'd they have 10 per Cent.[3]

[fasc. 4, f. 2r] The rest of the Country round is under the Government of the great Mogul, whose Deputies call'd No-Bobs or Kings of the Moors, are dispers'd here and there, to collect his Revenues, & for other Civil Considerations.[4] These I was inform'd live as grand as Kings, having constantly attending them 10 or 12 thousand men in arms; who however would not be a sufficient Match for So many hundred Europeans, as I am well inform'd by those who may be presum'd acquainted with their particular abilities; as indeed may be easily perceiv'd, by a very indifferent observer, of the Temper and Disposition of the People, who appear Naturally timorous and afraid of Strangers; besides that they are not near So robust or Strong in their Constitution, being generally of a More Slender Make.[5]

[fasc. 4, f. 2v] I had forgott to take Notice of their Catamarrans, for so they call a kind of Flatt upon which they go a fishing.[6] It consists only of half a Dozen of Sticks about ½ foot Diameter and 7 or 8 foot long, ty'd together at both ends with a chord. They are bound together So as to be Somewhat hollow in the Middle, Narrow or Sharp at the head, and broad at the other end or Stern, by which means they in Some Measure resemble a very Small boat. They in general are made only to bear two Men, tho Some will bear 3 or 4, and others only one. In order to row them or make them go, they have a kind of Padles, which are made of a long piece of Wood hollow'd all allong one Side, by dipping of which into the Water they pull themselves along. Frequently [fasc. 4, f. 3r] also they, use a Sail, with which they go very quickly along. Upon these Bundles of Sticks,[7] they go Sometimes a Vast way

---

[1] Fergusson means 'fee', however, he may have omitted a word.

[2] Meaning 'nabob', the anglicized version of *nawab*, a Mughal official. Later in the century, the word was anglicized as 'nabob' and came to describe Europeans, who returned from India with large amounts of wealth, which they made through lucrative private trade enterprises while serving the EIC in the East.

[3] Under the initial terms of the land grant, the Company agreed to pay as much as half of its customs and port revenues to the local authorities. Over time, as British power and economic influence grew, they were able to negotiate better terms with successive Indian rulers and dynasties. Under Mughal authority the Company paid an annual quitrent for the privilege of occupying Madras, a practice that was ended during the tumultuous events of the Second Carnatic War in 1752.

[4] Following the death of Emperor Aurangzeb in 1707, a series of successional crises and continued Maratha military incursions resulted in the devolution of Mughal authority into a series of successor states. When Fergusson visited, the region around Madras was under the authority of the Nawab of the Carnatic (Arcot), Dost Ali Khan (r. 1732–40). Nominally under Mughal authority, such nawabs exercised de facto sovereignty over their territories.

[5] This is an early articulation of the martial race theory that came to dominate recruitment in the British Indian army following the 1857 Rebellion. However, even mid-18th-century military regulations for South India stipulated that only certain castes and ethnicities were eligible for military service, such as Rajputs, Muslims, and certain Telegu groups. See Basu, 'Ideas, Memories and Meanings', p. 170.

[6] Catamaran describes a boat or ship of two hulls in parallel, joined by a frame. Traditional catamarans, like those in use along the Coromandel and Malabar Coasts of southern India, were constructed, as Fergusson describes, from several long blocks of wood hewn to shape and tied together, thus comprising the multiple hulls associated with the modern vessel. The word catamaran is Tamil in origin, being an amalgamation of the words *kattu* (to tie) and *maram* (wood, or tree).

[7] Meaning the catamarans.

out into the Sea, even when it blows pretty fresh. And what is Very remarkable, they Stand upon them erect, tho there be a pretty high Sea tumbling their catamarran here & there; So well have they learn'd to keep a steddy ballance, according to the Motion of their float. Besides, Should they happen to tumble off their Catamarran, or tho it Should be oversett with them, which sometimes happens, yet they are under no apprehension, Seeing they all Naturally sweem; So that when it oversetts with them, they quickly again tumble it up.

There are other Boats, in which the goods are carry'd to & from the Ships; These are Shap'd much like the Common fisher= [fasc. 4, f. 3v] =boats in Scotland, and are of the same bigness; but are built in a Very different manner, I mean with different Materials.[1] For instead of Iron Nails and Rivets to keep the planks together, they use a Strong tough kind of Straw or Rush,[2] with which, having holes bor'd along the Contiguous edges of the Planks, they bind them together. Neither do they use ockam[3] or Pitch to make the Seams tight; But all along the insides of the seams, they have, a Small bundle of the same or rather a Softer kind of Straw or Rushes, closely fastened.[4] This pretty well answers the end, tho I dont think they are Nigh so tight as our boats. Their oars are made of a long roundish stick,[5] and an oval piece of board fastened to its end, which last serves the same purpose as the oblong feather of our European oars.

[fasc. 4, f. 4r] **Saturday August 4th.** We Sailed from Madarass, and that Day Se'nnight[6] we came to an anchor in Pallisore Road, where we stay'd for a Pilot;[7] And Tuesday following being Supply'd with a Pilot and Sloup, we weighed anchor, and Next Day gott Safe to our Station at Rogues River in the Ganges.[8] As we came in to the Mouth of the River we Saw the Wreck of the *Ile*'s, one of our own Ships, who had run aground there about 10 Days before.[9] At our coming to an anchor we were Saluted by the three British

---

[1] Fergusson is describing a *masula* boat, a traditional vessel built without a frame or ribs, with stitching holding its planks together. The non-rigid design is useful as it is more flexible when breaking the surf to land along the Coromandel Coast.

[2] Likely coir, rope made from the rough fibre of coconut husks.

[3] Meaning oakum, a preparation of tarred hemp fibres used to caulk wooden European boats and ships.

[4] The wadding was made of a dried marsh grass, which is indeed softer than coir (Kentley, 'The Masula', pp. 123–6).

[5] Usually bamboo.

[6] Sennight is an archaic word for a week, or the space of seven days and nights.

[7] Meaning Balasore, in the state of Odisha. It was an important trading city until being supplanted by Calcutta during the 18th century. Ships sailing up the Hooghly River usually sought pilots here to navigate the various channels and treacherous shoals.

[8] See Plate 3. According to the *Britannia*'s logbook, they arrived on 15 August. Rogue's River was one of the channels along the Hooghly River and provided the first safe anchorage point on the route to Calcutta. The name was used throughout the 17th and 18th centuries due to the occasional presence of Portuguese and Rakhine rovers. It was located at the village of Kulpi, just a few miles below what is now the town of Diamond Harbour (BL: IOR L/MAR/B/285AA, entry for 15 August 1731).

[9] This is the ship *Eyles*, late in the Company's service. As Fergusson states, it sank after running aground in late July 1733. Its case set a precedent and became a textbook example of marine insurance dispute claims, referenced into the 19th century due to the circumstances of its sinking. The ship's owners had insured her for £500 for a voyage to London, commencing in Madras. However, upon arriving in Madras from Calcutta, the ship was found in a poor state of repair and returned to Bengal for refitting when it was lost. The insurers refused to pay, claiming that as the ship had not yet again reached Fort St George, that the terms of the policy had not come into effect. The ship-owners argued successfully that because the *Eyles* had already reached Madras, the policy was already underway (Steel, *The Ship-Master's Assistant*, pp. 182, 192–3).

Ships which lay there Viz. the *Decker*, *Royal Guardian*, and *Devonshire*, who gave us 7 guns each, which we answered with 21. There were likewise lying here two Dutch guardships but betwixt us and them there pass'd no Compliments.

Wednesday September 26. Our Longboat being Sent a few Miles up [fasc. 4, f. 4v] the River, in order to buy Paddy[1] for the Cattel at some of their small Towns or Villages; I went in her on purpose to divert myself and See the Country. Accordingly we went ashore at a Village call'd Deanstown,[2] where our De=Bash[3] enquiring at the Inhabitants if there was any Paddy (which Paddy is Rice unhusk'd) was told that there was plenty of it in the place, but that they Durst not sell any of it, because two or three Days ago the No=Bob or Ha no=Bob,[4] had Sent positive orders not to dispose of any of it to the Europe Ships, but that all they could spare was to be preserv'd for him; there being it Seems a Scarcity of it in those parts where he resides. And indeed the People were So afraid of disobeying his orders that We could not purchase one grain from them.

[fasc. 4, f. 5r] As I went through the Village, I heard a Noise of Drums and Small Bells, with people Singing, which keapt [*sic*] Tune together So as to make up a kind of Harmony, which I thought Not dissagreable [*sic*]. I ask'd our De Bash what might be the Meaning of it who told me that it was the Gentou people worshipping A kind of Idol, they call Jack of the Nutt.[5] As I came Nigh the place I Saw about 6 or 7 Men all Dancing in a Particular Manner. Two of them had hanging before them a Small kind of Drum, which was plac'd So as they might conveniently beat on each end of it with their fingers.[6]

---

[1] The ship's journal states this occurred on 27 September (BL: IOR L/MAR/B/285AA).

[2] Near the present village of Geonkhali, lying at the confluence of the Hooghly and Rupnarayan and Damodar rivers. It is thought that the names for the village and the nearby sandbar were derived from a previous Danish settlement. See Hamilton, *A New Account of the East-Indies*, II, p. 5; and Yule, *The Diary of William Hedges*, III, p. ccix.

[3] Meaning *dubashi*.

[4] This is Fergusson's version of 'annabob', the more common, but still incorrect English derivation of *al-Nawab*, meaning a Mughal governor or viceroy, as distinct from *nawab*, denoting only an official. At the time the governor of Bengal was Shuja-ud-Din Muhammad Khan (r. 1727–39). According to one later 19th-century anonymous author, 'the only dispute that is recorded to have happened during his time' involved customs receipts and trade regulations in the town of Hooghly (now Hooghly-Chinsurah), which was settled after Shuja Khan banned the sale of grain to any EIC forts or factories (Anon., *Historical and Ecclesiastical Sketches of Bengal*, p. 79). Fergusson's visit may have coincided with this episode. However, it is equally plausible that the ban on grain sales was due to drought leading to a scarcity in supplies.

[5] Fergusson is unclear as to what deity and associated rituals he witnessed. There are two likely possibilities according to historical regional Hindu practices, neither of which fits perfectly with what Fergusson described. One option, most similar sounding to what he calls 'Jack of the Nutt' is Jagannath, meaning 'Lord of the Universe' who is considered an avatar of Vishnu, one of the paramount gods of Hinduism, and is worshipped widely in north-eastern India and Bangladesh. Images of Jagannath are typically placed on a platform shared with the deities Balabhadra and Subhadra, and are venerated collectively. During the annual *Ratha Yatra* festival statues of these gods are each placed in massive chariots that are then are pulled miles in procession by devotees, a practice from which the English word 'juggernaut' is derived. However, in contrast to what Fergusson describes, Jagganath is not depicted with appendages, nor atop a tiger. The more likely possibility is that Fergusson witnessed the veneration of Jagadhatri, which is an aspect of the goddess Durga, which is worshipped predominately in Bengal. Jagadhatri is often depicted riding atop a lion accompanied by attendants, which fits somewhat more to the idol and ceremony Fergusson describes.

[6] The most popular of the Indian drums is a *dhol*, which is hung around the neck and beaten on both sides with the fingers, or also utilizing in one hand a *kanthi*, or cane stick.

The others, had fastened to their feet and Hands Small Bells, which by their Dancing and other Motions, were made to play Several Tunes in Consort with the two Drums and their own Singing. They were under [fasc. 4, f. 5v] a kind of Shade, which Stood before a Small House whose end opened into this Shade.[1] Within the House there Stood fronting of them three Images of Men finely dress'd after a particular Manner, each of them was Mountted [sic] upon Certain Animals;[2] The Midlemost [sic] Image was the largest by far being Jack of the Nutt himself. He was much finer dress'd and painted than the other two, besides he had a kind of Crown or Mitre upon his head, which was supported by the right hand of him who was at his left hand. He rode upon a Tyger which likewise was bigger than the other animals upon which his attendants Rode. The other two Images I was told were plac'd there as Servants or attendants of their God. Those Images were made of Clay; But the Richer sort I'm Told have their Gods made of More precious and durable Materials.

[fasc. 4, f. 6r] Within along with these Images there was their Bramminy employ'd in dressing and adorning them with Ringlets of Flowers, and other gay Materials. Before each of the Images was plac'd a Large Dish of Fruit & herbs of Different kinds, Neatly Sett out and Sprinkled with flowers; In which I observ'd that of the Midlemost much to exceed the other two in Bigness, Variety & Neatness. At each side were two large lamps burning. The Bramminy appear'd very intent about adorning his god, for when I look'd in and was pretty Nigh him a good while, he took no Notice of Me. The others that were without employ'd in Dancing, Singing &.C. appear'd not So devout, but Star'd at us now and then, tho all the time they continu'd their Motions & Musick, and sometimes devoutly look'd at their imaginary Deity.

Being fatigu'd with heat in the evening we return'd to the Ship.

[fasc. 4, f. 6v] **Thursday Nov*ember* 28.** Mr. Nairn our Third Mate[3] & I went into a Budgerow[4] in order to Sail for Calcutta, Where we arriv'd next Day in the Morning early. About 12 Miles above Rogues River where our ships lay, at a Place called Patna[5] I observ'd as we Saild [sic] along 13 Dutch Ships at their Moorings, they appear'd all as large if not larger than any of our Ships.

Calcutta is a large Town Situated in a pleasant Country along Side of the River which is a branch of the Ganges,[6] about 60 or 70 Miles from the Sea. It is not So populous nor So Regular by far as Madarass.[7] By the riverside Stands Fort Willi*a*m, which appears

---

[1] Fergusson is clearly in front of a temple.

[2] This statement adds further confusion as to what ritual, or *puja*, Fergusson witnessed. If a veneration of Jagadhatri, then the principal deity is female, whose attendants could be either male or female. Due to his own unfamiliarity with Hindu practices it could be that he is unaware how a female deity may be represented or indeed even that the veneration of female deities forms a central practice in Hinduism.

[3] William Nearn, according to the ship's logbook (BL: IOR L/MAR/B/285AA, f. 2r).

[4] A barge-like vessel that formed the principal mode of transportation for goods and persons along the lower Ganges and its distributaries. They were often described as sluggish and cumbrous in their handling.

[5] There is no record of a Patna south of Kolkata. Fergusson could mean Phalta, or Falta, a village in the area he describes.

[6] This is the Hooghly River.

[7] At the time of Fergusson's voyages, Calcutta was undergoing a massive increase in population. In 1710 there were an estimated 12,000 inhabitants, growing to around 120,000 by mid-century.

pretty Strong being well fortified with high Walls.[1] Its Situation Makes it have an entire command of all that pass and repass on the River, So that it has Much the advantage of both Dutch and French Factories which lie higher up,[2] and So are liable to be block'd up from any commerce from the Mouth of the River.

The Religion Manners & habit of the People much resemble those of Madarass, with some litle Variation of their Casts or Sects & Ceremonies.

[fasc. 4, f. 7r] **Saturday December 7.** After having purchas'd a few Goods and other Necessarys, Mr Lynd our Fifth Mate[3] & I came down to the Ship She bringing up anchor in order to fall farther down the River to a Place call'd India Lee,[4] Where we came to an anchor next Morning.

Thursday December 12. Our Captain having come aboard the Night before, and one of the Council at Bengal to clear the Ship, we Sett Sail and gott clear of the Mouth of the River, and Next Day our pilot having carried us Safe over all the shoals, went aboard of the sloup that attended & left us.

Tuesday December 24. We arrived in Madarass road, having had Contrary Winds and bad Weather in our passage. And Tuesday following I went ashore to do some business, being then ~~not Well~~ indispos'd, and on Monday went aboard again that the Surgeon[5] might go ashore.

Sunday February 2. We Weigh'd Anchor in company with the *Duke of Lorrain* having Saluted the Fort a[6] and afterwards the other Europe ship the *Prince Augustus*. The *Normington* having Sailed the Day before with a number of Soldiers aboard, to join a French Ship, who in conjunction were order'd to Cruise for the Swedish Ship that illegally had come into these parts.[7]

---

[1] Originally built near the eastern bank of the Hooghly River between 1696 and 1706. The fort was located in what is today B. D. D. Bagh (formerly Dalhousie Square) in the centre of old Calcutta. It was captured by the Nawab of Bengal, Siraj ud-Daulah (r. 1756–7), in 1756 and became home to the infamous 'Black Hole' incident after which it fell into ruin. Two years later Robert Clive rebuilt the fort in the Maidan, located immediately to the south of the main settlement, where it still stands.

[2] At the time the main Dutch factory along the river was at the town of Chinsurah, with the French situated at Chandannagar.

[3] John Lyn'de, according to the ship's journal (BL: IOR L/MAR/B/285AA, f. 2r).

[4] Sometimes spelled 'Indialee' or 'Indiyalee', this is an area located near present-day Pujali, to the south of Kolkata.

[5] William Gibson (BL: IOR L/MAR/B/285AA, f. 2r).

[6] Fergusson crossed out several words here, though missed this 'a' at the beginning of another 'and'.

[7] There was nothing illegal about it. The Swedish ship *Ulrica Eleonora* of the recently formed Swedish East India Company had arrived in India to participate in the Eastern trade. When the Swedes formed their own joint stock corporation, they received no opposition from European governments, however, their arrival in South and East Asia disturbed greatly the Dutch, British, and French companies, who themselves took illegal measures to discourage new European competition. The *Ulrica Eleonora* arrived in Porto Novo (now Parangipettai) on the Coromandel Coast, where no other European factory existed, and received from the Mughal *nawab* permission to trade, with the intention of establishing themselves permanently in the port. The ship then continued on to Bengal to conduct further trade, where it encountered no difficulties, before returning to Porto Novo. When Governors Pitt of Madras and Lenoir of Pondicherry heard of this development, they

[fasc. 4, f. 7v] Having had Very bad Weather with contrary Winds at the Cape which made us beat there 7 or 8 Weeks before we could Weather it, a great Many of our Men began to be much afflicted with the Scurvy, and other complaints.

Sunday June 1. We arriv'd at St Helena[1] to our great comfort, where Next Day about 16 of our Scorbutick Sailors went ashore, And by eating of Fresh Meat, Broths, and Greens, in a few Days were mostly recovered to a Miracle, altho Some of them were so extenuated and Lame with Large Scorbutick Swellings as not to be able to Walk. The Herbs they used as Most beneficial both as Salletts[2] and in their Broth, were particulary [sic] Purslain and Sallory[3] which grow wild there in great plenty. They used likewise plenty of Oranges which grow there. For those that had considerable swellings a Fomentation[4] of green herbs, Viz Rosemary, Wormwood, Agrimony &.C. was used.

Wednesday June 11. We Sett Sail from St Helena with the *Duke of Lorrain*, and Arrived at Gravesend in England on Tuesday the 12 of August 1734, and next Day having come up to Purfleet [fasc. 4, f. 8r] Mr Cuthcart coming down to see me I went with him up to London being Very much out of order, which had been my case the Whole of our Passage from India.

---

first attempted unsuccessfully to persuade the Nawab to revoke these privileges. They then sent out a joint naval force to stop the *Ulrica Eleonora* from landing in Porto Novo. When sighted, the Anglo-French fleet fired several warning shots at the Swedish ship, which was forced to return home without its cargo and personnel, who were abandoned in Porto Novo. The 'Porto Novo Affair', as it became known, caused a diplomatic incident among the European governments involved. The French, for their part settled with Sweden and did not give their backing to the position taken by the French company. In Britain the matter was more complicated as the primary concern was not that Sweden wanted to trade in the East, but rather that the Swedish company was primarily staffed by British-born former employees of the EIC. This was viewed as a direct assault on the monopoly privileges of the EIC, which could set a dangerous precedent for further British competition. Eventually the matter was settled with the EIC agreeing to compensate its Swedish rival for its losses, while the Swedish company agreed to no longer employ British subjects (Gill, 'The Affair of Porto Novo', pp. 52–62).

[1] St Helena lies close to the middle of the south Atlantic, approximately 1,210 miles off the coast of Angola. It was uninhabited when discovered by the Portuguese in 1502, who made use of its abundant supplies of fresh water and resources; however, their trade stations along the west coast of Africa were better situated, leading them to abandon the island. The Dutch VOC tried to establish a permanent settlement on the island but also abandoned it in favour of Cape Town in the mid-17th century. In 1659, the EIC sent its first governor there and the island became an important stopover for ships returning to American or European ports. By the time of Fergusson's visit, the population had reached just over 1,110. It is now a British Overseas Territory and hosts a population of just over 4,500. It is perhaps best known as the location for Napoleon's exile and death.

[2] Early modern English for greens or salad.

[3] This is not surprising considering that both purslane and celery are high in vitamin C.

[4] A poultice.

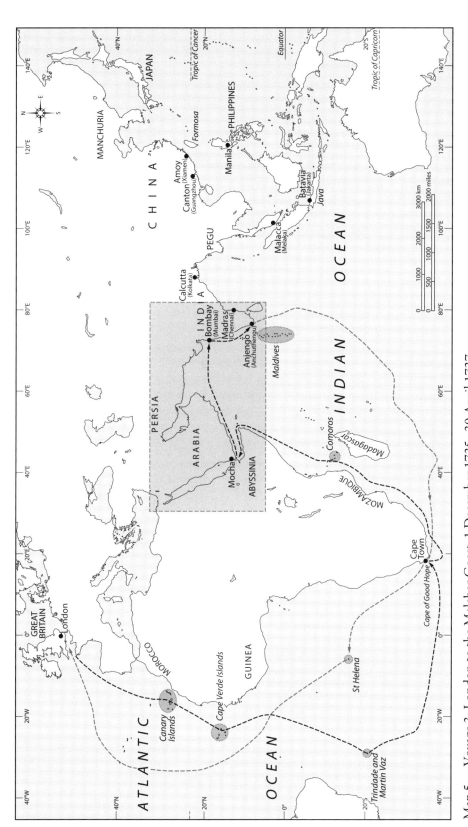

Map 5. Voyage 3: London to the Malabar Coast, 1 December 1735–30 April 1737.

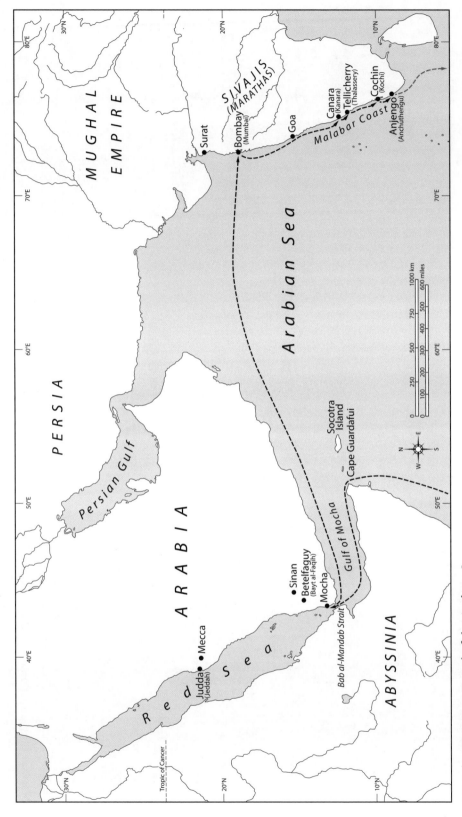

Map 6. Voyage 3: Detail of the Arabian Sea.

VOYAGE 3: FROM LONDON TO THE
MALABAR COAST
1 DECEMBER 1735–30 APRIL 1737

[fasc. 6, f. 1r][1] **Monday Dec*embe*r 1st 1735.** I Sail'd down the river [Thames] in a Small boat, and in the Evening gott aboard of the ship [*Britannia*] at Gravesend.[2]

Wednesday 3d. We Sail'd from Gravesend and gott into the Downs the Saturday following, where we Stay'd waiting a fair Wind till the 10th.

Wednesday Dec*embe*r 10th. We Weigh'd from the Downs, and friday [*sic*] following we gott out of the Channell, having lost Sight of Land that evening. Being favour'd with fair Winds & good Weather we came in sight of the Cape de Verd Islands on Tuesday Morning the 30th of Dec*embe*r. The Island we perceived first was that of St Nicholas which is pretty Large with high Land to the Westward of which lie 3 or 4 smaller ones which appear dry, barren & rugged Rocks.[3]

At six that Evening we gott in Sight of the Island Fogo or Del Fuego, which is very High in shape like a Sugar loaf.[4] In the Night we Saw break forth from the Summitt or highest [fasc. 6, f. 1v] peak frequent eruptions of Fire of a considerable bigness, this being a remarkable Vulcano. In the Morning when we were nigher it, we perceived at Several times large clouds of black Smoak come forth, but no percievable[5] [*sic*] fire. The part where this eruption appears is the Very highest point of the Island.

This Morning we found ourselves close in upon St Jago[6] being within a Mile & ½ of the Shore. This of all the Cape de Verds is the most fruitfull and best inhabited. We could observe the fields green, full of trees and bushes, and several pleasant plains. Toward the Southwest end, at Noon we Saw one of the portugueeze [*sic*] Towns, which seem'd to

---

[1] It seems either Fergusson misnumbered his diaries or a fascicle is missing, as there is no fifth volume. Probably the former since the narrative is not obviously interrupted.

[2] Fergusson was back aboard the *Britannia*, under Captain Phineas Frognall, this time as ship's surgeon, earning £50 16*s* 0*d* for his voyage of almost 17 months (BL: IOR L/MAR/B/285B, Pay book ledger, p. 4). Frognall had served as chief mate on Fergusson's previous *Britannia* voyage and would not survive this one, dying aboard the ship while at anchor off Mocha in July 1736 (BL: IOR L/MAR/B/285BB, entry for 21 July 1736).

[3] São Nicolau Island, one of the Barlovento (windward) Islands of the Cape Verde archipelago, has four islands lying to its west. The islands Fergusson describes are the islets of Raso and Branco followed by the larger Santa Luzia Island.

[4] Fogo is one of the Sotavento (leeward) Islands and home to the volcano Pico do Fogo, the highest mountain in the Cape Verde archipelago. Fogo means 'fire' in Portuguese.

[5] Fergusson spells perceive as 'percieve' throughout his text.

[6] Also within the Sotavento group, the island is now known as Santiago and is the largest in Cape Verde. Just as in Fergusson's day, it hosts the majority of the population and is home to the nation's largest city and capital.

consist of Many Stragling Houses, with a small Castle and Church.[1] The ground Neer it was level and full of green bushes & Trees.

Wednesday January 21st, 1736. In the evening we perciev'd the Island Trinida, and Next Morning found ourselves betwixt it and the 3 or 4 Small Islands called Martin Voz.[2] Trinidada is moderately high Land, of about 6 or 7 Miles in Lenth [*sic*]. Those of Martin Voz seem rugged Barren Rocks, being able to [fasc. 6, f. 2r] percieve No trees or bushes upon them. But about them we saw great Numbers of fowls.

Saturday February 21. At break of Day We Saw the Table Land of the Cape,[3] and at Noon we Anchor'd in Table Bay; But it blowing pretty hard we gott not quite in till the Wednesday following, When I went ashoar with the Cap*ta*in.[4] Here were in the road 7 homeward bound Dutch Ships [see Plate 1].

This Setlement of the Dutch is Situated in a Valley bounded almost on every Side with Very high rocks and Mountains, lying closs by the Bay which is a Small Sinus of the Sea that runs about a Mile or More into the Land, and appears to be a Safe harbour except that it lyes expos'd to the N*orth* W*est* Winds which Sometimes blow into it with great Violence. At the North Side of the Bay is a Small Island called Penguin, which contributes much to the safety of the Harbour.[5] On this Island the Dutch keep a great many Banditti employed in Making Chinam or Mortar & Bricks, with other laborious Work.[6]

[fasc. 6, f. 2v] The Cape Town is Moderately large, consisting of a good Many houses, built low, all thatch'd, except a few that are flatt, and Whitened curiously on the outside.[7] They are not crowded upon one another, but built Sparse; and their Streets are Wide and regular, with Several large Squares or openings here and there. In some of the streets are Canals in the Midle, on each Side of which are Trees, which make them look Very pleasant; And every Person has a sluice by which he confines the Water before his own door, and so keeps the Canal full or empty at pleasure. The Houses are not above 2 story at Most, a great Many being only of one. And 'tis observable that contrary to the Manner in Britain, they furnish the lower story alone leaving the Upper for Ware houses or keeping of Lumber, and for their Serv*an*tts to lie in.

Near by the Landing place or Bridge as it is called, is situated the Fort or Castile, which is built of prety Large Hard Stones which ~~appears~~ Makes the Walls appear Very Strong.[8]

---

[1] This is probably Cidade Velha, a former capital and one of the oldest settlements on the island.

[2] Fergusson is referring to the Trindade and Martim Vaz archipelago, about 680 miles off the coast of Brazil, by which it is administered today. Fergusson spells Trindade two different ways in this paragraph.

[3] Meaning Cape Town in Cape Colony, founded and administered by the VOC. It was an important resupply port for European ships.

[4] Phineas Frognall.

[5] Now Robben Island. The original penguin colony was extinct by 1800, but since 1983 penguins have recolonized the island.

[6] Deriving from the Italian, banditti was a common form of the plural for 'bandit'. Chinam is lime made of cockle shells or limestone by pulverizing the shells or rocks into a powder. Robben Island served as a penal colony and forced labour camp for centuries, only closing in 1996. Its most famous prisoner was Nelson Mandela who was held there by the apartheid South African regime, 1964–82.

[7] The population of Cape Town in the mid-1730s is thought to have been around 2,600 Europeans, with roughly another 2,200 enslaved residents.

[8] The Castle of Good Hope is a star-shaped fort built by the VOC, 1666–79.

It [fasc. 6, f. 3r] consists of Several ramparts, being in circumference not above ¼ Mile at Most, or rather less. Its Situation in No Ways contributes to its Strenth, being upon low ground, and not at all fortified by Nature. It commands the passage from the Town into the country, there being No other Way to gett in or out, but Near the Fort Walls. The Houses within the Fort are all low, Scarcely appearing above its Walls. It appears to be old and to Want repair; and I was told by Mr White[1] one of their Council, (being an Englishman at whose house I lodg'd) that in several parts their Walls are So crazy that they dare not fire any Cannon from them lest they Should tumble down. By this it might appear that the Dutch are under no apprehension of being attacked here; Had not they upon report of an ensuing War that Year before we arriv'd built a New Battery at about ½ Miles Distance from the fort in order the better to command the Road or Harbour, which gives grounds to think that they dont imagine themselves quite Secure.

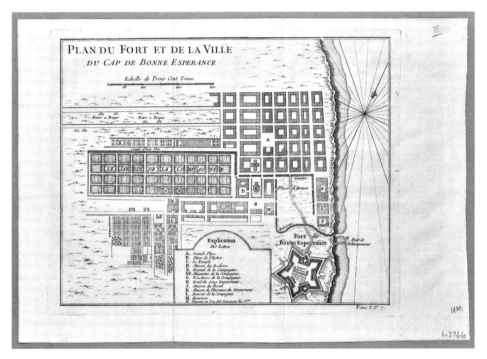

Figure 5.   Plan of the fort and the town of the Cape of Good Hope in the eighteenth century. Courtesy of the David Rumsey Map Collection, David Rumsey Map Center, Stanford Libraries, Stanford University, California (https://purl.stanford.edu/dq239ft9365). Cape Town as it would have looked when Fergusson visited showing the large VOC gardens in which Fergusson took a professional interest as a surgeon and apothecary.

---

[1] John White (c.1677–1755) was an English merchant and slave-trader who was born in New Amsterdam (now New York). After trying his hand at piracy, he arrived at the Cape in 1700 and later married into a Dutch family, changing his name to Jan de Wit. He was a prominent Cape resident, holding the position of Burgher Councillor (burgherraden) on several occasions (Upham, 'Hell and Paradise', p. 38). His townhouse is located along Strand Street and is now the Koopmans-de Wet House Museum.

[fasc. 6, f. 3v] The Garrison consists of about 100 or 150 Soldiers, which I think is but a Small Number for the place. But as all the Inhabitants of the Town are regularly Muster'd, and drawn out in Militia at Times, a smaller Number of Forces may probably Suffice.

There is near the fort A Very convenient landing place. They having built out from the beach into the Sea alitle Way, a kind of Key or pear [sic], of wood where boats putt out and take in their loading. And here the Water is most conveniently convey'd in 3 or 4 leaden pipes to the Very end of the Key. So that the Casks are fill'd without removing in the least out of the Long boats.

At the Upper End of the Town is the companies garden which is spacious, and has Many Very pleasant and regular Walks, with lofty Hedges on each Side, partly of Bays & Myrtle, but especially of oak which makes the finest Stately Hedges I have ever seen. Here grow in plenty all Manner of pott and Physical Herbs[1] with fruits of Several kinds. The Doors are allwise open, so that no body is hindered from walking [fasc. 6, f. 4r] in them; The litle rivulet that flows from the Table Land and which is part of what Supplies the whole Town with water is So curiously conveyed through the garden, that it can be Made to Water any part thereof at Discretion. And this I observe is done in all the private Gardens of other Gentlemen, which are So Situated as to admitt of it.

The Governor has a Small Country House which opens into the Gardens, which now and then he with his Family remove from the Fort into.[2]

Not far from the Gardens are the companies Stables where a good Many pretty litle horses are keept.

Here I saw two Wild asses which are certainly the finest Creatures to look at that are to be seen any Where.[3] They in Size resemble another ass, but are rather larger & of a More Neat and Sprightly Shapes. Their Head is not So Large or Angular; Their Body Shoulders and thighs are Well turn'd, and in Short they appear as lively Nimble and robust of their Size as any creature whatever; besides that they have a great deal of fire and life, which is plain from their never being Capable of [fasc. 6, f. 4v] being made so tame as to Submitt to bridle or bill. But above all their colour is most Curious and remarkable, their Skin, being most beautifully Variegated with alternate Strokes of White and Black, and so uniformly and regularly plac'd on the two Sides that there is not to be seen the least Variation of the Spotts or Waves of one Side from that of the other.

In the fields they are Said to be Very Nimble and Wild; it Seldom happening that any can be catch'd except when Very Young; tho' there are Severals of them shott by the Country people.[4]

From the Town all along Rivulett to the root of the Table Land, which is about 1 Mile & ½, are plac'd country Houses with Vineyards, Gardens and other planting, which make an agreeble prospect.

---

[1] Meaning medicinal herbs and plants.

[2] The governor at the time of Fergusson's visit was Jan de la Fontaine, (acting 1724–7, 1729–30; full 1730–37). He retired from the governorship after 28 years with the VOC.

[3] As will become apparent, Fergusson is describing zebras. He probably saw mountain zebras (*Equus zebra*), a species that lives in or around rocky and hilly regions of southern Africa in small groups of only a few animals.

[4] 'Country people' was a common method of referring to indigenous inhabitants.

The two principal Men here are the Governor and Fiscal. The Governor is the Chief, having the Direction of all the Company's affairs, the power of the Military, and the Disposal of all Lands[,] Plantations &.C.

The Fiscal is the Judge in Civil Matters, whose business is to take a Care [fasc. 6, f. 5r] that Nothing is done contrary to the Establish'd Laws or Interest of the Company. So that he Seems to have a powr [sic] independent of the Governor.[1]

The Inhabitants are Mostly Dutch with some French Refugees.[2] There being at present but one English family in all the Setlement. They Seem to have plenty of all kinds of Provision, their Water[,] bread and Mutton being the best I have ever tasted, besides they have all other kinds of Catle, fowl, Roots, Greens & Fruits that are to be had in Europe, and likewise plenty of Fish.

The People here are Neat enough in their clothing; and on Sundays &.C. they dress exceeding fine. The Women with all kinds of Silks and Jewells, and the Men all bedaub'd with Lace of Gold or Silver; So that indeed considering that they are not generally rich, I may affirm them to be the finest in Dress of any sett of people I know.

They have here a great Number of Slaves, which are chiefly brought from Madagascar, and Some from Several parts in India; None of the Hottentots being ever Made Slaves.[3]

The Companys Slaves which appear Mostly Women lodge in a Large building keapt on purpose for them call'd the Slave house.[4] [fasc. 6, f. 5v] They are employ'd in transporting of Goods from the Key to the Storehouses and from these to that &.C.

Most private Gentlemen in this place I'm told affect to have Many Slaves. They being look'd upon as the Most Splendid Livers,[5] who have the greatest Number. In Mr. White's house, there was at least 20 or 30, besides Many More that were employ'd in his gardens, and in the Country at his plantations. When once a Man has gott a competent Stock, he Seldom has occasion to renew it, it rather encreesing upon his hand, by the Slave Girls bearing of Children which in time Supply the place of their Mothers or Fathers.

---

[1] Under the Dutch, the fiscal was responsible for law enforcement and revenue matters. The position was created in 1688 in order to curb corruption and private trade among VOC servants. Fiscals were independent of the local government and reported directly to the highest body of the company, the Heren XVII in Amsterdam. When the governance of the Cape Colony came under British authority in 1795, and again in 1806, the office was maintained until it was replaced with an attorney general in 1827.

[2] Huguenots arrived in the Dutch Cape Colony as early as 1671 and in 1685, the VOC enacted a specific policy to settle French refugees at the Cape. About 180 Huguenots arrived in 1688 as a result. Eventually they were absorbed into the Dutch population, partly as a result of laws passed in 1701 that required official correspondence and education to be in Dutch.

[3] Indeed, it is believed that almost one half the population of Cape Town were slaves during this period. Bengal, the Coromandel and Malabar Coasts, Ceylon, and Madagascar supplied the majority of the slaves in the Cape in the decades before Fergusson's arrival. The local African population, the Khoikhoi, referred to, now pejoratively, as 'Hottentots' by early-modern Europeans, were not enslaved, due to the combined factors of them not being thought suitable to agriculture and early settler political weakness and reliance on them for livestock (Worden, 'Slavery at the Cape', *OREAH*). However, the growth of European settlement did result in their social, political, and economic destruction.

[4] Known more commonly as the Slave Lodge, this building is one of the oldest surviving structures constructed by the VOC in Cape Town. Originally built in 1679, it served to house VOC slaves, convicts, and the mentally ill until 1810, when it was converted into government offices under British rule. Today it houses a museum dedicated to the history of slavery in South Africa.

[5] Meaning lifestyles.

In this Town is a pretty little Church[1] as also a large Hospital for the Sick Sailors and Soldiers.[2]

In the Country the Dutch have Many Farms or Plantations, Some of which are at a Very great Distance from the Town. There are Severals I'm told above 18 Days Journey or 500 Miles from it. Mr. White has two about 350 Miles Distance. The Country as I'm inform'd at [fasc. 6, f. 6r] Some Distance from the Cape is Very fertile, and there are Many rich Pasturages here and there. All these within the above Mention'd bounds, the Europeans have expell'd the Hottentots from, and taken possession of. Their principle Stock in these remote plantations is Catle, with as Much grain as is Sufficient to Support them. The Butchers at times go or send into the Country & Buy the Catle from the Farmers, in order for Victualling. Nearer the Town besides Catle they have plenty of Grain, Vineyards and orchards.

The Method of Carriage to and from the Country is by means of Waggons of which they make Much Use, being drawn principally by oxen, and Severals by horses, both which they Seem to have plenty of. The roads into the Country I'm told are pretty good, and travelling easie Safe and Cheap. For you are in No Danger of Being Molested by the Natives, who Very Seldom are known to do any Injury to the Europeans. And there being no publick houses for entertainment, at whatever Bowers[3] house You putt up, You are recieved[4] [sic] kindly and treated greatly without any pay.

They have a good Many Slaves [fasc. 6, f. 6v] in the Country employ'd in looking after their Catle and Manuring their farms; besides Severals have Hottentots Servants, which are hir'd by the Year or So, and their Wages generally is a Young Cow or Lamb.

Of the Hottentots as to their Manner of living and other Customs I could not possibly be able to Satisfy Myself by ocular Inspection; there being but few who live Near the Dutch Setlements. The reason the Dutch give for their thinness in these parts, is that alitle after their Setlement here, the Hottentots who were then Very Numerous, were mostly Seized with the Small pox which kill'd incredible Numbers of them.[5] But another Very good reason I imagine may be given for it, is, that the Dutch who had some difficulty in encounters with the Natives at first, after they had it in their power, by killing many and Severely using the rest, oblig'd them to retire farther into the Country where they might live unmolested. And it has been too often practis'd of late, as I'm well inform'd, that the *Dutch* Bowers do drive away the Hottentots Catle [fasc. 6, f. 7r] and expell them from any agreable pasturages that they possess'd.[6] And the Dutch Governor himself, used

---

[1] This is now the *Groote Kerk*, or Great Church, erected in 1840, which replaced the smaller original church built in 1700–1704.

[2] Built by Cape Colony commander and later governor Simon van der Stel (in office 1679–99) in 1697. The hospital was located next to the VOC gardens, and was built with the expressed intention of treating sick sailors and soldiers who were en route from Europe to Asia.

[3] Or 'Boer', the Dutch or Afrikaans word meaning 'farmer', referring to the Dutch-speaking settlers in southern Africa.

[4] Fergusson regularly spells receive as 'recieve' throughout the text.

[5] A smallpox outbreak in 1713 virtually erased the Khoikhoi from the territories surrounding Cape Colony. It is thought that less than 10 per cent of the population survived. They were further decimated by subsequent epidemics in 1755 and 1767. However, as Fergusson makes clear, the impact and violence of settler colonialism should not be discounted.

[6] The Dutch found the Khoikhoi reluctant to sell or trade cattle. For the Khoikhoi, stock in cattle was the primary determinant of social and economic wealth, one which they were unwilling to part with for immediate financial gain.

to go or Send into the Country, and by force but under Shew of Justice, take away the best of their Catle, giving them in return a bitt of Tobacco or Some Such in considerable [*sic*] trifle. From these Causes, it is no Wonder if the Poor Hottentots chuse to retire from Such unjust oppressive Neighbours.

The Accounts that are generally given of this people, I have reason to think are in a great Measure false and Unjust.[1] And indeed we may make a Shrewd guess of the reason of Such a Conduct in the Europeans. For in order the better to Countenance or Vindicate the oppressions exercis'd against this people, they would endeavour to represent them as ~~quite~~ thoroughly Savage, Brutish and inhuman and So as not deserving to have justice or humanity ~~to be~~ exercis'd towards them. And this conjecture is Strongly confirm'd by what I had occasion to observe in the Various relations that were made me of the Hottentots. For upon enquiring at Some who had liv'd long in [fasc. 6, f. 7v] these parts, I had such a dismall account given Me of the Manners & Way of living of this people, that I was made to look upon them as the Most Despicable brutal and wretched Sett of Mortals that could possibly be conciev'd [*sic*]. Among other Inhuman Customs, I was told that it was Usual for them to kill all their aged Parents, alledging for So doing that they turn'd into the shape of Tigers and other Savage Beasts, and carried away their Catle in the Night.[2]

Another of the same Barbarous Stamp was told me Viz That if a Woman at a birth had twins, and if one prov'd Male & the other female; the last Viz the female was certainly thrown out to Starve or was otherwise destroy'd. These were affirmed to Me to be constantly practised by the Hottentots, and which at first I Verily believ'd tho' with some reluctance. But a Day or two afterwards, there coming to lodge at My Quarters, One of the Country Persons, being a German who was a Man of Good Sense & Learning and of an intire character, I had from him a quite different ac*coun*tt affirming all those to be [fasc. 6, f. 8r] in great Measure falsehoods. This Man liv'd in the Country about 50 Miles from the Cape, in alitle Village where he was Minister. He seem'd to have been at pains in inquiring into the Manners of this people, and gave Very good reasons for whatever he told. Our Discourse together was in Latin (he not understanding English) which he Spoke Very Well, and he Seem'd to be well acquainted with antient as well as Modern Learning. He had too good Sense to be a Bigott; and in Short Seem'd to Me the properest Person from whom I could have the Most Satisfactory account of what I wanted So much to know.

What therefore follows is what I learn'd from Him, and which he assur'd me with much appearance of Sincerity were true and to be depended upon, telling me with all that he was sensible how litle regard to truth Many had in their relations of things, which he had from his own experience found Since his being here.

The Hottentots are distinguish'd into different Nations, Tribes, or Clans; over each of which Tribes there is a Captain or Leader who is chosen by the Votes of the Chief among them; and he is [fasc. 6, f. 8v] commonly one who is distinguish'd by his riches, Strenth, or Some Superior Qualities. Him they Constitute Supreme in all Matters of

---

[1] This is a good example of Fergusson parting ways with his contemporaries. European descriptions of Khoikhoi were offensive in the extreme, and common enough that some simply relied on pre-existing imagery. One contemporary wrote in 1712: 'having been so frequently describ'd by others, I shall only add, that I found the Character of the *Hottentots* to be very true, and that they scarce deserve to be reckon'd of the Human Kind, they are such ill-look'd stinking nasty People' (Woodes Rogers quoted in Merians, *Envisioning the Worst*, p. 122).

[2] Shapeshifting is a common element in the religion of the Khoikhoi and related San peoples.

whatever kind, his commands being Laws, and they having no others but that are establish'd by Custom or use among them. He can order delinquents to be punish'd with Death or otherwise as they are thought deserving.[1]

The Natural Disposition or Temper of the Hottentots is by no means cruel or Barbarous, as is plain from their innocent living among themselves and with Europeans; altho' betwixt the Different Nations or Tribes, there Sometimes arise Disputes, which are carried to blows and bloodshed.[2] Of their Humanity and Honesty there was lately a remarkable Instance, by a Dutch Ships being Shipwreck'd upon the Coast a Distance from the European Setlements. When whatever Goods were Sav'd or came ashore, the Hottentots who liv'd there carefully assisted the Sailors to gather together, and afterwards carried Whatever they could upon their backs into the Dutch Setlements, without the least thing being [fasc. 7, f. 1r] loss'd or a missing, or without looking for Any reward for their trouble. Instances Such as this of Humanity and kindness I'm afraid are not frequently found among Christians.

They prove the Most faithfull Servants, and may be Safely trusted with whatever charge of Value, and have Seldom or never been found to be guilty of a breach of their Trust. They are punctual in keeping their engagements to the time they Serve; and if any do happen to leave their Service before the time of agreement is expir'd, by flying away among their own People, if application is made the Delinquent is carefully Sought for and deliver'd up, or otherwise punish'd as requir'd, even sometimes with Death. In Disputes betwixt Europeans & Hottentots the Dutch Governor or Fiscal are judges; But betwixt Hottentot and Hottentot their own Captains judge.

The Features of the Hottentots are by no Means bad; and of those I saw there were Some comely and Sagacious enough. One Girl particularly I saw at My lodging who had been [fasc. 7, f. 1v] for Sometime in the Service of a Dutch family, and was dress'd in the European Manner, look'd to be as well Shap'd and well look'd a Woman as I have readily Seen.[3]

Their Complexion is not quite black but Swarthy as in India. Their Hair not short and Wooly like the Guinea Inhabitants; but of these I Saw it resembled Much the Long friz'd Hair that Hangs from the Hips of a Black ram.

Their clothing Mostly is made of Sheeps Skins, the leather of which is Some how dress'd or prepar'd So as to become Soft and pliant, but with the wool upon it. Two or three of these are Sowed together, of which a kind of plaid or covering is made which

[1] Khoikhoi society was organized in villages, or clans, consisting of individuals linked through a common patrilineal ancestor. Groups of these clans related through marriages formed larger social and political units, known as a tribe or horde, which comprised several hundred or thousand members. The leader or headman of each clan was a hereditary position passed on to the eldest son of the founding ancestor, who mediated conflicts and made legal decisions as the head of a council of other elders and wealthy members of the clan.

[2] Raiding among Khoikhoi groups was a method of redistributing resources such as livestock herds, procuring marriage partners, and expressing masculinity, which are common among pastoralist peoples. Complex systems of conventions and rules governed these interactions. Initially the Dutch, viewed as neutral parties, were asked to mediate raiding disputes. However, their continued and growing interference in Khoikhoi social relations undermined traditional authority and organizational structures.

[3] European men held a long fascination with Khoikhoi women, ascribing them with a racialized form of exotic sexuality that reached seemingly insatiable and disturbing heights. For example, by the early 19th century, a Khoikhoi woman known to Europeans as Saartjie (Sarah) Baartman (1789–1815) was (in)famously labelled the 'Hottentot Venus' and exhibited across Europe. See Holmes, *The Hottentot Venus*.

they wear by throwing it round their Shoulders, from whence hanging down it covers their back and belly. With a piece of Skin is made a Small apron purse like, which being fastened to a girdle before, hangs over and covers their privy parts. Their Legs are wrap'd round with fresh Skins, which by drying there turns hard and stiff, so that when they [fasc. 7, f. 2r] go along, they sometimes make a ratling Noise. Their food is mostly greens, fruits and roots, Some of which require a particular way of Dressing before they can be Safely eat;[1] which has Made Many Europeans suffer by attempting to eat them, without knowing the proper Method of Managing them. Some of them eat Sheep and other Catle. But of their Cows they chiefly use the Milk.

They do not live together in Cities or Towns, neither have they in general any setled Houses or Habitations. They build alitle hutt or Shade in any convenient place where they remain for Some time; and then remove as they find it fitting, for their Sustenance or the pasturage of their Catle.[2]

Their Language is Somewhat peculiar but not so hard to be learn'd as Some others; Seeing Several Europeans understand it Very Well.

They punctually observe that of Marriage, or every Mans having his proper Wife, with whom he lives till Separated by Death.

Whoring, I'm told, is by them punish'd [fasc. 7, f. 2v] with Death, even altho' the parties be both Unmarried or Single. This Seems Severe Discipline, and Somewhat incredible, but the above Gentlemen affirm'd it to be true.

The account of their killing their old parents, I before observ'd, is false; But it is true that when they are turn'd So old, decrepid & Infirm, as to be quite a burthen to themselves, they then out of compassion Sometimes Shutt them up in their Hutts, or otherwise confine them by hedging them round in Some convenient place where they are Suffer'd to expire; after which they carefully bury them. Hence 'tis plain, has arose that other report of their barbarously killing them.

They have a great opinion of the power of Magick or Some Such enchantments, and look with much reverence and esteem on any they imagine Skill'd therein, of this was told me a pretty odd Story. At the first Setlement of the Europeans here; The Hottentots made Some resistance, and would not easily permitt them to go up into their Country, upon which there happened Seve= [fasc. 7, f. 3r] =ral Skirmishes.[3] Sometime afterwards when Matters were better agreed, The Dutch Gover*nor* from Some political Views, made a Tour a considerable Way into the Country carrying with Him about 100 Men with Some Carriage Guns, ammunition &.C. At an Interview with the Hott*ento*ts, having Interpreters between them, he was told by their Chief or Captain, that of all the

---

[1] This could be cassava or manioc (*Manihot esculenta*). Originally from South America, it was spread around Africa in the 16th and 17th centuries by the Portuguese. Now a staple across much of the global south, its tubers require a special preparation before being eaten as they contain cyanide.

[2] Known as a *matjieshius*, meaning mat-house in Afrikaans. These small dwellings were made by laying reed mats over a dome-shaped wooden frame. Their practicality led them to be adopted by European settlers, and Khoikhoi descendants continued to use them into the early 1900s.

[3] The VOC first settled the Cape in 1652. Tensions quickly rose between Dutch settlers and the Khoikhoi who lost important pasturages to the newcomers. In 1659 open warfare broke out, known as the year-long Khoi-Dutch war, which resulted in the fortification and fencing off of the Dutch settlement and the restricted movement of the Khoikhoi. In 1673 and again through 1674–7, wars broke out between the Dutch and Khoikhoi, culminating in the dispossession of land for the indigenous population, and the paying of an annual tribute of 30 head of cattle to the Dutch.

Hott*entot*s he was the greatest and most Skillfull Leader, being able to perform what none besides could do. The Dutch Gov*ernor* in answer told him that he of all Europeans was the most knowing & powerfull; and upon that challenged the Hottentot Leader to a Tryal[1] of Skill, telling him that as an Instance of his Abilities he could make water itself which quenches fire, to burn; which he defied the Hott*entot* Capt*ain* to Do. Whereupon were brought to the place two basons, the one full of Water which was Sett before the Capt*ain* and the other full of Spirits plac'd before the Governor. A road [*sic*] of red Hott Iron being brought [fasc. 7, f. 3v] to each. The Gov*ernor* immerging his in the Bason sett fire to the Spirits which flam'd about. But the poor Hott*entot* following his example had the Mortification to See his rod extinguish'd by the Water. The Consequence was the publick Disgrace and reproach of the poor Capt*ain* who went off in great Shame and confusion. Whilst the Governor was loudly applauded and extravagantly admir'd by the Ignorent Hott*entot*s who immediately Submitted themselves, and granted what ever he required. Thus we See by how Silly and Mean artifices 'tis possible to impose upon a gâping Simple Multitude.[2]

Their arms are Lances, and Bows and arrows. These they commonly poison by first besmearing them with a Certain Gum and then dipping them in a particular poison, for without the Gum the poison wont adhere.[3] Whatever they wound with these most certainly dies Soon after.

The report of its being Death for any European to lye with a Hottentot is evidently false. For the Minister [fasc. 7, f. 4r] told me of a Dutchman in his Parish, who taking a liking for a Hott*entot* Girl his serva*nt*t, had first a child or two with Her; after which he took Such pains that he taught her to read so as she could understand the Bible; and instructing her in the principles of Christianity he married her; and has Since had Several children; She having profess'd her belief in Christ, and desiring to be baptiz'd, which was not Yet done, but would quickly be.

~~Their~~ Religion, has been by most affirm'd, to be unknown to this people. But from what I can understand, they certainly have Notions of Some Supreme or Superior Being. The reason I imagine of their being thought Void of all Religious opinions, is that they have no priests or persons devoted to religious Service; and their Ceremonies being either few and Simple or none at all. besides [*sic*] that their Customs are not easy to be learn'd by the Europeans who I Suppose are at no great pains in their Inquiry's about them.[4]

Their opinions or Notions of Ma= [fasc. 7, f. 4v] =gick evidently proves what I here alledge, Seeing it Shows their Believing that there are Some Beings possess'd of extrordinary Wisdom and power above themselves.

At the New Moon they make extrordinary signs of Joy and Veneration by Dancing Singing, and other More Devout Gestures, which are certainly a kind of adoration of it as some excelling Being.

---

[1] Fergusson spells trial both with a 'y' and 'i' and it is transcribed according to the original.

[2] This event does not appear in the European historical record of Dutch-Khoikhoi relations.

[3] Still in use for traditional hunting methods by the San people today, the poison is made from the larvae or pupae of the *Diamphidia*, or the Bushman arrow-poison beetle. It is applied to the arrow or point using the sap of the common black-thorn acacia (*Acacia mellifera*).

[4] The Khoikhoi and San peoples had a complex religious belief structure, with rituals performed by priests or shamans. There is a pantheon of deities, and one supreme god known as Cagn, the creator of the world.

Besides I'm told that being ask'd concerning God, altho' they can give no Distinct account of their belief, Yet they give plainly to Understand that they have Notions of Something great and powerfull above them which they know not how to expresse.

To conclude they are certainly both in Natural Genius, Temper and Disposition, as also in Manners and Customs, Very different from what they have been commonly represented, and are generally believ'd to be. In short in their Natural Capacity they seem Not to be inferior to the rest of Mankind, and are far Superior to Most in Native fidelity and Integrity of Life. [fasc. 7, f. 5r]

They indeed have no arts or learning among them, and are remarkably ignorant of all these things, which So Very Much exalts humane Nature above the Brutal part of the Creation. But those who affirm them to have no More of Humanity than the Exterior form are either much Mistaken themselves, or would willfully impose upon others; as is plain from the Matters of Fact before observ'd which are no Small reproach to these Nations, who have So far the advantage of them in Arts and knowledge, but fall much Short in Native Honesty and faithfullness.

And 'tis no wonder, that the generality of Europeans consider the Hottentots as a Monstrous Sett of Men, Seeing they differ So much in Manners & Customs from them.

For we Very well know that among Europeans and Christians themselves, the Very difference in points of Religion or the like, is Sufficient to make one another be look'd upon by the Common people, in a Very [fasc. 7, f. 5v] Savage or Despicable light, & even as unworthy of the common offices of Humanity & Compassion. So far our pretended Knowledge contributes to root out of our Minds the most amiable Virtues of charity, Kindness and Fidelity, which are the Most essential characteristicks of Humanity, and in which I dare affirm, the generality of us are Much excell'd by these despis'd Mortals the Hottentots, who have knowledge ~~Sufficient~~ and Religion Sufficient to dispose them to the practise of these Virtues towards all Mankind; but not enough, it seems, to teach them to be treacherous, Cruel and inhuman to those of a different profession from themselves. Happy Ignorance! when Such are its amiable effects.

[fasc. 7, f. 6r] Here I must take Notice of a Race of Animals that are Very Numerous in these parts, Call'd by the Hottentots & Europeans Bavians, or by others Babians or Baboons.[1] The following Description of them I had from Severals, which was confirm'd by the above Mentioned Gentleman who at times has Seen Many thousands of them.

Of all earthly animals The Bavians in Shape, features and Sense come nearest to Mankind. Their Description Seems to answer exactly that of the antient Satyrs;[2] and from them I make no doubt, the antients took that opinion at first; they being I'm told to be found in Most parts of Africk [sic].

Their face and Hands are Very like those of Men. Their Nose & Cheeks are flatter, but their forehead Eyes and Ears are precisely ressembling the humane. The colour of their face is Swarthy. Their Bodys are Covered with hair except their Breasts, which in the females [fasc. 7, f. 6v] do not differ much in likeness from those of a Woman. They have a Short tail of 3 or 4 Inches lenth. Their hinder parts and legs come near to those of other beasts.

---

[1] Bavian, or more correctly *baviaan*, is early modern Dutch, from the Middle French for baboon. It was used by the Boer and Huguenot populations at the time of Fergusson's visit.

[2] A humanoid creature in Greek and Roman mythology. In the former they were represented with equine features, and in the latter with those of a goat.

They walk frequently erect, but when in haste they use all four with which they run Very Swift.

They take great care of their young by taking them up in their arms, and often transporting them with them upon their backs.

They are reckoned Very Strong, no Man or Dog being a Match for one of them full grown. In bigness they are near as Tall when erect as a Short Man, and Some of them higher.

They, when hurt or oppress'd make a Moaning not unlike the humane [*sic*] Species under Such Circumstances. And to their hurts they are Seen to Make applications of plants & the like, and for want of other things they often hold it cover [*sic*] the wound [fasc. 7, f. 7r] with their hands.[1]

They are frequently Seen in flocks of 1, 2 or 3 hundred together. They chiefly in habit [*sic*] the Mountains and inaccessible unfrequented places, except when they come down to the plains in order to forage for themselves and Young.

Their food is herbs, roots and fruits, which they often Steal in great quantities from the Country Bowers by breaking into their gardens and Vineyards. And their precaution and adress in this is Very remarkable; for When a party of them Sett about an expedition of this kind to rob an orchard or Vineyard. They first carefully place one or more of their Number in proper Stations for Watches to forewarn them of any approaching Danger, which they do by making a particular kind of hooping Noise, upon which those in the Gardens preceipitantly [*sic*] take to flight. And if the Watch Should neglect their Duty So as to Suffer the rest to be Surpris'd, it has been observ'd that [fasc. 7, f. 7v] they Severely punish them, Even Sometimes by tearing the offenders in pieces. In Stealing of Fruit from gardens, when the Walls are high, Some keep on the outside, others Stand on the walls and others gott into the garden, and after plucking the fruit, they throw or hand the Grapes, aples [*sic*] or Melons to these on the Walls who in like manner convey them to those on the outside, and So on till they have gott enough; after which they grasp each of them a bundle in their arms, or by leying them on their Shoulders or backs carry them away.[2]

Their Sagacity and activity is farther confirm'd by many other parts of their conduct. A remarkable Instance of which had lately happen'd. Three or four Bowers had gone out one Day a hunting and Shooting, and having kill'd a Young Bavian, Some of the old ones were Seen to follow them a great Way, but at a Distance. [fasc. 7, f. 8r] At last they happening to go into a Narrow place or glen, betwixt two Steep hills, they found themselves like to be kill'd by large Stones and pieces of Rock, which the Bavians taking this opportunity threw down upon them in great plenty and with much force, in order to be reveng'd upon them for Killing one of their Young.

One thing in these Creetures is Very remarkable, and Seems peculiar to them of all other animals that are known, and that is, their fondness for Women, whom they have been known to force So as to copulate with them which is alitle horrible to think of, and Should not be easily Credited, were it not confidently affirm'd, and too well testified by

---

[1] While contemporary populations of South African baboons are known to practise zoopharmacognosy, or self-medication through ingesting certain plants, they have not been observed to tend to open wounds in the manner here described.

[2] Residents of Cape Town still consider baboons a nuisance. The animals are known to frequently enter homes and gardens in their search for food.

Several Instances.[1] For if they happen to find a Woman alone in the fields in a convenient place they often have been seen to pursue them, and when overtaking them, after throwing them down they make Strong efforts to Satisfy [fasc. 7, f. 8v] their Inclinations; but the Instances of their Succeeding therein I'm told, are but Very few. And the poor Woman who has thus Suffered retires Somewhere where She is not afterwards heard of or known.

It is a pleasant enough Story which is told of the Hottentots Viz That they affirm the Bavians to be real Men, but that they are So Very cunning as not to Speak, lest they Should be forc'd to labour or work. And in reality I don't wonder considering their figure; And sagacity, that the Hottentots reckon them to differ So litle from Mankind.

These Creatures, I think are a Curious Instance of that Wonderfull gradation of Beings, which is so beautifully conspicuous in all the parts of the Creation with which we are acquainted; they seemingly to be plac'd in the Distinction, and to form the link betwixt Mankind and Brutes.[2]

[fasc. 8, f. 1r] **Tuesday March 10th.** Afternoon we Sail'd from the Cape of Good Hope, and directed our Course So as to pass betwixt Madagascar Island and the Main Land.

Friday the 9th of April[.] we Stood in for the Main Land of Mosambique, and at Night discovering Some Lights from that [p]art, we knew ourselves not to be far off the Shore which we discovered Next Morning.

This Land lies betwixt 14 or 15 Degrees South Latitude. Here the Portugueze have a Setlement with fortifications &.C.[3]

The Day after at Sunrising we saw the Island Mohilla, and next Morning we discovered that of Comaro, which are two Small Islands at alitle Distance from one another, which I was told were both inhabited, there having been Several Ships boats ashore there who Saw the Natives, but they were So afraid as to run away into the Woods upon their landing.[4]

---

[1] It has been documented that baboons and some other primates will show their genitals and grope women to taunt and force them to flee from gardens or homes where the animals seek food. However, baboons committing rape against humans has never been documented, though it continues to persist in the popular imagination. Most recently in 2018, a satirical news article first published in the *South Africa Morning Post* titled, 'Gay baboon terrorises African village, Rapes 5 men', went viral and was shared widely across social and news media platforms in southern Africa by those who believed it to be a genuine story. See *Africa Check*, <https://africacheck.org/fbcheck/gay-baboon-rapes-men-in-african-village-story-just-money-making-hogwash/>.

[2] In referencing Creation and the gradation of beings, Fergusson is pointing to the Aristotelian concept of the Great Chain of Being, or *scala naturae* that was the dominant paradigm for the classification of the world and its organisms. It was a hierarchical system that placed God at the top and all plants and animals in descending order. Linnaeus used the system as the basis for his own *Systema Naturae*, which was being written during Fergusson's voyage. The concept eventually fell out of favour as the theory of evolution took hold in the 19th century.

[3] The Island of Mozambique was settled by the Portuguese in 1507 and was the capital of their east African territories until the end of the 19th century. Construction of the Fort of São Sebastião was begun in 1558, though not completed for several decades.

[4] The ship's journal has this occurring on Monday, 12 April (BL: IOR L/MAR/B/285B). Mohilla, now Mohéli (also Mwali), is the smallest of the three main islands of modern Comoros, the others being Grande Comore (Ngazidja) to the north-west, and Anjouan (Nzwani) to the south-east. By the mid-18th century, the islands had become a regular source for slaves to supply the plantations on neighbouring islands such as Réunion and the Seychelles. This may explain why Fergusson describes the inhabitants as fleeing from ships.

[fasc. 8, f. 1v] The 27th of this Month we Made the Main Land a few Leagues to the Southward of Cape Gardafoy,[1] and next Day we rounded the Cape and entered into the Gulf of Mocha.[2]

Tuesday May 4th. In the Morning we pass'd the Narrow Straits of Babel Mandel,[3] into the Red Sea, and with a Very fresh Gale that evening gott into Mocha[4] Rode, where lay at Anchor betwixt 20 and 30 Sail of Large Ships besides many Small grabs and gallivats.[5]

From the Rode the Town [of Mocha] has a pretty enough appearance by Means of Some large Houses that Stand Next to the Sea, which being all plaister'd over with White Mortar makes them look like building of plain stone. And the Spires of 3 or 4 Mosques, especially of the largest, contribute to Accounts of the View of the place to advantages; which not alitle decieves [sic] our Expectations at [fasc. 8, f. 2r] going ashore; for then the place has quite another look. The buildings are Some of them indeed large, but have So mean an appearence [sic] in their Structure, Materials, and ill Situation with want of repair, that it appears but a Very despicable place. They are Mostly built of Small kind of Mouldring Brick except the foundation of the greater houses, which are laid with a kind of coral rock or Sea Stone for 2 or three foot above ground. The roofs of them are all flatt with a kind of rail built letticelike with many Small openings, all around them. This is partly for the Convenience of the air, and also, I'm told, that the Women may look through the Lettice without having their features distinguish'd by those from without.[6] The Houses of the Rich or better Sort of people are commonly 3 or 4 Story's high.[7] The floors are all made [fasc. 8, f. 2v] of reeds, Cajan,[8] or pieces of board plaister'd over with a Very Strong kind of Mortar, as are all the walls plaister'd over with the Same on both Sides, wood for Lining of rooms &.C. being Very Scarce here. Some of their Houses in the inside have their ceilings Very curiously painted in an irregular Manner. Their Doors, and Windows which are have all a small projecting part from them of Wood, are Very Nicely Carv'd and perforated for the air. Here it is they Most commonly Sitt upon their Carpetts and Cushions to take the Air, but in the other parts of their houses there is Nothing Nice to be Seen.

---

[1] Cape Guardafui, or Ras Asir, in the Puntland region of Somalia.

[2] Now known as the Gulf of Aden.

[3] Bab el-Mandeb, meaning 'Gate of Grief' in Arabic, due to its difficult waters.

[4] Mocha, or al-Mukha in Arabic, is a Red Sea port in Yemen. Until supplanted by Aden in the 19th century, it was one of the region's most important trade centres and most famous for coffee exports. The EIC established a trading factory there in 1618, which operated intermittently into the 19th century. Fergusson's visit came in the waning years of 'Yemen's coffee era', which ended due to Dutch success in smuggling coffee plants to the Indonesian archipelago and elsewhere (Um, 'Foreign Doctors', p. 263).

[5] These ships were commonly found across the Arabian Sea in the 18th century. The grab, or *ghurab*, was a broad low-lying, double-masted vessel of between 150 and 300 tons and could carry 150–200 men. The gallivat, or *galevat*, was a smaller vessel often described as a large rowing boat with a single or double mast and no larger than 70 tons. It could be rowed by 50 oars and carried a crew of about 100.

[6] At the time Yemeni cultural practices of Islam held that women usually remained in the home out of public view. Windows were thus covered with a lattice so that women could observe the goings-on in the streets while maintaining standards of modesty.

[7] Yemen is famous for its traditional mud-brick architecture that allowed buildings to reach many stories high, accommodating residents on the upper floors and storage and livestock on the lower.

[8] The pigeon pea plant, *Cajanus cajan*, is a perennial legume grown primarily as a food source. Its woody straight stems are also used as building material, as described here, for flooring, thatch, or fencing.

The Cape of Good Hope.

Plate 1. 'The Cape of Good Hope', print by Gerard van der Gucht, 1736. Courtesy of Yale Center for British Art, Paul Mellon Collection, Yale University. A contemporary view of the approach into Cape Town showing the prominence of Table Mountain as Fergusson would have seen it.

Plate 2. 'Fort St. George on the Coromandel Coast', etching by Jan van Ryne, 1754. Courtesy of NMM, Greenwich, London. A view of Madras enclosed within the walls of Fort St George. What was then called Black Town was to the right just beyond the city walls. The city is as it would have appeared during Fergusson's visits.

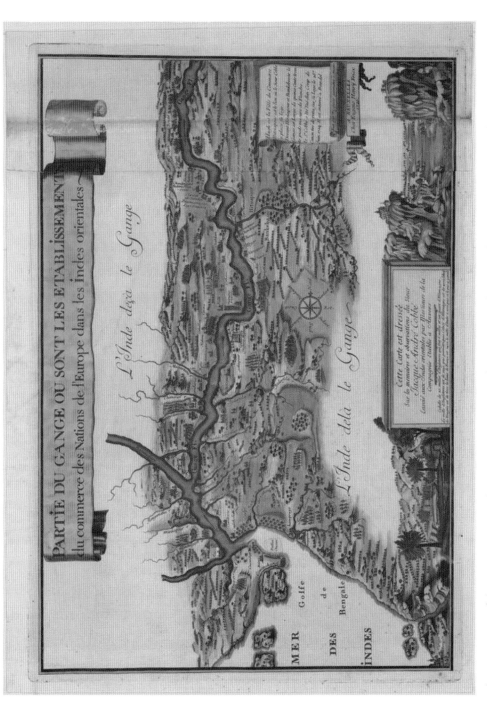

Plate 3 'Part of the Ganges River where European nations have their trade establishments in the East Indies', 1726. Courtesy of the Barry Lawrence Ruderman Map Collection, David Rumsey Map Center, Stanford Libraries, Stanford University, California (https://purl.stanford.edu/rx436fg4986). The Ganges and Hooghly rivers were an important centre of international trade. Calcutta, shown here just right of centre and recognizable by the square shape of Fort William, had not yet reached the prominence it would by the end of the eighteenth century.

Plate 4. 'Tellicherry', print by Gerard van der Gucht, 1736. Courtesy of Yale Center for British Art, Paul Mellon Collection, Yale University. Showing the EIC factory as Fergusson would have seen it in the 1730s.

On the Tops of their Terrasses Some of them build Small rooms with Cajans and a kind of Straw for the convenience of Sleeping cool, and of enjoying fresh air.

Of Cajans, and a kind of long Strong Straw, the Sides and ends of the Houses of the poorer Sort are [fasc. 8, f. 3r] built, and their roofs Slopping[1] are cover'd with a kind of Short rush or Hay, as the Small Hutts in Ireland or the Highlands of Scottland are thatch'd.

The Town is Surrounded with a Wall, built partly of brick, and partly only with pieces of hard earth or clay. Its circumference is about a Mile and half English. The Houses Stand close together, and their streets are Very Narrow, Very irregular and Very Nasty; all filth, and impurities being thrown from their houses into the Streets, which makes them Smell Very dissagreeably. Neither are they at all pav'd.

It [Mocha] stands close by the Sea Side upon a Dry Sandy ~~Desart~~ plain, which is extended all along by the Sea Shore I'm told for Some hundred Miles.[2] But this desart is bounded by high ground 25 or 30 Miles from the Sea, from which Hills they have all their grain fruits &.C. brought them.[3] [fasc. 8, f. 3v] In Short there is nothing to be Seen without the Walls but a Very Wild, dismal, barren desart, excepting only closs by them a few Date Trees, which are made to grow there with much ado. Here are likewise to be Seen no rivulets or Springs of Water, only there are about ¾ or ½ Mile from the Town 3 or 4 draw Wells by which the Place is Supplied with a Sorry kind of Saltish Water.[4] This is brought to Town upon asses, in Goat Skin Leather Vessels, they are Made by Sewing together the ~~Skin~~ intire Skin after it is dress'd, only leaving the Neck open by which they take in and empty the Water. Those Skins which hold 4, 5, or 6 Gall*on*s are Sold for a Camassie or penny the piece, an ass carries three or 4 of them, and a Man or Woman only one. These last employ'd in carrying of Water are Mostly Slaves from the Abbassine Coast.[5] [fasc. 8, f. 4r] They likewise bring water in Very Large leather Vessels, upon Camels.

However the Richer and Nicer people who can afford it, have all the Water they Drink brought them from Mosa Wells a place 20 Miles off; and this last Water is indeed Very good.[6]

The Climate exceeds Most others of the World in the Sultriness and excessive heat of the Weather, which when it is calm is almost intolerable; and especially when Warm gusts of Wind blow from Land, neither Man Nor beasts are able to breath but with Difficulty, however this happens but Seldom.

Here it rains but rarely, there having fallen No considerable rain except once for above 3 Months We were there. But 30 or 40 Miles Inland among the Hills I was told it rain'd

---

[1] Meaning sloping.

[2] The Tihamah coastal plain indeed extends almost the length of the western Arabian Peninsula, from the Gulf of Aqaba in the north to the Strait of Bab el-Mandeb in the south.

[3] These are the Haraz Mountians, known for fortified settlements, and the rich agricultural terraces hewn into the slopes where khat and coffee are commonly grown.

[4] This was a well-known problem in Mocha. Its water sources within the town proper were notoriously brackish, becoming sweeter the further away from the coast one travelled. To the east, outside of the gate of Bab al-Shadhili, was a neighbourhood where most residents would collect their daily water supplies. This is likely the location to which Fergusson refers. Water supplies were precious for Mocha and the town's defences also included these sources. See Um, *The Merchant Houses of Mocha*, pp. 116–17, 174.

[5] Meaning Abyssinia, now Ethiopia and the neighbouring coastal state of Eritrea.

[6] This could refer to Mawza', a small town and region inland from Mocha.

Very frequently, as [fasc. 8, f. 4v] it appear'd indeed by the blackness and cloudiness of the atmosphere from that Art.[1]

Here are ~~pretty~~ frequently Sudden Gusts of Wind resembling a Whirlwind, which tears up the sandy Desart, and Carries the Dust and Sand up into the air So as quite to obscure the Light, which I have More than once Seen, and am persuaded, that to Travellers there, it Must be Very Dismal, and sometimes fatal.

Here likewise I Saw at Several Times amazing flocks or Swarms of Locusts. These animals are Much resembling a ~~large~~ grassoper [sic], but larger, being about the thickness of ones Small finger.

They covered the Whole Heavens with a black Cloud for Many Miles farther than We could See. And from there [sic] flying all one way along, and being some hours [fasc. 8, f. 5r] before they pass'd, one Must Necessarly be persuaded that they extended a considerable Number of Miles. When these Vermin Sette [sic] on any fields of Corn, or fruits, they inevitably Destroy all that they cover, which makes the people at their approach have recourse to their prayers in order to have the Evil averted from them. And in Short from their Number and largeness of Size, they appear a Very Destructive Swarm.

I have been inform'd by these[2] Who have Seen it, that Sometimes it happens, that they are Driv'n by the Wind into the Sea, Where they float'd upon the Surface for Some Leagues, and omitted a Very Stinking putrid Stench. And it is reported that there once happened a plague Nigh the Head of the Red-Sea occasion'd by the putrid Steams from a Vast Number of those Locusts that were drown'd there.[3] Hence it appears that Locusts in [fasc. 8, f. 5v] these parts of the World are No Unusual plague.

There is one thing which I thought Worth the remarking, and that is That the Cocks here crow all Night long; but especially the first part of the Night, about 9, 10, and 11 o'clock they crow even More frequently than in the Morning, contrary to what happens with us in Britain.

The Native Arabians here are of a Brown or Tawny Colour, a kind of Medium betwixt the Whiteness of Europeans, and the blackness of the Western Inhabitants of Africk. Their Features are Human enough; But the Faces of the Better Sort of the Men appear Very Much to Disadvantage &, I think, diminutively, by reason of the excessive Largeness of their Turban, which buries their Head. [fasc. 8, f. 6r] The Dress of the Men consists of a pair of thin Breeches open and loose at the Knees, of a thin White Kind of Bannyan instead of a shirt with a large Wide and long Sleeves, which come all over their hands; Above this they have another Small Bannyan which lapps over on the fore part where it is keept fast by a Girdle; This Bannyan reaches down to the Midle of their Legs and is Made of Silk or courser cloth according to the abilities of the Wearer. Upon their Head they Wear a Very large Turban which is Much broader and made in another Shape than those of the Turks or other Mahometans. They Wear no Stockings, but on their feet they have a Slipper made of colour'd Leather.

---

[1] The Haraz mountains receive annual monsoonal rains from March to May and June to September, making the region an important agricultural centre. It seems that Fergusson meant 'part'.

[2] Fergusson has clearly written 'these' but meant 'those'.

[3] 18th-century medical science believed that some diseases were caused by vapours of bad air, known as miasmas or effluvia. For other instances where Fergusson makes similar remarks, see below, pp. 93, 121.

They Wear ~~Sticking~~ in their Girdle a short Dagger (or Jumbier as they Call it).[1] And in this and their [fasc. 8, f. 6v] girdle, the better sort are Very Nice, having them Curiously Made with Gold and Silver ornaments, But Many of the poorer have only a large common Knife sheath'd; For Men of all Ranks Wear a Jumbier or something under their Girdles in its Stead.

The Women Wear Drawers and a Bannian or Gown different from that of the Men. They likewise wear no Stockings but only Slippers. When they come abroad they are covered with a large Cloth which they Wear Much in the Same Manner that the older Women in Scotland wear their Plaids;[2] for it covers their head and all their body as far down as their Midlegs. And all of them except the Very poorest Sort, never appear abroad without being Veil'd with a thin kind of colour'd cloth through which they can See, but not be distin= [fasc. 8, f. 7r] =guish'd by others.

The common Coulys or Porters and others of the poor, I mean the Men, Wear nothing but a piece of course cloth wrapt round their loins and fastened betwixt their legs So as to cover their Nakedness, with a rag wrapt round their head instead of a Turban.

All the Arabs here have a Method of blacking the Cilia or edges of their Eyelids with some kind of black Dye.[3] I suppose as an addition to their beauty; and their Hands, and feet they rub with the juice of an Herb which Tinges them of a reddish or flesh colour, which juice they Say is of a Very cooling quality.[4]

Many of them have a Custom of hanging round the Necks of their Children Small packetts or pouches containing Scraps of the alcoran[5] & other Whimsical things, which they look upon as charms to preserve them from Evil.

[fasc. 8, f. 7v] This Town, which is a place of considerable Trade being the greatest and almost only Port on that part of the Arabian coast, is Subject to the Emâm or King of All that part of Arabia, whose Capital is Sinan or Sinam which lies 15 or 16 Days Journey to the North-East of Mocha.[6] Here [Mocha] is a Governor appointed by the Emâm who Superintends all affairs in the place without controull; but He is answerable to the Emâm for all his proceedings, and is deposed at his pleasure.[7] The Governor lives in a grand

---

[1] Or *janbiya*. These daggers are still worn today by men in Yemen. As Fergusson mentions, they also serve as a marker of social class, through the knife's handle and sheath. The best ones having handles made of rhinoceros horn or ivory and sheathes of precious metals.

[2] Fergusson is describing the *niqab* and comparing it with the *arisaid*, a traditional article of clothing worn by women in Scotland, which also covers the body head to toe.

[3] Kohl is an ancient eye cosmetic used to line and shape the eyelids. Its use is still popular across the Middle East, much of Africa, and South Asia. Part of the reason for its continued popularity in Islamic countries is its association with the Prophet Muhammad, who regularly wore kohl.

[4] Henna is the eponymous dye prepared from the flowering tree (*Lawsonia inermis*), which is used to colour the skin or hair, and dye cloth and leather. It is frequently used on the hands and feet to create delicate patterns for cosmetic and ceremonial purposes.

[5] Meaning the Quran, the holiest text of the Islamic faith. People would not wear 'scraps' of the book, but rather pieces of paper upon which a passage, or *sura*, from the Quran would be written. In other Islamic traditions entire miniature versions of the Quran or other holy texts are worn as talismans to ward off evil.

[6] Fergusson means Sana'a, the capital of Yemen. The ruling house of Yemen was the Qasimids, who ruled under the religious title of imam, as they were also the religious leaders of the Shia sect known as the Zaidiyyah. At the time of Fergusson's visit Yemen was ruled by Imam Al-Mansur al-Husayn II (1696–1748). He ruled during a period of economic transition that saw declining coffee exports to European markets, due to the crop being grown in ever greater quantities outside Yemen.

[7] Faqih Ahmad (born Yahya) Khazindar was governor of Mocha 1721–4 and again in 1730–37. While popular and well-regarded by contemporary Arab chroniclers, European sources depict the governor as a 'Tyrant', even

Enough Manner according to their Customs, all persons paying him Submission and Respect. But his Grandeur especially appears every Friday, when in the Morning all the Inhabitants of Note Wait upon Him to kiss his Hand and Show their respect. At Noon he Rides to Mosque[1] on [fasc. 8, f. 8r] a Horse richly furnish'd attended by Severals of the grandees well Mounted, and all the Military or Soldiers in arms in Number about 5 or 600 accompanying, who in like Manner conduct Him Back to his own House before which, there being a Large open place, all the foot Make Vollies, with their Small arms and file off; After which the Governor with the other Grandees on Horseback Show their Dexterity by pairs, in running, riding the ring in opposition, and exercising their lances which are Very long and unwieldy. This they continue for an hour or less as the Governor pleases, the Drums beating, and other Musick playing in the Mean time. Their Horses here Seem Very Nimble, and appear Very Sprightly and Well Shap'd in general, and the Horses furniture[2] is really grand enough, neither does it in any great Measure differ [fasc. 8, f. 8v] from the well accoutred furniture of our British Gentlemen, I mean in Shape or Manner of putting on.

Besides the Governor there are other officers commission'd by the King, who have considerable power independent of the Governor, tho' all of them are Subordinate to Him; As, the Kings Shroff[3] who collects the Revenues and pays the Military; the Merbâr[4] who superintends all affairs at the Seagate or that belong to the Shipping; the Captain of the Soldiers whose office is known from its Name; and other Inferiors of less Note.

There is here a large prison but of No Strenth. Any person being able to break through it if unfetter'd. But as Most of the Prisoners have their legs fetter'd with Strong Iron chains, and their [sic] being a guard of Soldiers to Watch it, the place answers its intention Well enough; [fasc. 9, f. 1r] Besides did they escape from prison, they could find no reception any Where but Must be unavoidably discovered. This prison they call the Hobbs.[5]

They seldom or Never, as I'm inform'd, punish any Crimes by Death; not even Murther itself; perpetual chains and imprisonment being the punishment; which to Me Seems Worse than Death by Many degrees. To the common people for Small crimes they Use bambooing, which is done by having them held fast down extended with their bellies on the ground, while one beats Severely their legs, Hips and Back with a large Cane or bamboo.

The Natural Disposition of the common Arabs Seems Somewhat insulting and abusive. For in Walking out, Europeans are apt to be justled or Mouth'd at, and

---

calling him 'Mocha's Nero', due to what they perceived as his arbitrary treatment towards European merchants. Khazindar's second tenure as governor came to an end when French warships bombarded Mocha in retaliation for being overcharged customs duties. See Um, *The Merchant Houses of Mocha*, pp. 68–76.

[1] Friday is the holiest day of the week in Islam and is marked by the *Jumu'ah*, or Friday sermon delivered at mosque during midday prayers.

[2] This is an archaic usage that means the trappings, or decorations attached to the bridle and saddle of mounts.

[3] Shroff is a derivative of the Arabic *ṣarrāf*, meaning treasurer or money changer.

[4] This is the Amīr al-baḥr, which was usually transliterated as mirbar and sometimes as meerbar. It combines the Arabic words for commander (*amīr*) with sea (*baḥr*) and is thought to be the origin for the word 'admiral'.

[5] Hobbs, or more accurately *habs*, is not the name of the prison, but rather the Arabic word for imprisonment. One reason for the lack of security or guards at the prison could be that more serious criminals were imprisoned on the island of Zayla', situated across the Gulf of Aden, now a part of Somalia. See Um, *The Merchant Houses of Mocha*, pp. 114–15.

frequently Stones or Dirt thrown at them by the Boys. But by [fasc. 9, f. 1v] people of Distinction those insults Seem no way to be countenanc'd but on the Contrar discourag'd. However in the Country I understand Travellers pass unmolested and without any Danger except in those parts that are frequented by the Wild Arabs.[1] These are a people who have Never Subjected themselves to any Government, but herd in flocks, and take what booty they can lay hold on.

The Religion of this people is Mahometan intirely in its Strictest form; This being Arabia Felix the Native Country of that Prophet as they call Him.[2] They are in general Very much bigotted or extravagantly fond of their Religion; And to this is owing that contempt they Show for those who differ from them; Especially the Jews are here much despis'd, tho there are Many families of them living together in a certain place without the Walls; because the Arabs won't Suffer them [fasc. 9, f. 2r] to inhabit among them.[3] These Jews here appear truly a Wretched people, and with Much ado they procure a Miserable livelyhood by doing all the Meanest and Most abject offices for the Arabs, Such as emptying their Necessary houses[4] & the like; Neither could I understand that there was among them one of any Substance, or above the lowest rank of Mortals.

The Christians however I find are more respected among them, tho' they reproach them for Many things; and in Religious Matters What they chiefly lay to their charge are these following particulars as I was inform'd by some Christians who understand their language and have liv'd and convers'd for some time among them. First they accuse the Christians for not believing in Mahomet seeing he was foretold and prophecy'd to come, by their own Prophet Jesus Christ, (as they alledge), tho' the prophecys they [fasc. 9, f. 2v] Say, have been eras'd and otherwise Vitiated by Christians.

Again they find much fault with the presumption of Christians in calling God their Father with other familiar appellations, which they esteem as a kind of Blasphemy against the Majesty and Greatness of God.[5]

But the strongest charge of all against the Christians, and that which they triumph Much in, looking upon it as that whereby the Religion of Mahomet has So Much that transcendent purity above the Christian and all other Religions, is, That the Christians have destroy'd the Unity of God, and perverted the True, Just, & Natural Ideas of the Supreme Being, By exalting other persons into an Equality with Him, or dividing the

---

[1] A common European reference for Bedouins into the 20th century.

[2] Arabia Felix, meaning 'Happy Arabia' is a Latin name for the Arabian Peninsula used in early modern English. The lush mountainous interior of Yemen lent itself to the image of the region as rich and fertile, hence 'happy'. The religion of Islam was founded in the early 7th century, when Muhammad, a merchant from the city of Mecca, received revelations from God. Islam spread rapidly across the region and North Africa, reaching as far as the Iberian Peninsula by 711.

[3] Judaism and Islam have a long, and at times tumultuous, relationship. Adherents of Judaism, along with Christians, are indeed accorded protected status under Islam due to their shared monotheistic faith and traditions descended from Abraham. However, even during the lifetime of the Prophet Muhammad, relations between the two communities could be strained. One of these periods of discord occurred in 1679, when Imam al-Mahdi Ahmed put into place his predecessor's plan to expel the long-standing Jewish community from Yemen. He exiled them to the small town of Mawza' situated on the dry Tihamah plain a day's travel from Mocha. Many died due to the harsh conditions of their forced journey. They were later allowed to return to their homes in Sana'a and elsewhere.

[4] Meaning privy.

[5] Indeed, as Fergusson is about to explain, for many Muslims the Christian doctrine of the Holy Trinity, with the existence of God in the Father, Son, and Holy Spirit, goes against Islamic ideas of monotheism.

Deity into Different Personages So that No Notions of Him can be form'd but Such as are confus'd and unsatisfying to the Mind, whereby the Most evident, the Most [fasc. 9, f. 3r] amiable and fundamental Truth of all Right Religion is Subverted and betray'd. These are the Most Material objections they Use against the Christians in General.

They are Very fond of Making proselytes to their Religion and lay hold of all opportunitys of that kind, as it appear'd in an Instance When I was there. For, three of the Companys[1] Soldiers Who among others had been Sent ashore for their health, not caring to go aboard again after they recovered, for some reason or other they apply'd to the Governor expressing their Willingness to be converted to the Mahometan Religion.[2] Upon which they were immediatly entertain'd, Shav'd and Dress'd in an Arabick Habit; and the Same Day underwent the initiating Ceremony of Circumcision. So precipitantly did they admitt, in less than one Day, these three into their Religion, lest by a longer conside= [fasc. 9, f. 3v] =ration they Should have altered their Minds.[3] And thus the Company lost three of their Men without being in the least able to recover them.

The Devout people among them are Very assiduous in reading the Alcoran and in praying. The Doors of their Mosques Stand allwise open Where the people go in as they have a Mind and perform their private Devotion, at which I have Seen Many of them, by looking in as I pass'd by at Some little Distance (for they wont admitt any Christians to enter their Mosques). This they perform by falling to their Knees, bowing down with their faces towards Mecca, and Muttering with Seeming Devotion. One thing commendable among them is the assiduity and Diligence of their Muftis who Say prayers in the Mosques publickly several times a Day;[4] and by themselves or other church Servantts from the Steeple of their Mosques call aloud [fasc. 9, f. 4r] exhorting the People to Mind the Hours of prayer, this they do both Night and Day.[5] And their yearly Income as I'm inform'd is Scarce Sufficient to afford them a Very Sorry Maintenance, tho' all of them live exceedingly temperate & Mean. They are in their ordinary habit no Ways different from other Men. Neither do they here, (as I'm inform'd) intermedle at all in Worldly affairs; but Spend their Life in the Exercises of Devotion, and an abstemious Retirement, which I think is a course Very Agreable to their office; And happy had it been for other parts of the World, if Priests of another Denomination, had So carefully

[1] Referring to the EIC. The soldiers' desertion is confirmed in the Mocha Factory records. Their desertion may not have bothered the *Britannia*, considering that, whilst in Mocha, Captain Frognall referred to the 39 soldiers aboard as 'extraordinary mutinous & troublesome' (BL: IOR G/17/2, Goodwin and Frognall to Benyou, 20 January 1736, p. 336v; ibid., Goodwin to Board of Directors, 15 August 1736, p. 352r).

[2] Turning renegade was relatively common in the late medieval and early modern periods. Many Europeans are known to have converted to Islam and served Muslim rulers. Shipboard conditions for sailors and soldiers and the opportunities for advancement in their adoptive lands likely played a role for the men Fergusson describes.

[3] Religiously, conversion to Islam is a relatively simple process. One must recite the *Shahada*, often translated as 'the testimony', which is a declaration of belief in the oneness of God and in Muhammad as his prophet. It is one of the 5 Pillars of Islam that the faithful must practise, along with praying five times a day, the giving of alms (*zakat*), fasting during the holy month of Ramadan, and performing the Hajj religious pilgrimage to Mecca, should one have the means to do so. Fergusson mentions most of these practices in the following pages.

[4] Fergusson is a little confused on the titles and roles within Islamic societies. What he is describing here is an imam. Perhaps his confusion stems from the use of the title of imam by the rulers of the Qasimid dynasty. Nonetheless, a mufti is a legal jurist who rules on religious matters as they relate to the law.

[5] Before being replaced by speakers and recordings, five times each day muezzins would announce the call to prayer from atop mosques' minarets, which Fergusson calls a steeple.

pursued this Innocent Manner of Life, So Suitable to the Character of Those Who have devoted themselves to the offices of Religion: They had certainly thereby done More Honour to the Religion they proffess'd and made their own Characters More Valuable with Men. [fasc. 9, f. 4v]

Tho' by the Alcoran all Mussulmen are prohibited to drink Wine, Yet I find in this Many of them at times do not fear to transgress, tho' they are liable to be Severely fin'd and otherwise punish'd by the Secular power When discovered to be guilty of this offence.[1] Of this there happened an Instance when I was at Mocha. For, One who being acquainted at our Factory, happened to come there one Night While we were drinking a botle of Wine after Supper, and He being desired to sitt down join'd with us by taking a glass in his Turn, as he had frequently done before. But some one or other who was not his Friend getting Notice thereof acquainted the Governor who fin'd him in 500 Dollars which is above 120 £ Sterling.[2]

Nevertheless there have been Governors here who More than once [fasc. 9, f. 5r] have Ventur'd to gett drunk with Wine at the English and other European Factories without Notice being taken of it.

They carry that point of Hospitality to a great lenth, which teaches people to offer no Insults to Those that are in their own Houses. For, 'tis reported, that they Will not allow any, not the greatest criminals to be assaulted in their own Houses. But the Method in these cases when an offender takes Sanctuary at Home, is to putt a guard Upon the House so as not to allow any Water or provisions to be carried in, by which effectual Means the Criminal is soon [fasc. 9, f. 5v] forc'd to deliver Himself up. And relating to this there happened an Instance where the English Factors were concerned, whilst I was at that Place. It was this; One who had listed Himself in the Companys Service as a Soldier for Bombay, aboard of our Ship, and who all along had pass'd for an Italian, a few Days after our arrival at Mocha, understanding the Arabian Language, discovered Himself to one of the Arab fisherman who came aboard to Sell fish, as a Musselman who had been taken captive by the Spaniards, and Now Wanted to be reliev'd So that He might live among those of His own religion. The Case in the Sequel appear'd So as he represented it Viz That he was in a Turkish Galley taken by the Spaniards from whom he [fasc. 9, f. 6r] Made His escape to England, where he listed in the East India company's Service, in Hopes by that Means to gett into Some Mahometan Country again.[3]

The Governor being inform'd of this by the Fisherman, immediatly Sent to the English chief & Captain, desiring they Might allow that Mussulman that was aboard to come ashore. The Chief represented, that this Man had cost the Company considerable expences, and that tho' he was a Mussulman, he might enjoy his own religion as Many others in the Companys service. This was all in Vain, for the Governor Without delay

---

[1] Fergusson is referring here to the government. However, in many Islamic countries political and religious authority were inseparable. The title of Yemen's ruler, imam, offers a clear example of this. In many Muslim countries the consumption of alcohol by members of the faith remains a criminal offence.

[2] If this is true, it is an astronomical sum of roughly £14,200 in 2017 figures, *TNA*, 'Currency Converter: 1270–2017'. Available at <https://www.nationalarchives.gov.uk/currency-converter/>. Dollars here refers to the Spanish dollar, a major 18th-century Indian Ocean trade currency.

[3] The mutual raiding, capture, and enslavement of each other's shipping and people by Christian European and Muslim powers of the Mediterranean was a common practice dating from the medieval era, ending only in the first decades of the 19th century.

sent another Message thus. That He would immediatly order the Factory Gates to be Shutt up by a guard, if they did not give orders for relieving the Mussulman, which accordingly was done; He however promising to repay his Expences. [fasc. 9, f. 6v] By this Instance We See their regard for those of the Same faith.

I forgott to Mark another considerable objection which they use against the Christians with Much Triumph and contempt, and which is owing to their Ignorance of that in comprehensible [*sic*] Doctrine of the Trinity which is Such a Stumbling Block to Human Understanding. They Say, it is impious and absurd to affirm, That God is capable of having Sons, or of joining Himself in any Measure to Human Nature; This they Say is degrading the Supreme Being in a Very gross Manner. But with Those of the Romish Religion[1] they have still a greater Quarrell for their Worshipping of Images; by which Means they Rob God of his Due by applying His adoration to Such Sensless things.

Here as in most Countrys intirely Mahometan are no Hogs, this being forbid to be eat; tho' in this as in drinking of Wine, the Gentlemen among [fasc. 9, f. 7r] them don't Scruple Sometimes to transgress. By this it appears they are Not so bigotted in general to the Ceremonial part of their religion as is imagin'd.

The Manner of paying their Submissive respect to their great ones is by kissing their Hands. And some of the Meaner Sort who are Not allow'd this Honour fall down and kiss the Couch where on their Grandee Sitts.

The ordinary Method of Salutation among equals of the Men is by grasping each others Hand which they Mutually Stoop to kiss. Women of the better Sort are but Seldom seen abroad and then allwise cover'd up and Veil'd; but the Common sort are oblig'd to come abroad often for the Necessitys of a Livelihood, and they [fasc. 9, f. 7v] except the Very poorest, are allwise Veil'd.

Here are an incredible Number of Poor or Beggars by profession. These are a Race propagated from father to Children who live by begging; for the Children of Beggars allwise follow the profession of their forefathers, looking upon it as reproachfull or Irreligious to do otherwise. They go about the Streets & call aloud for charity for Godsake; And there is atleast[2] a considerable show of Charity among the better Sort of People, for Many of them Night and Morning allow a Number of small loaves of bread to be distributed among the poor.[3] And twice a Day before the Governors House there are Some Hundreds of poor gathered together to recieve Bread by the Governors appointment.

Besides those Poor that belong [fasc. 9, f. 8r] to particular parts, there are a Vast Number of Itinerant Beggars called Fuquiers who Wander all their Life from place to place begging their Sustenance.[4] Of these a Vast Number were at Mocha alitle before we left it, who had come down from the Hodge, as it is called.[5] This Hodge is the pilgrimage to Mecca the Native place of Mahomet, which Most part of Mussulmen look upon themselves as oblig'd to perform once in their Life; But Many especially the Fuquiers and other Enthusiasts of this religion go Much oftner. Those of India go thither by Sea to

[1] Catholics.

[2] Fergusson runs these words together throughout his text.

[3] See above, p. 84, n. 3.

[4] More commonly fakir, the word is derived from the Arabic *faqr*, meaning poverty, and was used to describe travelling Sufi Muslim ascetics who lived on alms they collected.

[5] See above, p. 84, n. 3.

Judda which is a Sea port town up the redsea and but 30 Miles Distant from Mecca.[1] Thither Europeans and others from India drive an advantagious Trade; For I find the Pilgrims dont Scruple to Mind the affairs both of the Next and this World at the Same occasion, Seeing [fasc. 9, f. 8v] Many of them, I'm told, bring sums of Mony with them in order to purchase Goods for their Home Trade, so that this Hodge May be look'd upon as a Very great Fare for the Body as well as the Soul.

At Judda by reason of its Vicinity to Mecca the People are Vastly abusive to Christians who trade there; and by the Mobb a few Years ago, all the Christians they found ashore Were Murthered; purely from suspicion of their having Maltreated a Mussulman aboard of their ship.[2] And upon this account it is that they Seldom dare to Stir from their Houses for fear of Insults from the Rabble. Besides, Should any but Mussulmen be found Nigh that Gate which leads to Mecca they would run the Most imminent hazard of their lives. This I am well inform'd of from Many Who have been more than once there.[3] How absurd it is, and how Much to be deplored! That these Systems of [fasc. 9, f. 9r] Religion, who pretend So Much to purify the Minds of Man and to exalt the practice of all the Moral Virtues above what the Religion of Nature of itself could do, Should Yet have Such direfull effects as to corrupt the Minds of Men in Many Cases, by banishing from them the Most Sociable and amiable Virtues of Humanity & Hospitality, and filling them with Enmity and Cruel Hatred against all those Who happen to be of a Different persuasion from theirs! So truly May the Poets Lamentation when Surveying the terrible effects of ambition and avarice, be apply'd here to Religion[:]

Quid non Mortalia pectora Cogis? Religio![4]

[1] Jeddah was the primary gateway to Mecca during the age of sail, as it lies just 41 miles from the holy city. Due to the pilgrimage traffic, the port established itself early on as a centre for Red Sea trade. It remains one of the Arabian peninsula's largest seaports.

[2] The incident to which Fergusson refers occurred midday on 6 June 1727, when an incensed mob broke into the home of two British supercargoes, killing them and five of their guests, while at dinner. Arab fishermen had discovered two bodies lying on a sandy islet, near to where a British ship lay, and soon rumours spread throughout Jeddah that Muslim lascars were murdered aboard the EIC ship, which had just arrived from the Malabar Coast. Angry locals demanded investigations into the deaths of their co-religionists. Ottoman governor Ebubekir Pasha discovered that the lascars died of natural causes and were buried with due ceremony on the small island, which was too rocky to dig deep into. As a result, a rising tide washed away the sand covering the bodies, leaving them exposed. The Pasha was satisfied with this explanation and told the British that if other Muslims died aboard their ships that their corpses ought to be brought ashore to be buried properly. The British agreed; however, when another Muslim lascar died and his body was brought ashore, a mob formed around the corpse and rumour spread that it showed signs of beatings, broken bones and other abuses. Again demanding retribution, the mob took the body to the Pasha who was unable to calm the crowd, who attacked the British in their residence and carried away all their valuables as retribution. The Ottoman government of Jeddah apologized for the incident and paid restitution to the EIC (Firminger, 'The Massacre of Jiddah', 158–9).

[3] According to *surah* 9:28 of the Quran, polytheists are forbidden from approaching the Masjid al-Haram, or Sacred Mosque in Mecca, which surrounds the Kaaba, Islam's holiest site. While there has been theological debate as to the exact meaning of what constitutes polytheism, generally it is accepted historically and today, that it is forbidden for non-Muslims to enter the holy cities of Mecca and Medina. It is unsure if Fergusson is referring to Muslims or Christian Europeans when writing about those 'Who have been More than once there', as European Christians were known to attempt to reach these forbidden cities. The best-known of these was Victorian adventurer Richard Francis Burton, who wrote about his travels in his three-volume *Pilgrimage to El-Medinah and Meccah*.

[4] Fergusson is paraphrasing from Virgil's *Aeneid*. A version of the full quotation and translation is: '*Quid non mortalia pectora cogis Auri sacra fames*!' 'Cursed Avarice, on what desperate Wickedness thy Influence drives the Minds of Men!' Fergusson's response to this is 'Religion!' Virgil, *The Works of Virgil*, I, p. 305.

In Mocha besides the Native Arabs live Many Abbasines, and Bannians from India.[1] These first came from the opposite coast of Africa, and are a people of larger Stature & Much blacker in colour than the Arabians. Of these the Governor [fasc. 9, f. 9v] and others I'm told haves [sic] Most of their Whores or Concubines. The reason of this I guess is, that they are much easier procur'd, being to be bought for a Very Small Sum, or because they are generally of a better Stature and features than the Arabian Women. Many of the Abbassines both Men and Women come over I'm told Voluntary in order to Work for their bread, rather than live in their own country, Where, 'tis reported, they are at continual Wars and Quarrells one Small tribe with another.[2] These Abbasines, I'm told are generally Very barbarous and inhuman. No Strangers dare Venture to land on their coast; for fear of being immediatly [sic] destroy'd: as it happened lately to a Small French ship, and another Tranquie with Bannians,[3] who were cast away upon the Coast, for those that gott ashore in the Boats and Wreck, all except a Very few who found Means to escape [fasc. 9, f. 10r] were kill'd by the Natives.

These People have a Very Strange and particularly odd custom, as is credibly affirm'd, tho' it appears so base and Whimsical as not to be easily believ'd. It is this, When they are at War and have kill'd or taken Captive any of their Enemy, they cutt from them their privitys which they carry home and present to their Wives. These are after being prepar'd by Drying, hung round their Womens Necks in a String and there Wore for an ornament. He being in greatest Esteem among his companions whose wife is adorn'd with the greatest Number of Such Jewells & This is confirm'd by those who were Sav'd of the above Wreck, for venturing again ashore, to find their companions they saw some of them lying dead with their privities cutt off.[4]

However this be, the features and Looks of the Men are somewhat fierce and Cruel, tho' the Women are comely enough according to their complexion which is exquisitely black.

The Banians from India residing at Mocha are to the Number of 3 or 4000. They carry on the greatest part of the Trade of this place. And all the Kinds of Curi= [fasc. 9, f. 10v] =ous Mechanicks are of this People, by which it would appear that the Arabians are a

[1] In the Indian Ocean trading-world, the Bania, (also Banya) are members of a Hindu and Jain occupational caste, famous as merchants, moneylenders, and brokers. Throughout the late 17th and 18th centuries, they provided the bulk of the financial capital behind both Asian and European trade across the Indian Ocean.

[2] Various competing dynasties, not tribes, vied for power in Ethiopia during the 18th century, most famously during the *Zamana Masafent*, or 'Age of the Princes'. The power of the monarchy was destabilized through regicide, rebellion, and a series of rapid successions to the throne, which led to the rise of local warlords, eclipsing the power of the monarchy.

[3] A *tranki* is a dhow-like type of boat used most commonly in pearl diving, the name derives from *trankeh*, the Arabic name for the pearl diver's net bag.

[4] Historically Ethiopia was a source for eunuchs who served many Islamic imperial courts throughout the medieval and early modern periods. It was well-known that Ethiopian armies engaged in the genital mutilation of their slain and wounded enemies on the battlefield. However, it seems that Fergusson's story of presenting mutilated genitals to wives to adorn themselves with is an embellishment, as other Europeans who were actually present at the Ethiopian court had other explanations of what happened to the war trophies. For example, Remedius Prutky, a Czech Franciscan who was vice-prefect of a mission to Ethiopia in the mid-18th century also mentioned this practice, stating that the trophies were carried back to the emperor to be presented as evidence of the number of slain enemies. See Arrowsmith-Brown, *Prutky's Travels to Ethiopia*, p. 151. Scotsman James Bruce also recorded witnessing the practice and subsequent trophy ceremony in the Ethiopian court at the end of the century (*Travels to Discover the Source of the Nile*, IV, pp. 176–8).

people of No great Industry or application else they Would Not allow the Most beneficial Trade of their Country to be enhanc'd by Strangers. However The Governor from Time to time finds occasion to Squeeze from them large Sums of Money at his pleasure;[1] Neither are any of them allow'd to Send away any of their Money or effects, or to go away themselves without paying a considerable Toll according to their abilities.

The Bannians are Not allow'd to bring their Wifes along with them from India; or possibly the reason they do Not, is for fear the Governor and others Should take them to themselves. Tho' in this I should think there is not great Danger, Seeing the Arabs will not upon any acc*oun*tt offer any Violence to one in his own House, not even to the greatest Criminal, but besett the house and Starve him till they comes [*sic*] out.

[fasc. 10, f. 1r] I should have observ'd that the Arabs like most of the Eastern People, use much Perfumes of all kinds of fragrant Spicy Plants & Woods by Way of Fumigation, inspersion, Irroration[2] &.C. in which the Rich are Sometimes at incredible Expence by consuming Quantities of Agalloch wood, spikenard, ambergrease and other perfumes of great Value, in their fumigations.[3] Whilst at the Same time Rose Water and other Liquors impregnated with fragrant ingredients are plentifully and daily us'd in order to Sprinkle upon their Hands faces and cloths; of all which I have frequently shar'd, when upon any occasion I happened to go to their Houses. For there The Serv*an*tts, when any Stranger comes allways bring in a chofing Dish[4] of perfumes to place in the room, and another Small one of Silver or the like, which is given into our bosoms in order to perfume Our cloths;[5] and at going [fasc. 10, f. 1v] away we have Rose Water from a Curiously made flask pour'd upon our Handkerchiefs and into our Hands that we may Sprinkle our faces therewith.[6] These Customs appear well adapted to these Hot Countries, where from Such profuse Perspiration or Sweating, disagreeable Smells must Necessarily [*sic*] be Occasioned, especially when Several people are together in a closs Room. And hence we easily percieve the reason of the frequent Washings which are us'd by all the Eastern Nations of whatever Religion; which least certainly contributes much to their Health;

---

[1] While the Bania were not the only group of foreigners subjected to Governor Khazindar's exactions, as a community they were traditionally called upon to provide loans to the Yemeni government, which were rarely repaid. They were also required to pay a poll tax whilst resident in Yemen and had to pay fees upon arrival and departure from Mocha, and occasionally violence was used to exact additional sums from them. Their community in Mocha is not thought to have been as large as Fergusson estimates, instead numbering only 200–700 throughout the 1700s. Only in the rarest of circumstances did Banian traders settle with their wives and families. See Um, *The Merchant Houses of Mocha*, pp. 70–71, 164–7.

[2] Meaning to sprinkle and to spray, respectively.

[3] Agalloch wood, also agar or aloe wood (*Aquilaria malaccensis*), is a tree native to South East Asia which, when infected with a mould, produces a dense dark resin in the wood that offers a distinctive fragrance when burned. Spikenard (*Nardostachys jatamansi*), from the Himalayan regions of India, China, and Nepal, is prized for its roots which are crushed to produce an essential oil, used in Ayurvedic medicine and across the ancient Mediterranean as an essential perfume ingredient. Ambergris is produced in the digestive tract of sperm whales and is highly valued in the perfume trade as both a scent and fixative.

[4] Fergusson means chafing dish.

[5] This is likely referring to the *mabkhara*, the Arabian vessel in which incense is burned using charcoal. It remains a custom across the Arabian Peninsula that specially blended and prepared fragrances, known as *bakhoor*, are burned and passed amongst guests as a gesture of hospitality.

[6] These, known as *qum qum* in Arabic, are found across the Islamic world and still in use today. They stand upright, are usually crafted of chased silver and have a bulbous base and long vertical spout, through which rose or orange water is sprinkled.

And therefore it is, no doubt, that frequent Washings of the Body are enjoin'd by the Mahometan Religion as well as by the Numerous Sects of the Pagan.[1]

The goods exported from Mocha are chiefly Coffee of which Several thousand Tons are Sent to Europe, & different Ports in Persia, India &.C.[2] Some Drugs as Olibanum or Frank= [fasc. 10, f. 2r] =Incense, Myrrh, Dragons Blood[,] Aloes Succotrina, Jeera, Balm of Gilead & ~~probably~~ a few others.[3] They recieve [sic] from Europe few Goods. A very litle thin cloth, some Glass & Cutlery ware, & a few other Trinkets are the Chief. But from India Several Sorts of Cotton cloth & Silks &.C. The Coffee is all brought from Betelfukee a town about 100 Miles from Mocha where the great market for all the Coffee is held.[4] It is carrid [sic] on Camels Backs to Mocha. Each Camel carrying 2 Bales of about 250 lb Each. It is very remarkable the Docility & Patience of labour in these Animals. For in coming to our Factory Door 50 or 60 at a time, they kneel down and deliver their load, and after it is taken off, they gett up & go on in order till all of them are unloaded.

These creatures Seem perfectly adapted to be Beasts of Burden in Such a country & Climate as this of Arabia Where the Excessive Heat in these [fasc. 10, f. 2v] Sandy Desarts, and the Scarcity of Water & Provender requires animals like Them that can bear both Hunger & Thirst longer than any others.

Tho' all the Sea Cost [sic] adjoining to Mocha is quite a barren Sand as has been before observ'd, Yet on going in to their Herb & Fruit Market in a Morning, you See Such a profusion, of Fruit, Herbs & Flowers as to make you believe the Country really deserv'd the appellation it has of Arabia Feelix, in spite of the Desart Barren appearance it has wherever you cast your Eyes in the Neighbourhood of the Town. For here you see Grapes, Peaches Apricots Quinces Almonds all in abundance & to be purchas'd at an easy rate, as are their Pott Herbs sallads & Flowers for perfuming & adorning their Rooms.

All these come from beyond the [fasc. 10, f. 3r] Hills that lye about 20 or 25 miles from the Sea Coast, where the ground is good, & where they have frequent Showers.[5] There is also to be gott Beef, Mutton & Poultry at reasonable Rates. The Beef is indifferent but the Mutton is Fatt & good. The Sheep here have most remarkable large Tails round & thick, So as to weigh as Much as one of the Quarters, being a lump of Fatt that is Sweet like marrow. The Tails of many of Them are So heavy & Unwieldy as to trail on the

---

[1] This is a reference to the many Gujarati Hindu and Jain merchants present in Mocha at the time.

[2] Mocha was at this time the world's primary port for coffee, exporting an estimated 12,000–15,000 tons annually during the 18th century. The Dutch were the largest European purchaser of Mocha coffee until 1726, when they developed their own production in Java. Throughout the remainder of the 18th century, the British were the main coffee exporters at Mocha. See Tuchscherer, 'Coffee in the Red Sea Area', pp. 54–6.

[3] Dragon's Blood is the common name given to three different species of plants producing a deep red resin used for dyeing or medicinal applications. Historically throughout the Mediterranean and Indian Ocean regions the species used was *Dracaena cinnabari* and later *D. draco*. The former is native to the Socotra archipelago and the latter to Morocco and the Canary Islands. Fergusson is also referring to the common aloe plant (*Aloe socotrina*) and cumin by its Hindi name *jeera*. Balm of Gilead is a fragrant, resinous medicinal gum made from the *Commiphora gileadensis* tree, commonly found in southern Arabia.

[4] The town of Bayt al-Faqih (archaic Betelfaguy), is the most famous of the three coffee-growing regions of Yemen. The coffee from here commanded a better market price and was thus more sought after. As one French merchant related in 1709: 'It was in our Power, when we were at *Aden*, to have loaded ourselves with *Coffee* of *Sanaa* and *Galbany*, which were are pretty near at hand: But they are not so much esteem'd or enquir'd after, as those of Betelfaguy' (italics in original, La Roque, *A Voyage to Arabia Felix*, p. 102).

[5] The Haraz Mountains, today containing Yemen's third largest city Ta'izz. It is still the region's foremost agricultural area.

ground, which obliges their Owners often to make Small wooden or Bamboo Carriages to Support the Tails from trailing on the ground & hurting them.[1]

I was frequently desir'd by the Arabians to give advice in their Diseases, which at first I did willingly and undertook the Cure of Several of the better Sort, particularly of the Merbaar[2] or High Admiral Judge of all matters relating to Sea affairs. [fasc. 10, f. 3v] He had long labour'd under a Chronical Disorder, which in 4 or 5 weeks I cur'd by a Mercurial alterative Course.[3] I often had the honour of drinking Coffee with Him when he Sate in Judgement on his Sopha or Scaffold cover'd with a fine Carpet under the Arch at the Seagate when every Arab that pass'd kneeld & kiss'd the Place he Sate on; and my Sitting thus with Him in State procur'd me much Respect from the Natives; and I hop'd also after I had cur'd Him to have been handsomely rewarded. But on my going with my Interpreter to take leave after he was quite cur'd; all the Return I had was that he honour'd me and allways Should with the Name of his Friend.[4] I desir'd My Linguist to tell him that the Medicines I had us'd were expensive, and the attendance and care I was putt to requir'd Some other Sort of acknowledgement; But He plainly told me he darst not tell Him what I Said for fear of Severe punishment. This and other Instances made me decline all business of this Sort; which also was dangerous in case of miscarriage.

[fasc. 10, f. 4r] **Monday, Aug*ust*: 16, 1736.** We Sailed from Mocha, and having a tolerable passage we came to an anchor a few Miles from Bombay road the 6th of Sept*ember* following. Here we were Surpris'd by an order from the Gov*ernor* and Council prohibiting us from coming into the road, until we clear'd ourselves from a Report that had been Spread at Bombay of our having the Plague aboard of us.[5] But a Declaration being drawn up and Sign'd by the Principal officers affirming our Ships Company all to a Man being in health, nor one dead in the Passage, And the Same being confirmed by the Chief of Mocha that was aboard of us; we were Soon cleared from all Suspicion and admitted into the Road, the 8th of Sept*ember*.

Bombay is a Small Island intirely belonging to the Crown of Britain, Situated near the Continent in 19 Deg*rees* North Latt*itude*.[6] Here is a Very large and Strong built Fort Situated [fasc. 10, f. 4v] closs by the Sea on that Side of the Island that looks toward the

---

[1] The tail fat from sheep, called *allyah*, was a staple in Arab and Persian cooking. The sizes of sheep's tails were often commented upon by foreign travellers, the earliest known being Herodotus, who also noted that 'little trucks' were placed under the tails (Rawlinson, *History of Herodotus*, II, pp. 415–16).

[2] According to VOC records, an unnamed *amir al-bahr* was replaced in early July 1736, by a new one, recorded only as Suleyman. However, Fergusson is not clear when or whom exactly he treated. I am grateful to Nancy Um for her assistance and the reference for this information (National Archives of the Netherlands, The Hague, Dag Register, VOC 2415 Amsterdam kamer, entries for 4 July 1736 and 1 November 1737).

[3] Fergusson's vague reference to 'Chronical Disorder' and the use of a mercurial treatment suggest the High Admiral Judge suffered from syphilis. See Wilson, 'Exposing the Secret Disease', pp. 74–6.

[4] Foreign doctors, especially Europeans, were often sought after by Yemeni officials during this period. Their services were usually well-rewarded, either directly with trade commodities, through commercial perquisites, or other benefits for their trading companies. See Um, 'Foreign Doctors', pp. 278–80.

[5] Indeed, Bombay officials had heard the plague 'was raging' at Jeddah and had struck Mocha and that some of the *Britannia*'s 'Company were very sick and a great many dead'. As Fergusson states, the following day they were cleared to approach Bombay (BL: IOR L/MAR/B/285BB, entry for 7 September 1736).

[6] Prior to European entrance into the Indian Ocean, Bombay was one of seven islands that were sparsely inhabited under the Gujarat Sultanate. In the early 1500s, the islands were ceded to the Portuguese, who gave Bombay to the British as part of Catherine of Braganza's dowry when she wed King Charles II in 1661.

Figure 6.   'The English Fort of Bombay', etching by an unknown artist, 1703. Courtesy of NMM, Greenwich, London. Bombay Castle was the seat of the EIC in western India and did not change much in appearance from the beginning of the century, when this image was produced, to when Fergusson visited some thirty years later. What was different was that by the time of Fergusson's arrival a substantial settlement had grown up around the fort.

Continent, at the back of which Stands the Town.[1] That part inhabited by Europeans to the Southward; and that by Natives and others to the Northward. The Limits of the Town are of considerable Extent, and Surrounded by a well built Strong Stone wall with many large bastions, except towards the Sea where the fort and other Small ramparts command that part. The Circumference of the Walls I Suppose is ~~about~~ betwixt 2 and 3 Miles. The Houses of all the Europeans are exceeding low consisting only of one ground Story. And all of them have a large projecting Shade or Virando paved below.[2] This Serves to keep off the Water in the rain time,[3] and in hott weather it is a fine cool shade to Walk under. Their Houses are Situated in no regular order, every one building according to his

[1] The fort is Bombay Castle, the headquarters of the EIC for western India and the Arabian Sea, and seat of the Governors in Council. During Fergusson's visit the President of Bombay was John Horne, who was in office 1734–9.

[2] Veranda entered English through the Hindustani and Bengali words *varaṇḍā* and *bārāṇḍā*, respectively.

[3] Bombay is subject to a monsoon season from June to September each year.

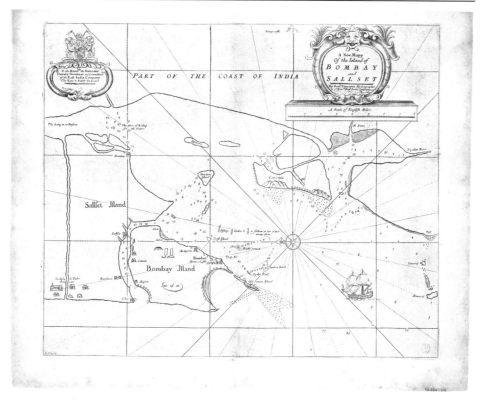

Figure 7. 'A New Mapp of the Island of Bombay and Sallset', engraving by Samuel Thornton, 1734. Courtesy of NMM, Greenwich, London. When Fergusson visited Bombay, it was a small settlement and fort at the south-eastern tip of its eponymous island. The Portuguese occupied the neighbouring northern island of Salsette, until it was taken in 1737 by the Marathas (Sivajis).

own humour their [sic] being plenty of room. Every house has a garden adjoining [fasc. 10, f. 5r] it, with rows of Trees on all Sides that cover and overshade it, which indeed Serve to keep off the rays of the Sun, but likewise keep off the cool breezes; and Serve Very Much to harbour the Musquettos and other troublesome Insects.[1] Their rooms Within look Very Well, being exceedingly Neat plaister'd, and pav'd with a kind of Mortar which looks like one Uniform piece of Marble; and the furnishing of Most that I Saw is Very Neat and genteel. Here they Use No glass in their Windows, but instead thereof a kind of Shell that is wash'd in, in plenty by the Sea. It is cutt into Small Square bitts of 2 or 3 Inches. Its colour is Somewhat like Mother of Pearl, and transmitts the

---

[1] Bombay was an infamously unhealthy island for Europeans. One visitor in the 1750s wrote, 'for as fast as Recruits came from Britain, they died in Bombay' (Cope, *A New History of the East-Indies*, p. 255). Mosquito-borne diseases were the likely culprits for high European mortality. Malaria, meaning 'bad air', was the name originally given to what was thought to be illness due to miasma, or the unhealthy tropical humid atmosphere. Contemporary accounts credited high death rates in Bombay to the 'unwholesome vapour' created by fertilizing coconut palms by covering their roots with a mixture of dung and small fish called 'buckshoe' (Grose, *A Voyage to the East Indies*, I, pp. 30–31; Hamilton, *A New Account of the East-Indies*, I, p. 181).

light tolerably well, but intirely excludes the Sun Shine; Upon which accountt it is preferred to glass, or any other lattice Work.[1]

The Black Town consists of Much Smaller Houses, but built contiguous and regularly Situated So as to form Several long Streets.[2] Here live Many Small [fasc. 10, f. 5v] Merchants, Shopkeepers; Artificers[3] and others, all asiaticks [sic]. And contiguous to the walls without live incredible Multitudes of People of the poorer sort.

The Island of Bombay is said to be one of the Most populous Spotts probably in the Whole World.[4] This I imagine is chiefly owing to its Situation and government; For all religions are allow'd off, and the Neighbouring parts being Subject to Many petty Princes, who are constantly at War with another, makes it impossible for the People to live with out Much trouble and oppression, which determines Many to Seek an asylum Here, where if industrious, they will easily find a livelihood.[5] And this I guess, is the Reason why So Many of the Ancient Sect of the Persee live here;[6] because their own Country in general having embrac'd the Religion of Mahomet; Those who Still adhere to ~~ancient~~ that of the ancient Persian Magi, find it troublesome to enjoy their Religion at Home with freedom.

[fasc. 10, f. 6r] Another probable Reason why So Many People flock to Bombay, is that as the British are oblig'd to concern themselves in the Quarrells of these petty Princes, Those of their Enemies who are disgusted at Home fly here for protection or out of Resentment. Those princes adjacent to Bombay are chiefly the Suviaja, the two Angrias, the Sangarian, the Sedi &.C.[7] One of the Angrias and the Sedi are our allys, and the rest

[1] Window screens of nacre, or the inner lining of the shells of molluscs, particularly the windowpane oyster (*Placuna placenta*), were common throughout the west coast of India. It has the same colour as mother of pearl, because it is a thinner version of the same product. Its use was frequently commented upon by European travellers, including French navigator François Pyrard, who visited the region a century earlier (Gray and Bell, eds, *The Voyages of François Pyrard*, II, pp. 15, 63).

[2] The 'Blacktown' of Bombay was an area designated for Indian settlement to the north of Bombay Castle. It is now known as the Borabazar Precinct of Mumbai, located at the northern end of Fort district.

[3] A skilled craftsman or artisan.

[4] Estimating population figures for the early modern period is notoriously difficult, and Fergusson gives no specific numbers. He is clearly impressed with the number of people, but it surely was not the most populous place in India, let alone the world. Robert Cowan, who governed Bombay 1729–34, estimated there to be 30,000–40,000, living on the island, of whom only 900 or so were Europeans (Barendse, *Arabian Seas*, I, pp. 424–6). By comparison, one contemporary estimated nearby Surat's population in 1704 to be 200,000 (Hamilton, *A New Account of the East-Indies*, I, p. 147).

[5] Indeed, during the early 18th century Bombay's population was soaring as it supplanted Surat as the principal trading entrepôt in western India. Fergusson is correct that the political situation on the Indian mainland was fraught with war and conflict, mainly the result of the Maratha (Sivajis) and Mughal Empires, who were war with one another.

[6] The Parsis are adherents of the Zoroastrian religion whose community originated in what is today Iran. A large group migrated to western India following the Arab invasion of Persia in AD 650. The community was initially attracted in large numbers to Bombay in the early 1730s for employment in the EIC's shipbuilding industry. Their population continued to grow throughout the 1700s, as Parsis entered a variety of occupations, becoming one of the city's largest merchant and business communities. See White, 'Parsis in the Commercial World', p. 187.

[7] 'Suviaja', also commonly Suvaji, were contemporary European variations for referring to the Maratha Empire (1674–1818), stemming from the name of Shivaji Bhonsle (d. 1680), the founder, and first Chhatrapati (king), of the Marathas. The Marathas successfully challenged Mughal authority and by 1707, had established their independence over a large swathe of western India, with their capital in Pune. The empire was ruled through local notables (*deshmukhs*), who controlled regions (*paganas*), levying tribute and supplying troops to the

our Enemies. All these are Revolters from the great Mogul, and daily Strive to encroach upon the Dominions of their Neighbours in order to encrease their own.[1] The Sedi alone pretends the greatest Submission to the Mogul & is called the Moguls admiral. Upon *whi*ch account we are oblig'd to protect him from Angria and the Suviaja which cost is much, the powerfullest, and the greatest Enemy to the Mogul. And by Him[2] Angria is protected, He calling Angria his admiral, because Angrias country being Situated near the Sea Coasts is more convenient for Shipping; And of all the other Indian [fasc. 10, f. 6v] Princes he is much the powefullest at Sea; and of late is become formidable to Europeans, having taken many of their Ships with rich cargos as well as exceeding many Moremen's Ships, their allys.[3] The Minority of the present Mogul and his remoteness from these parts encourages these Revolters in their usurpations whilst either want of power, bad conduct, or private views hinder us from putting a stop to their proceedings which so much stagnate the present Trade of Bombay and partly of all India.[4] Neither will the just policy of Trade allow the East India Company to make a peace with Angria and the rest, which might be attended with Some advantages; but would inevitably ruin their trade at Surat and other places Subject to the great Mogul.[5] So that there appears No proper remedy in the Case but power Sufficient to incapacitate Them from doing Mischief at Sea, which one would think Should be No hard thing to be effected. But the

---

chhatrapati, and later the *peshwa*, or head minister. Thus, there were varying degrees of local autonomy under the suzerainty of central Maratha authority, an Indian political formulation Europeans did not always understand (Gordon, *The Marathas*, pp. 34–5). The two Angrias Fergusson refers to were Maratha *deshmukhs* who controlled territories along the Konkan Coast. Manaji Angria ruled the north from *c*.1733 until his death in 1759. Fearing being overpowered by his half-brothers Sambhoji and Tulaji, who successively ruled the south, Manaji, as Fergusson notes, nominally aligned himself with Bombay, despite all the Angrias operating under the same Maratha fealty (Elliott and Prange, 'Beyond Piracy', pp. 107–9). The Siddi were regional potentates, meaning monarchs and rulers. Mughal sovereignty at the time was fragmenting allowing several local dynasties to appear. Siddi power was centred around the coastal fortress of Jangira, and in the early 18th century they were the maritime arm of Mughal authority. The Sangarians, or Shankadhors, were a loosely formed polity based in the ports of Dwarka and Beyt in the Gulf of Kutch.

[1] Fergusson is describing the period of the Mughal successor states. Regional powers exercised increasing autonomy in the wake of Emperor Aurangzeb's death in 1707 and subsequent successional crises, which saw 6 emperors enthroned over the next 12 years. This permanently reduced Mughal central authority.

[2] Fergusson means Shivaji. At the time, the chhatrapati was Shahu Bhosale (1682–1749), who greatly expanded Maratha territory across India by the time of his death.

[3] By 'Moremen's Ships' Fergusson is likely referring to 'country ships', or vessels owned and operated by Asian traders, some of which were protected by Angria, and others which were seized, depending on the ever-evolving political situation. In December 1735, Sambhoji Angria made the most lucrative capture of a ship in their history, taking the EIC's *Derby* along with its crew, £32,000 in cash and other valuable cargo (Anon., *A Faithful Narrative*, pp. 55–6). Indeed, Angria was likely fresh in the minds of the crew of the *Britannia*, as they learned of the 'unwelcome' news of the *Derby*'s capture while in Mocha (BL: IOR L/MAR/B/285BB, entry for 5 May 1736).

[4] The Mughal Emperor at the time of Fergusson's voyages was Muhammad Shah (r. 1719–48). Coming to the throne at 17 years of age, he was a patron of the arts and is generally viewed as an effective ruler. However, he reigned over a period of precipitous decline due to growing Maratha power and continued incursions. This weakened state attracted foreign invaders, such as Nadir Shah (1688–1747) from neighbouring Persia, who infamously invaded and sacked Delhi in 1739, from which the Mughals never recovered.

[5] Local powers, including Bombay, vied for sovereignty over regional maritime trade, which was articulated by the pass, also known as *dastask* (Hindustani) or *cartaz* (Portuguese), which permitted, or forbade, merchant access to particular ports. Failure to produce a pass or carrying the pass of the enemy could result in the seizure of a ship, its crew, and cargo. See Elliott 'The Politics of Capture', pp. 190–91.

European Governors probably fix'd their account in the Trades[,] being thus obstructed[,] by which with the Companys arm'd Ships they are able to convoy their own [trading vessels].

[fasc. 10, f. 7r] On the North End of the Island of Bombay is another Small Fort which commands these parts. Here the Governor has a pleasant Country Seat. It is called Meum.[1] And indeed the whole Island has a pleasant enough aspect; being either covered with Paddy grounds or Trees especially coco Nutt. The last is probably of the most extensive use of any one Tree or Plant in Nature. And Those who have been at pains to observe them, I have heard recount, an incredible Number of Usefull things made from it; a few of which are worth the Noticing. From the Branches is Daily extracted a great quantity of Juice, which drank without preparation is pleasant & Nourishing. And by fermenting, it makes a Liquor called Toddy of the Strenth of Small beer, from which they distill great Quantitys of a spirituous Liquor called by Europeans Pariar arrack[2] wherewith the Natives and common Soldiers and Sailors gott often drunk. And of this, more Nicely prepar'd is made [fasc. 10, f. 7v] the Goa Arrack; and in a great Measure the Batavia.[3] In Short I know no Spirituous Liquor of the product of India or us'd by the Natives, but that which is the product of this Tree, except Paddy & Sugar may sometimes be us'd. The Nutts which they bear in great plenty, contain in their Cavities a large Quantity of a Milky Liquor of a pleasant taste reckoned very wholesome, as also their cavitie is lined with a thick Kernal of a Sweet pleasant taste resembling an almond, which is reckoned Nourishing if eat [sic] moderately; But if in large quantity, burthensome to the Stomach by reason of the great quantity of oil they Contain. And of oil these Nutts yield the greatest Plenty, which is known to be of extensive use. Besides round the outer Shell of the Nutt when ripe, grows a great deal of a Tough fibrous Substance, which answers all the uses of Hemp. For of it are made all their Strongest cables & rops [sic] large and Small, besides some Coarse cloths for parti= [fasc. 10, f. 8r] =cular uses. The toughness of this is incredible, far exceeding that of Hemp. There are many other lesser necessitys Supply'd by this tree, not considering these it has in common with others, but it is needless to enumerate them. In Short the Usefullness of these Trees is plain from this, that those on the Island of Bombay which are all farm'd out bring to the Company a greater revenue than any other branch of Customs that they have; I mean without cutting down.[4]

On Bombay I saw a very particular kind of Tree, which is large and remarkable for this, Viz From Several of its Branches Sprout forth roots which grow perpendicular towards the ground with their Shaggy fibrous extremitys, without any leaves but exactly

[1] The original fortress at Mahim was built under Gujarati control of the island in the 14th century. What remains of the present structure, however, dates from the British period in the late 17th century. It was one of many defensive structures, along with Worli, Sion, and Riwa fortresses, built to defend the northern island from Portuguese and Maratha attacks.

[2] Meaning Pariah-arrack, or rather, 'low-caste' or 'untouchable' liquor. This was an extremely cheap, potent, and even dangerous alcohol commonly sold to European sailors and soldiers.

[3] Batavia arrack is a type of rum originating in Java made from sugar-cane molasses and fermented rice.

[4] This is probably not true. Even if it was, it would not last for much longer. The year after Fergusson's visit, the EIC ordered 3,200 coconut palms cut down to improve their line of sight in nervous preparation for a Maratha invasion of Bombay that never materialized. The Marathas had just driven the Portuguese off the neighbouring island of Salsette, and Bombay feared they might be next (Mumbai, The Maharashtra State Archives: Bombay Public Department Diaries, 10, Consultation of 4 April 1737, n. p.).

resembling a root tore out of the ground, and clear'd from the adherent Earth.[1] These enter the ground and after rooting deep those emitt fresh stocks from them, which grow up to large Trees.

[fasc. 10, f. 8v] On Bombay live a great many of the Gentou Religion, which ~~is~~ Seems to be the most antient of any in India; and is yet Strictly adher'd to by far the greatest Number of the People. Altho' the Mahometan Religion Seems to make great Progress over all India; partly by the Industry of its propogators, [sic] and because it is a receptacle for all those of the Different Sects of the Gentou, who upon Some Delinquency forfeit their Cast, to which it is not easie for Them to be again return'd, without much Expence and trouble. And another Reason why this Religion Seems to be much embrac'd is because it is That of the Great Mogul and of all those princes over which he has an Immediate Influence. So that in those Countries the Gentou Religion Seems to decline Much; But in these remoter [parts] on the coasts of India it still flourishes and has more [fasc. 10, f. 9r] numerous adherents than the Mahometan.

The Antiquity of the Gentou Religion is Certainly very great; as appears evidently from Many Circumstances. For it Seems to exceed all their Records and Traditions, of which they have Some of Very long Standing. Besides those are many of their Pagoda's (which is the name for their Place of Public worship) of some thousand years standing. And I saw a very remarkable one of this kind at Tullycherry built mostly of Brass in a very curious tho' antique manner, which is reported to be above 2 thousand years old.[2] The Pagoda itself was not large. But it was surrounded with an [sic] high Stone wall of considerable extent which Seem'd to bear plain marks of its age; from the Stones being blown or wasted almost quite away in many Places; and in other Parts it was overgrown almost with Earth, Shrubs and grass.

Within the wall adjoining on End of [fasc. 10, f. 9v] the Pagoda was a large Tank or pool of considerable Extent, with Stairs at Several places, by which they go down to Bath. All within the outer wall is esteem'd Sacred neither must any of a Different Religion Presume to enter thither. Within the Limits of some of these Pagoda's which are of greatest antiquity, and held in greatest esteem; or rather in the Pagodas themselves, are conceal'd immense Riches, by the Princes and others who have Much Money and a great deal of Devotion. They bury it under ground, and the Place where it is putt is known only to a few; So that it must Sometimes happen that great Quantities of Gold and Silver are forever lost.[3] The Sums Said to be in Some of them are indeed incredible. And I was told by an English officer who had been assisting one of their Princes at war against another, That from one Pagoda, for fear of its being Surpris'd [fasc. 10, f. 10r] by the Enemy, was remov'd as much gold as loaded Ten Elephants. An immense Sum! if we consider how much one of these animals is able to carry. However, I'm told that it but Seldom happens that the Victors ever are So prophane [sic] as to rifle the Pagoda's of the vanquish'd, except they be of a Different Cast or Sect, even tho' they are persuaded that there are immense

---

[1] This is the banyan tree (*Ficus benghalensis*). Ubiquitous across South Asia, it is the national tree of the Republic of India.

[2] In what is now called Thalassery, the Thiruvangad Sree Ramaswami temple, dedicated to Ram one of the incarnations of Vishnu, has copper sheeting on its roof giving it its colloquial name, the Brass Pagoda. Its exact age is unknown, though records date it to at least AD 826.

[3] Indeed, this has happened. In 2011, a hidden treasure of unknown provenance valued as high as £811 billion was discovered in the vaults of Sree Padmanabhaswamy temple in Thiruvananthapuram, India.

Riches contain'd within them. So great Influence has the Principles of their Religion over those we call Pagans, as to putt a Stop to their Rage, and what is more to their Love of Money; for which they Seem ready to Sacrifice every Moral principle upon all occasions, and every other consideration except their religion to which they are addicted in a very Strong manner.

It were impossible almost for one to give credit to the accounts given of the Stupendous Instances of the force of Enthusiasm in many of this Religion; did not daily examples remove all grounds of doubting of [fasc. 10, f. 10v] their Truth. These Miraculous Examples of Patience and resolution are occasion'd by religious Vows which many of them make upon Some account or other. e.g. Some Shut their Hands in the usual way by folding their fingers into the Palm, and vow never again to open it while they live, which they so religiously observe that the Nails of their fingers pierce thro' betwixt the Bones of their palm, and are Seen growing thro' the Back of their Hands, which it is plain must at first occasion exceeding great pain in So tender and Sensible a part. Others extend their arm and vow never to alter its posture, others hold it up; others Vow never to Shut their fingers; by which means in Time all these joints turn immovable; and they become thereby Subject to a Natural necessity of keeping their vow. Some looking up, vow never more to look down, others[1] [fasc. 11, f. 1r] Others bending down their Heads towards the ground, vow never more to look upwards, of all these & many More There are daily Examples to be Seen. And it is observable, that all the Devotees of this kind are held in much respect, and are look'd upon as holy men, which possibly is one great reason which determines Many to enter upon Such Vows, and which enables them to Undergo them with So much resolution. Another of these kinds of Religious Vows I can't help mentioning by reason of its Singularity, and its being pretty common as I'm told, It is this. Some Men take upon their Vows of perpetual continency, and in order to testify their Veracity & Sincerity, or it may be to enable them to the effectual performance of their Vow, they have a very large Iron ring putt through the opposite Sides of their foreskin, and the two ends of the ring rivetted [*sic*] together, which indeed next to St [fasc. 11, f. 1v] St Origens Method, or Castration, Seems to be the most effectual prohibition of their Enjoyments that way.[2] These People go quite Naked without the least covering, by which means the Proof of their continence is conspicuous to all. These likewise are held in more than ordinary esteem by the religious People; and their Persons are look'd upon as Sacred, and Undefil'd. Upon which account they imagine there is Some Virtue in them, but especially in the confin'd Member, for curing of particular Diseases. And, what to Me is a litle [*sic*] Strange, I'm told, The women more especially have an extrodinary Esteem for these Devotees whom they often Visit, & look upon it as a great happiness when they can kiss and hug the brïdled Member; and after handling it, they touch over their Eyes ~~with~~ thinking its efficacy is great for the Diseases of this organ; or probably [fasc. 11, f. 2r] from another Motive, Viz that they may be thereby influenc'd or assisted to the Practice of the Same Self denying Virtue. But this last is but conjecture; and 'tis possible curiosity is the

---

[1] Fergusson has followed, unusually for his style, the common 18th century practice of writing the first word on the following page at the bottom of the preceding one. He will employ this occasionally throughout the remainder of the text.

[2] Origen (*c*.184–*c*.253) was an early Christian theologian and scholar who was rumoured to have castrated himself over a misinterpretation of Biblical verse.

greatest motive of any. There are Many other Strange Customs to which People of this religion are addicted; which denote how Strongly they are devoted thereto, and to what Pitch Enthusiasm of any kind in any Religion will carry Men. For Some of these People take upon them incredible Pilgrimages on foot to Some Noted and remote Pagoda's: Some from the farthest distant Parts will go to the Ganges in order to bring with them a flask of that Water, which is held among Many as Something Sacred. Upon which account botles [*sic*] of the Ganges Water in some parts is Sold for great Value, providing they are assured of its being genuine.

Upon the Malabar Coast in a particular District, they celebrate [fasc. 11, f. 2v] the anniversary of Some remarkable Saint in a very odd Manner. For it Seems this Saint was ~~putt~~ upon Some occasion or other putt to the Torture by having a hook putt through his back whereby he was hoisted and Swung round for Some time.[1] Upon which account Those who have a great Veneration for his memory, on such an [*sic*] Yearly Day after other Ceremonies and oblations, have a Machine built, by which they have themselves hook'd up by the back and turn'd round in the Same Manner. Many of these Examples are to be Seen in one Day, for they hire for Money Severals to Undergo this which be no ordinary torture. Seeing the hook is putt thro' So much of the flesh of their back as is necessary to bear their Weight; tho' it Sometimes happens that the part gives way and they drop down So as they break Some of their bones, they being hoisted up so very high. [fasc. 11, f. 3r] But what is most to be admired in this affair is the Seeming cheerfulness and gaiety they Mantain [*sic*] while they are thus Suspended; For I am told by those who have More than once Seen the Ceremony, that they who undergo this, continue all the time Singing Some cheerful Song, and brandishing a Sword which they hold in their Hand. This I Imagine they do in Imitation of their Saint, who probably Suffered after the Same cheerful Manner.

These foregoing Examples, I think, may Serve to Show, that The resolute and Patient Sufferings of Enthusiasts Should be of No force to demonstrate the Truth or Divinity of any Religion whatever; Seeing we find that the Bigotted professors of the worst Religions are fully as capable of Showing Miraculous Influences in this way, as those of the Very Best Religion. So Strange is the force of Enthu= [fasc. 11, f. 3v] =siasm of whatever Stamp, that when deep rooted it Seems to occupy of itself the ~~whole~~ intire [*sic*] command of the Mind, having either all the passions and affections there of blindly Subservient to its Dictates, or those that Seem most averse to its Extrevagancies [*sic*] So over power'd and extinguish'd, as not to be able to resist or contradict its Influences over the Human Mind. And as all the Passions or affections of Men are apt to be extravagant and Petulant in themselves, when not under the Direction of Reason; So this Strange affection of Enthusiasm in Religious Matters, having for its objects Those things that are reckoned to be above the reach or without the Compass of Human Reason, and consequently determining its Votaries to Disregard or Despise the Wholesome admonitions of Reason,

[1] Hook-swinging was a widespread devotional practice amongst Hindus in South Asia. The ceremonies held different origin-stories and varied according to region. All of them, however, were associated with the veneration of particular deities, not saints, as Fergusson understood. The practice in South India is historically associated with veneration of the goddess Kali, who is often represented holding a sword. Devotees in South India were thus, usually swung while also holding a sword. European travellers almost always commented upon the practice and often held it up as one of the 'strange' or 'barbarous' customs of India. See Oddie, *Popular Religion, Elites and Reform*, p. 7.

leads Mankind wheresoever the fortuitous impulses of Such an unaccountable, blind, and Enormous Passion determines Them.

[fasc. 11, f. 4r] Hence we find what contradictory and inconsistent actions Men commit thro' the Influences of Enthusiasm. The World, yea, all parts of it are pregnant with terrible Influences of the direfull effects of this Monstrous Passion; Neither need we go So far as the remote parts of India in order to be convinc'd of this.

Christians, tho' pretending to a More rational Religion than these blind Pagans, have I'm afraid, been as much Subject to this Irrational Passion or affection of Mind, and have done & daily do as Monstrous, inhuman, & inconsistent Actions as the most Ignorant of the Pagans; Witness the Cruelty and Barbarity exercis'd towards one another, for Some trifling differences in the Ceremonial part of Faith; the Indignities and Barbarities committed upon their own Bodies from whimsical and ridiculous Motives; the Childish, Stupid and inconsistent Forms as well as objects of their Worship. I mean those of Images[,] Relicts &.C. All which [fasc. 11, f. 4v] discover as much Barbarity, Ignorance & Stupidity, as Those Actions or Ceremonies of the Despis'd Blind Pagans. So true it is that Blind Enthusiasm or Bigotry makes dreadfull ravage in the Best Religions, as well as in the best naturally dispos'd Minds, once they have blindly given themselves up to its Dictates, by renouncing the Plain and wholesome Directions of Calm Reason which is the genuine Governess of our Minds, and ought to be the Sole examiner of ~~all~~ our Thoughts and Directrix of all our actions. How inconsistent it is for Creatures who derive all their Excellence from Reason, thus industriously to renounce her, and establish another Mistress in their Souls. By So doing they evidently cease to be Reasonable Beings, and in justice Should be regarded as Such who are divested of the Use of Reason; and were it possible, ought to be dispos'd of (in order [fasc. 11, f. 5r] to prevent ~~harm to Society~~ their doing harm to themselves and others) as in all well regulated Societys, Mad men of another kind are. But this Madness is too Universal and of too Serious a Nature I'm afraid, to be thus treated, however much in itself it may deserve it.

These are reflections which every unprejudic'd Man can't help making, when he Surveys with Some attention the effects of blind Enthusiasm. But to return to our account of this people.

Among all the Customs of the Gentous, there is none I admire or approve more than their abstaining to Eat animal food of any kind.[1] This is Strictly observ'd by all those of the Superior and most esteem'd Casts, they looking upon it as inhuman and injust [*sic*] to take away the Lives of any Creatures who do us no harm, but more especially of those from [fasc. 11, f. 5v] whom alive we reap many benefits and advantages as, Cows especially and a few others. For Say they, Nature has Supply'd us abundantly of wholesome Nourishing food from the fruits of the Earth, & from the Milk of animals; So that we are Under no necessity of taking away the Lives of others to Save our own.

This reasoning, in my opinion, carries no Small weight with it. For I own, I cannot See what Title we have or necessity, for butchering So many of our fellow Creatures, Seeing we can be plentifully and more wholesomely nourish'd, by vegetable food.

Of all the animals the Cow kind are most valued by the Gentous; And they carry this So far that the Cows are Said to be worshipped by many of them. But I could find no authentick proofs of this kind; and if there be any Such custom of paying adoration to

---

[1] Fergusson is referring to the vegetarianism practised by many Hindus.

this animal, I believe it [fasc. 11, f. 6r] is only among a few of the Most ignorant and of the meanest or lowest Casts.[1] The reason for their valuing this kind of animal Most is from the consideration of its extensive Use. For with them they till their ground where they Sow their Cotton for their Clothing, & their rice and other grain for Sustenance; And from them they have the most part of their best Milk from which they make their finest butter. So that it appears by means of this animal both their clothing & food is principally procur'd. And those are the very Reasons I have heard Several Sensible People among them give for their regarding this animal So Much; But they utterly denied that they in any manner worshiped it, tho' they Said, it might be Some of the poor Ignorant people among them thro' Mistake might fall into that way.

[fasc. 11, f. 6v] Besides this the Gentous Show their Regard for animals by their feeding many of them whom they think they are neglected or Seemingly want food; Thus at Mocha where there are vast Numbers of Dogs, and but little Sustenance for them, The richer Banians who reside there allot [sic] a Certain quantity of loaves to be distributed among the Dogs daily. And I have Seen a Banians Servantt [sic] with a Baskett [sic] of Small loaves, and Some Scores of Dogs attending him, until he had distributed them all. They are in like manner carefull [sic] of the Birds and fowls by throwing out on the Tops of their Houses grain and the like for them.

Thus it appears that the Gentou Religion teaches its Followers Charity of a More Extensive and disinterested kind, than is commonly observ'd by the greatest part of Mankind of a Different Religion.

[fasc. 11, f. 7r] **Thursday Sept*ember* 30th 1736[.]** We weigh'd Anchor from Bombay and arriv'd in Tully Cherry[2] road the 12th of Oct*obe*r [see Plate 4]. Tully Cherry is a Settlement belonging to the English Company, upon the Malabaar [sic] Coast in [   ] Deg*ree* N*orth* Lat*itude*.[3] The fort is Situated upon a Small ridge or Rising ground hard by the Sea Shore, and has for its garrison in ordinary about 100 Soldiers; But at the time I was there, above 250 or Near 300 Soldiers belonging to it. This increase of their Number was occasioned by Wars they were engag'd in. Upon acc*ou*ntt of the Prince of the contiguous Country[4] with whom they drive[5] all their Pepper Trade. For His Country being invaded by a Neighbouring Nation called the Cannary's,[6] who had overrun and taken possession of the Greatest part of it, whereby the Trade was obstructed; and the

---

[1] Hindus do not worship the cow. However, it is considered a sacred animal as a symbol of life that is associated with Aditi, the mother of the gods in the Vedas.

[2] Now Thallassery. This region of the Malabar Coast was a major centre for the pepper trade, attracting foreign merchants and powerful local rulers. Tellicherry itself was established as a trade factory by the EIC in 1683. Construction of a fort followed in 1708. Fergusson interchanges his spelling of the town, sometimes following the more common contemporary practice of writing the city's name as one word, or here as two. At the time of his visit Stephen Law was the chief of council and was engaging in a complicated series of treaties with regional rulers, resulting in the British receiving the most favourable terms of trade amongst rival European powers.

[3] Fergusson has left a wide space here before his contraction 'Deg:N.Lattd', presumably intending to return and fill in the coordinates for Tellicherry at a later date.

[4] This was Udaya Varman (d. 1746), a prince regent of Kolathunadu, a kingdom neighbouring Tellicherry.

[5] Fergusson clearly meant derive.

[6] Or rather, the Canarese, meaning people from Canara, a kingdom in the predominately Kannada-speaking region in what today is the Indian state of Karnataka. In 1732, they invaded and seized most of the rich coastal territory of Kolathunadu.

Prince their Friend refus'd to allow them to trade any longer, unless they as= [fasc. 11, f. 7v] =sisted Him to expel these his Enemies.[1] Upon these accounts the English with the assistance of a few Dutch belonging to a Neighbouring garrison,[2] were oblig'd to take the field; and tho' in all they did not exceed 500 Men, they engag'd and defeated 10000 of the Enemies foot and 6000 Horse, and 6 or 8 Elephants, killing Some thousands of them.[3] This may appear Somewhat Strange, and the more if we consider What indifferent Men the Company have for Soldiers in India, besides there [sic] being enervated by the climate and bad Diet. But our wonder Ceases when we on the other hand consider the Quality and Disposition of their adversarys; for their Horse will not Stand the Fire, & upon them all their Hopes are built. Again tho' Some of the foot have firelocks,[4] yet they know not that greatest part are arm'd only with Lances, Scimiters [sic] and the like; and those who have firearms, [fasc. 11, f. 8r] know Nothing of that Method and order of arrangement and firing in Platoons; But discharge their Pieces without order of time or Place, So that they become an easy Prey to those who are under better regulation, and who by keeping in a closs body, and firing in regular Platoons Secure themselves from the irregular assaults of their adversarys, the greatest part of whom are not capable of hurting them at any Small distance; And it was observ'd by Some of the chief among the Captives, That the Method of the Europeans fighting intirely astonish'd them; for they expecting to fall upon them after their first firing was over; they were immediately Surpris'd to be intercepted by another, and another, and So on without end, contrary to what they had ever experienc'd before.

And indeed their warlike preparations for their Small army which was to Sett out again from Tully=cherry[5] [fasc. 11, f. 8v] in a Day or two, did not alitle Surprise me. For there was ready to be carried with them above a Dozen of field pieces of Six pounders, and 2 or 3 Larger, with a considerable Number of Smaller ones, all fitted with exceeding convenient

---

[1] It is unclear where Fergusson received his information as the British records tell a slightly different story. The EIC factors at Tellicherry cautiously observed the progress of the invasion. They grew increasingly alarmed as their main European rivals, the French, allied with the Canarese in an attempt to push them out of the region's lucrative pepper trade. By early 1736, the situation was untenable, and the British entered into a treaty of friendship with Udaya Varman and expelled the Canarese and, with them, their trade concessions to the French. The cost to Kolathunadu was high, however, as the prince carried the burden of British expense, which indebted him to the EIC. The victory and alliance were initial steps in ultimately securing British hegemony along the Malabar Coast by the end of the century (Nair, *Records of Fort St George*, IV, pp. 66–7).

[2] The garrison was stationed at St Angelo Fort, which was built 1505–7 by the Portuguese and captured by the VOC in 1663. It stands outside the port of Kannur (formerly Cannanore) 13 miles to the north of Thallassery.

[3] Fergusson is certainly using exaggerated figures. The battle he refers to is the taking of the fortress of Cadalay, near Kannur, on 1 April 1736. The Canarese General Gopaljee had positioned himself there with the aim of taking the neighbouring Dutch Fort St Angelo. According to Bombay's report of the battle, the enemy's forces of 'about four hundred Horse, all their Foot, whose Number we are Uncertain of, & three Elephants' were met with a combined allied force of about 300 soldiers under the British, 300 under the Dutch, along with 6,000 Indian troops, supported by EIC ships and marine forces to soften the defences. The Canarese were finally expelled from the fortress after a gruelling 6 hours of pitched battle (Nair, *Records of Fort St George*, IV, pp. 107–9).

[4] Firelock refers to firearms that contain a lock, a firing mechanism that is used to strike and ignite powder to propel the ball through the barrel of the gun. In Fergusson's day the flintlock was predominant.

[5] Fergusson hyphenates Tellycherry, though he placed the last half of the word on the same page, likely as an afterthought.

carriages. Besides those, there were Machines called chevre defrizes[1] contrived to keep off the Horse from falling in upon them at an Unawares, with other preparations, which Show'd in my opinion much Conduct and Industry in the Managers. And their Success [in] the foregoing Campaign was very great and unexpected, having taken all the Fortified Places that the Enemy possess'd, excepting only one on the frontiers, which they were then going to attack. The Last of these, which they had taken and demolish'd I saw; it being a few Miles distant from Tully Cherry.[2] This was a very strong fort, and contain'd 8 or 10 thousand men. Yet with [fasc. 12, f. 1r] their Small army, they block'd them up; and when their general opened the gates and was forcing out his army, The Europeans advanc'd and fir'd so constantly that the Very gates were so chock'd up with dead bodies that None could possibly gett out; So that they were oblig'd to Surrender at Discretion.[3] Yet tho' the English Commander design'd to Save all the Captives, The Naïrs[4] or Subjects of the Prince the ally of the English, a great many of whom attended the Army, falling upon them with their Scimitars and Lances, massacred all they could have power over; So in tolerate [sic] seem'd they against those who had endeavoured to Subdue their Country, that had they not been prevented, there would not one of the Captives been left alive.[5] This Much of their wars, may help to lett us know, the Conduct & Courage of these people in Warlike Matters.

[fasc. 12, f. 1v] And from these late Examples we may be taught, not to admire and extoll so much the Exploits of Alexander the Great, and others who with a hand full of well Disciplin'd Men, overcame Such Numerous armies of those who were undisciplin'd in the true Arts of war. For nothing is more Certain and plain from many Instances, that knowledge and conduct in military affairs infinitly [sic] more contributes to Success, than the Bare Number or Strenth [sic] of Men. And I am well assured, from what I myself have observ'd of these Eastern people, and More especially from What I have heard from others who had the best opportunitys of knowing, that Ten Thousand Europeans of the regular Standing forces, providing they could endure the heat and other Inconveniences of the [fasc. 12, f. 2r] Climate, would be Sufficient too oververrun [sic] and Conquer the greatest part of the Moguls Dominions, atleast those that lie to the Southward, which are Very populous and of great Extent.[6]

The People round Tully Cherry for a Considerable Extent are Subject to their own Prince, whose Ancestors for a long Date, I'm told, Were Kings of that Country, and

---

[1] Meaning the *cheval de frise*, or Frisian horse, which was an anti-cavalry obstacle composed of wooden or iron spikes attached to a frame, used to block enemy advancement.

[2] This is Cadalay Fortress. Fergusson goes on to narrate the battle, which he likely heard about from soldiers garrisoned in Tellicherry.

[3] Indeed, according to EIC records, twice the Canarese tried to surrender by hoisting 'a Flag of Truce'. However, the lack of coordination among forces made it impossible to stop the battle (Nair, *Records of Fort St George*, IV, p. 111).

[4] Nairs (also Nayars) are a diverse family of matrilineal caste groups in Kerala, traditionally associated with the military and landownership.

[5] The Canarese had been waging a war of attrition along the Malabar Coast for years, and it seems that the Nairs took the opportunity to offer no mercy to their enemies. The governor of Tellicherry, Stephen Law, wrote to his superiors in Bombay following the taking of Cadalay that 'we cannot sufficiently express our detestation at the Barbarity of the Nairs exercised even on Women and Children' (ibid, p. 75).

[6] Fergusson would be proven correct within his lifetime. In 1757, EIC troops under Robert Clive, with the help of local allies, defeated the forces of Bengali Nawab Siraj ud-Daulah at the Battle of Plassey, thus becoming, for the first time, major territorial powers in India.

Never acknowledged any Subjection to the Mogul, except once when forc'd to a Verbal Submission by the approach of a Numerous Army against them.[1]

Tho' I find there has been considerable Provinces or Portions of his Small kingdom dismembred [sic] from the rest, by the Invasions of his Neighbours, and Some again reunited; they being almost constantly at Variance one with another, endeavouring to watch all [fasc. 12, f. 2v] opportunitys of taking advantage, So that they might extend their own and lessen the Dominions of their Neighbours; A Custom we find peculiar to all Princes, and Potentates in all ages and Countries.[2]

In this Country their Nobility, or Great ones are distinguish'd, by their carrying in their Hand a drawn Scimitar, tho' in nothing else do they Seem to differ from the Rest.

The Braminy's here, I observ'd, did wear a white Large thread round their Neck, which hung over their Shoulder and upon their breast.[3]

The Dress of their Women in this Country is different from that I have observ'd in other parts of India; For here they have only a cloth which is wrap'd round their lower waste which covers them down to their legs; but their breasts, Belly, & all the rest of their body is Naked.[4] [fasc. 12, f. 3r] This appearence [sic] in Girls or Young Women is not So disagreeable [sic]; but in the old or those that are big with Child it appear'd to me No pleasant Sight. The Contrary fashion to this, appears in the Habit of the Natives at Bombay; for there the women are mostly covered from the Neck down to their thighs, which of the Common Sort of People are intirely bare; they having only a piece of cloth which goes betwixt them, and is fastened closs to their girdle or belt before & behind. So that it appears, that in different Places different opinions of Modesty or decency in Dress concerning the parts that ought to be covered, obtains;[5] tho' all Seem to agree about the Suitableness of covering one particular part. Which Universal Custom, whether it is owing to Native Modesty, or to Some other political reasons at first, which Custom has confirm'd, [fasc. 12, f. 3v] is I think hard to determine; tho' I am inclin'd to believe it is owing to the first; for We observe that these Parts in all other animals have a Covering from Nature, or are generally So Situated as not to be obvious to the Sight of their fellows of the Same Species, especially in the Females. So that we may justly conclude, that these Parts in mankind, tho' without a Natural Covering, were not design'd to be expos'd, Seeing that defect was to be easily Supply'd, by the reason or Modesty of Man prompting them thereto. This I take to be the most Universal reason; although others of a Political kind may probably had Some Share in it.

---

[1] Kolathunadu was situated in the heart of the Kerala region and was buttressed from the Mughals by Mysore, which Fergusson may be referencing as the latter paid tribute to the Mughal emperor at the end of the 17th century to preserve its autonomy. The Nawab of Arcot and the Nizam of Hyderabad were the largest representatives of Mughal power in the South, but these were far removed from the Malabar Coast.

[2] Indeed, Kolathunadu was in a near constant flux during this period due to successional disputes, breakaway regions, and the Canarese invasions.

[3] This is the *upanayana*, or sacred thread. The wearing of it marks a rite of passage into formal education in the Hindu tradition.

[4] This tradition is now most associated with the princely state of Travancore, whose dynasty was descended from the same lineage as the Kolathiri, the ruling house of Kolathunadu. 19th-century British missionaries waged a well-publicized campaign to cover the upper bodies of low-caste Travancore women, in what was known as the Breast Cloth Controversy. It does not seem that Fergusson shared the same reservations as his later compatriots.

[5] This is the older more formal meaning of the word, meaning established or customary.

I cannot help taking Notice of a very Strange & remarkable custom, which I'm told is us'd at times among the Gentou's and others [fasc. 12, f. 4r] in most parts of India; But is Very Much practis'd in the Country Near Tully-Cherry. It is, a Method they have of trying the Innocence or Guilt of Persons accus'd of any grievous Crimes. For it is permitted by their Laws for any Person who is accus'd of a Crime, if he is willing, to appeal to this Tryal in order to clear his Innocence; after which he must inevitably Stand or fall by the Event of the Experiment; no witnesses or other Circumstances being admitted for or against them afterwards. The Experiment is this; The Person accus'd & who in clines to putt his Fate upon this Test, putts his hand or Fingers into a vessel of Boiling Lead, oil, or Butter, three Several Times Successivly [sic], lifting out in the hollow of his hand or fingers Some part of the Boiling matter; And if afterwards [fasc. 12, f. 4v] there appears no Sign of burning upon the Part immerged, he is Esteem'd Innocent & clear'd; and on the other hand if the Parts are in the least burnt, he is condemn'd as guilty, and recieves his Punishment accordingly.[1]

By this it would appear that None who made the Experiment could possibly escape, unless by an immediate Miracle, or by Some Trick or Chicane. But the ~~Thing~~ Ceremony has been So often Seen with all its Circumstances, by Men of Good Sense (I mean Europeans) who have had the best opportunitys as well as Inclination to examine accuratly [sic] into the matter, that one could have no room to doubt of the fairness of the Experiment; were it not a Thing in itself So incredible, That one Should putt their Hand into Such Burning Materials without its being burnt. The Ceremony of the Tryal is [fasc. 12, f. 5r] perfom'd with a great deal of Solemnity, as I'm well inform'd, by the Gentlemen at Tully Cherry who Saw a remarkable one of the kind but three Days before our arrival there, which I Shall Sett down as it was represent'd to me by many that were present.

The Case was this, A Young woman married about one Year or more, was accus'd by her Husband of lying with another man. The Husband mad with Jealousy or Some other Passion, apply'd to the Judge complaining of the Injustice that was done Him. It is necessary to observe that Adultery, with this People is punishable by Death.[2] The Woman protested her Innocency [sic], and without Undergoing any other tedious forms of Tryal, immediatly [sic] declared She was willing to prove her Innocence in

---

[1] Trial by ordeal was not uncommon in India, particularly the south, in what is now Tamil Nadu, and was often commented upon by European travellers. This appears to be a later version of the *taptamaṣa*, or 'The Ordeal of the Hot Piece of Gold', one of many methods of establishing innocence or guilt by ordeal articulated in the *Nāradasmṛti*, one of the *Dharmaśāstras*, a Sanskrit collection of legal maxims attributed to the 6th century CE Hindu sage Nārada. Accordingly, a coin is placed into a pot of boiling ghee, or other liquid. The accused is then required to retrieve the coin by hand and if found uninjured by the ordeal, is pronounced innocent (Jolly, trans., *Minor Law Books*, pp. 119–20). News reports from as recently as 2018 demonstrate that the practice still occurs, albeit rarely and extrajudicially. See *The Times of India* article, 'Woman Guard Forced to Dip Hand in Boiling Oil'. Available at <https://timesofindia.indiatimes.com/city/rajkot/woman-guard-forced-to-dip-hand-in-boiling-oil/articleshow/67293730.cms>.

[2] The *Dharmaśāstras* are of various views on punishments for adultery, often depending on who and what classes of people were involved. Most punishments required the ritual purification and period of penance for the adulterer. Islamic law as it was practised under Mughal authority did prescribe stoning to death for adultery, however, the punishment was almost never carried out (Baer, 'Death in the Hippodrome', pp. 61–2).

the abovementioned manner. [fasc. 12, f. 5v] It being thus determined, The woman was carried before Mr Law the Chief of Tully-Cherry. She living hard by,[1] and the matter being related, they begg'd, that they might be allowed Some convenient Place to Secure this Woman in before the Trial, which was granted. And particular Care was taken of Her for a Day or two, till the time fix'd for the Experiment was come. Then a Fire being kindled in the open place, and a Large Ladle full of Lead being Sett a boiling, the woman was brought out, and her Hands being Carefully washed to take away Suspicion of any Trick; She was told, by the Judge or officer appointed to Superintend these things, to consider well what She was going about, and to take Care not to putt herself to the Trial, if she was not conscious of her Innocency; Seeing the Consequence of her Miscarrying in it, was to be an ignominious Death. But she persisting in her [fasc. 12, f. 6r] first Declaration, Her Sentence which was drawn out was read in her hearing, determining her Death or Acquittance [sic] according to the Success of the Trial; after which the Leaves on which it was wrote were tied round her waste. Then Stretching out her Hand towards the Vessel of Boiling Lead, She Said; according to the Laws of my Country I come here to clear myself of a crime with which I am accus'd, and therefore I do this to prove not only that I never was guilty with the Man I am charg'd with, but that I never knew any man but mine own Husband; and with that, She putt her hand into the boiling lead three times Very deliberatly [sic], and lifting out Some of it every time in the hollow of her fingers. After this immediatly her Hand was examin'd and not the least Sign of Burning appearing on it, it was wrapp'd carefully Up with a clean cloth, which being tied fast round, it was Seal'd up, and She return'd to Prison till Next Day; when [fasc. 12, f. 6v] being again examin'd and found Still intire without Blemish, She was pronounc'd Innocent, and dismiss'd with applause; and her Husband with much Disgrace: And, if I remember, she was ordered no more to cohabit with Him.

This is the True Relation of this Fact which was So Recent, and Seen by Severals who being Strangers there, were very Incredulous and Consequently Curious to observe the Procedure; who all besides these that had Seen it So often before, Sincerely assur'd me that the matter happened in the Very Manner it has been represented; which Struck them all with no Small astonishment, and the More that the woman being under their own Custody in the Fort, they had no reason to Suspect that any Methods were us'd to elude the Experiment.

This is done in Boiling oil & Butter by those of another Cast; And there is a Noted Story there related of one of the Princesses [fasc. 12, f. 7r] of this Country, Called the Princess of Callastria,[2] who being accus'd of adultery, appeal'd to this Tryal of her Innocence; And the more effectually to Show it; when A Large Vessell of Boiling Butter was prepar'd; instead of her hand, She at once plung'd her whole head into it and yet was not in the least Scalded or blemished; tho' the Drops which Shak'd off from her long Hair upon raising her head, Scalded Severals of the Bystanders. This Last Instance, if True, is a miracle, in my Judgment, not of the least kind; But of this I had only a

---

[1] Here Fergusson is using nautical terminology meaning nearby.
[2] The Kolathiris of Kolathunadu.

Distant Report, having convers'd with none who Saw it; tho' most people there Seem to believe it.[1]

When I first heard of this Custom, I could not at all entertain any Belief, that Such Things could happen in the manner related; But that there was Some hidden trick or chicane in the Matter, invented by their Braminys or others to elude the force of the Laws. But [fasc. 12, f. 7v] when I found the matter related to me so punctually by those who had often been Eyewitnesses both of the Fortunate and Unhappy Events of the Ceremony; and in particular in an Instance So late, I found My Mind under no Small Difficulty what to determine in the affair; ~~neither~~ Of the Fact I could not possibly doubt, without at the Same time doubting of every other thing which I had not Seen myself. And how to give credit to it with all its Circumstances as represented in the Late Instance, without alledging [sic] Some occult Manner of preparing the Hand against the Impression of the Fire, or some dextrous Way of immerging it in the boiling Substance, was equally difficult;[2] Seeing I could suggest to myself no other Rational way of accounting for it, Unless by Supposing the immediate Interposition of Providence Suspending the Natural Powers or force of Fire, [fasc. 12, f. 8r] in order to Vindicate the Innocent from Unjust Punishment. But this is going a very great lenth, and does not Seem analogous with the ordinary conduct of Providence So far as it can be trac'd by Us. Though after all, Who ever believes the thing to happen in the foresaid manner and does not Suppose Some Trick in the Case, has not, I think, any other possible Way to Satisfie [sic] his Mind concerning it. And those Gentlemen at Tully=Cherry Whose Opinions I ask'd, and who Seem'd to be fully persuaded that there was no manner of Deciet [sic] or fraud in the Tryal, all told me that they verily believed, that the clearing of the Innocent after this manner could be imputed to no other cause but the Interposition of Providence.

This Ceremony, I think, is a matter which deserves a very Carefull Inquiry; And I'm persuaded lett the Event thereof happen as it will, the Satisfaction attending it, if pursued with diligence and Suitable accuracy, [fasc. 12, f. 8v][3] would not be Small. For if found to be an Imposture carried on by preparing the Member by Some Means against the Impression of the Fire, the Discovery of Such a Secret, 'tis plain would be of great

---

[1] This story does not appear in the other records. However, it may be a variation on another regional story concerning a princess of Kolathunadu who, upon having an affair with a person of lesser social standing, lost her nobility and was married off to a rich Arab merchant. In the port of Kannur, the princess and her husband established the city-state kingdom of Arakkal in 1545, which lasted until the early 19th century. In English sources, the dynasty was commonly called the Ali Rajas (Galletti, Van der Burg, and Groot, eds, *The Dutch in Malabar*, p. 38). It was they who encouraged the Canarese to invade Kolathunadu in 1732.

[2] There is something known as the Leidenfrost effect, which was eponymously named for a German doctor who first described it in 1751. The effect explains how, if a person were to dip their hands in cold water before submerging them in boiling oil, the evaporation of the water off the skin creates a short-lasting vapour barrier that protects from scalding. There is no way of knowing if this is at play in these examples that Fergusson's sources claim to have witnessed.

[3] On the inside back cover of this fascicle, is a stamp that codicologists, filigranologists, and others concerned with the history of paper refer to as a ream wrapper (see Figure 8 overleaf). It was the manufacturer's mark that was placed at the end of a quantity of paper made. This particular design is known as the Strasbourg Lily and was commonly used at the time. While upside down in the fascicle, one can see the initials 'I. H.', which correspond to one of the Honig families of papermakers in Holland, who sold their wares across northern Europe in the 18th century. Particular thanks are due to Paul Love, who identified the mark (Churchill, *Watermarks in Paper*, p. 15, figs 204, 417).

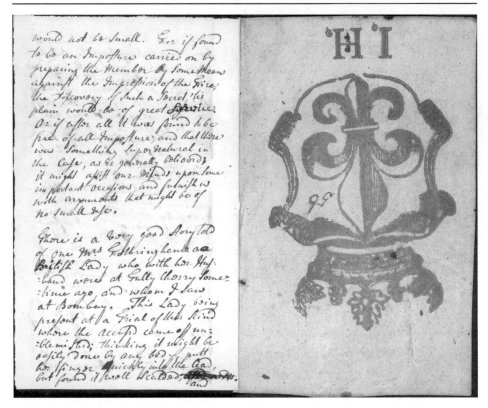

Figure 8.   Sample from Fergusson's diary (fasc. 12, f. 8v, and back inside cover) showing the papermaker's red (in original) ream wrapper mark with the upside-down initials 'I. H.', belonging to the Honig family who manufactured paper in the Netherlands during the seventeenth and eighteenth centuries. Reproduced with kind permission from Andrew Gladstone and The Centre of South Asian Studies, University of Cambridge.

Service. Or if after all it was found to be free of all Imposture, and that there was Something Super Natural in the Case, as is generally believ'd; it might assist our Minds upon Some important occasions, and furnish us with arguments that might be of no Small use.

There is a very good story told of one Mrs Fothringham a British Lady who with her Husband were at Tully Cherry Sometime ago, and whom I Saw at Bombay. This Lady being present at a Trial of this kind where the accus'd came off unblemish'd; thinking it might be easily done by any body, putt her finger quickly into the lead, but found it well Scalded; and [fasc. 13, f. 1r] and was afterwards much jested with, as one whose virtue would not Stand the Test.[1]

---

[1] It is unsure who this is exactly as there were several Fothringhams serving the EIC along the west coast of India in the early 18th century. This event was also related two decades later by the EIC ship's captain John Henry Grose, who said in his travelogue that it was the then governor of Tellicherry Robert Adams who exclaimed humorously to Mrs Fothringham after her finger was scalded, 'The trial [...] I suppose, madam, was for your virtue.' See Grose, *A Voyage to the East Indies*, I, p. 199.

Altho' These People appear So Strict observers of the Matrimonial Ties, So as to punish adultery by Death; Yet I'm told, there is a Custom us'd among them which Seems not So consistent with their Strictness in this Matter; For it is allowed for one woman to be married to Several men, but So as every one knows of it.[1] All of her husbands cohabit with her by Turns, as it is agreed among them or Setled [sic] by Law, but So promiscuously, as it cannot be known to which of the Husbands the offspring really belongs, or who is the real Father of any of the Children. And therefore it is, that Inheritance or Succession goes by the womans Side; for Example: A Man does not leave his Inheritance to the Children of his wife, but to the children of his Sister. For in the [fasc. 13, f. 1v] first Case, he cannot be Certain that it descends in his own blood; But in the last, by leaving it to his Sisters Children, he is Sure it is in the family. But I know not if this be the Rule or Custom, when a man is married to a Woman who has no other Husband.

This is probably one of the Strangest Customs that is to be heard of any where in Matrimonial affairs; For in most other Instances of Polygamy among many different People as the Turks & others, We find the men have the only liberty, and advantage over the women, Seeing they can Marry Several Wives, and cohabit with them at Pleasure, or turn them away upon easie terms.[2] But Among this People, the Women appear in good earnest to wear the Breeches, Yea More than one pair; and to have intirely the better of the men, Allmost [sic] in every Case that Concerns matrimony. And I imagine [fasc. 13, f. 2r] These Laws or Customs were first instituted among them, at a time when Under the Government of a woman or of some silly Prince who was Guided by Women.

Of all the Customs concerning matrimonial affairs that I have either read or heard of, there none pleases me more, or appears So just and equitable as well as conducive to the happiness of mankind, as that which I'm inform'd prevails among the Inhabitants of the Maldivee Islands. There, Every Man has no more than one wife; But upon just occasions the Marriage may be easily dispos'd, and each allow'd to enter into Marriage with any other they please. As in Case of perpetual differences, disagreement of Tempers, Diseases of Particular kinds, as Madness Ideotism,[3] or any other tedious Disorders which makes any of the Partys unfitt for the Duties of marriage. Upon these and Such like accounts [fasc. 13, f. 2v] the Woman may take another Husband, or the man another wife, making what allowance is judg'd proper for the Party forsaken in case that Disease is the cause.

Could this Custom be allow'd of in other Countrys, I'm convinc'd that many terrible Inconveniences attending the marriage State would be in a great Measure remov'd. Nor need we fear that any Confusion or other mischiefs greater than are undergone in the usual manner, would follow upon it; Seeing proper Laws, ~~would~~ determining what alone are Sufficient Reasons for parting; and the manner in which it ought to be done; with requisite allowances being made for the offspring &.C. would very much remedy or prevent these Inconveniences. Atleast they would be fewer and of less consequence, than

---

[1] Polyandry was practised by certain groups in India. The practice is most associated with the Himalchal region in the north. In South India, however, women belonging to matrilineal Nair castes, some tribes of the Nilgiri Mountains, and the Vellalas of Nanjanad in Travancore could take multiple husbands. Indeed, polyandry is even found in the *Mahabarata* in which the daughter of a king is married to 5 brothers.

[2] In Islamic law men may generally take up to 4 wives.

[3] Meaning idiotism.

those attending Marriage for Life in many Cases which are Sometimes [fasc. 13, f. 3r] of the Most insupportable kind.

A Gentleman acquainted of the reasoning of these People about this Custom of theirs; who being told that Such was not allow'd among Christians, but that as long as the Married Couple liv'd they could not so be Separated So as to have the Liberty of marrying again except in a very few Cases; They were Surpris'd that Such wise People as the Europeans Should bind themselves to Such hard Laws. For Say they, [']I marry a woman whom I think very Good; by and by She becomes froward[1] or foolish, allways [sic] giving one much plague, or She can have no children, or She has Some loathsome Disease which cannot be cur'd or the like; What? Must I Suffer Upon her accountt without being able to do her any Service by it; and because She becomes unfitt for marriage must I likewise become uncapable [sic] of the Matrimonial functions. [fasc. 13, f. 3v] No! I take Care of Her, or give her back again to her Friends, and take another Wife. And if any other Cares to Marry her, She May if She pleases.['] This reasoning with proper restrictions, certainly carries a great deal of force with it. But Religion and inveterate Custom have consecrated the Contrary. It may be observ'd; that this people is esteem'd the most strictly honest of any in India.

At Tully=Cherry the [East India] Company have tolerable pleasant Gardens, but not kept in good order. There I Saw Several of the Cassia trees which are in plenty enough upon the Coast. The Smell of the Leaves when rubb'd is pleasant and aromatick [sic], and the Bark is of a fine Cinnamon Taste.[2] The trees are not very high, but Spreading and bushy resembling an apple Tree. And I find the Natives and others there, make no Difference in the Species betwixt this and the Cinnamon Tree, only it is allow'd that in Ceylon from Whence [fasc. 13, f. 4r] the greatest part of the Cinnamon comes, it is of a Stronger & better kind which makes it So much more valued. [A]nd it is observ'd upon this Coast of Malabar, that the further to the Southward, the Cassia is much Stronger and Nearer to the true pungency of the best Cinnamon, than to the Northward. And we know that Ceylon lies to the Southward of this Coast, So that we may hence Suppose the true reason why this Cinnamon So much is preffer'd to the rest.

Thursday Oct*ob*er the 14th. We weigh'd from Tully Cherry, and the 18th we anchor'd in Cochin road.

This is a Setlement[3] [sic] belonging to the Dutch lying almost in the middle betwixt Tully Cherry and Anjango. It is a pretty litle Town Surrounded with a Strong wall and Trench, Situated upon a corner of Land that is [fasc. 13, f. 4v] Surrounded with a kind of River of Water which communicates with the Sea in two places So as to form this portion of Land into a kind of Island.

---

[1] An archaic word meaning contrary or difficult to deal with.

[2] *Cinnamomum cassia*, or Chinese cinnamon, is also used for its aromatic bark. Fergusson is distinguishing this species from *Cinnamomum verum*, which is considered by some, as the Latin name implies, as true cinnamon.

[3] Cochin (now Kochi) was the seat of Dutch Malabar. It was captured from the Portuguese in 1663, during a joint expedition between the VOC and the Samoothiri (king) of Calicut (now Kozhikode) Puratam Tirunal (r. 1662–6). Their aim was to expel Portugal from the Malabar Coast, in which they were ultimately successful. At the time of Fergusson's visit the Dutch Commander was Julius Valentijn Stein van Gollenesse, who went on to the governorship of Ceylon in 1743 and was VOC director-general in Batavia from 1751 until his death in 1755.

The Dutch who at first took this place from the Portugueze have fortified it very well and have a pretty strong Garrison in it. The river will admitt boats and Small Ships or Sloops, but none of much burden.

This Setlement is design'd chiefly for the pepper trade, and for venting of their Sugar and arrack from Malacca and Batavia.[1]

There is a particular Disease to which the Inhabitants of Cochin are subject. Viz an insensible hard oedematous Swelling of one or both Leggs, which when it has been of any Standing is reckoned incurable and commonly remains during Life without any conside= [fasc. 13, f. 5r] =rable pain or Seeming Injury to their Healths [sic]. I Saw Several people especially the black Natives with this kind of Legs; and one especially a Young Lad, had both his Legs So Swell'd from the knee downwards, that each was bigger than his waste, neither could there any Distinction of Toes be Scarcly [sic] perciev'd. This Disease is imputed to the water they Drink.[2]

After three Days we Sail'd from Cochin, and the Sunday[3] following we anchor'd in Anjango road about 4 Miles from the Fort, opposite to a rivulett [sic] where we design'd to fill up our Water Casks for the passage to St Helena.

Anjango[4] is a very Small Fort belonging to the English Company Situated upon a Sandy Bank closs by the Sea in 8 & ½ Degree North Latitude. It has for its Garrison a Captain, an Ensign and about 100 Men [fasc. 13, f. 5v] White and Black; Besides the Chief and two others with a Writer, & other Servantts.

Nigh the Fort along the Beach is a Small Village on the Companys Bounds.

The Fort Seems to Stand on an advantagious [sic] Ground and free from the Danger of any assaults from the Natives. For on one Side it has the Sea; and on the opposite a River Running along and discharging itself into the Sea alitle below the Fort that Surrounds it So as to leave no passage but from that Side where the village is Situated. This River runs a considerable way up into the Country, in a very pleasant irregular way leaving many Small Islands by its crooked windings; and being Smooth without much Current [fasc. 13, f. 6r] is easily Navigable by Small boats:[5] Here Mr Wake the Chief had a very pretty Barge in which they often go to take their Diversion by Sailing up Some Miles into the Country & entertaining themselves with Gunning or the like.[6]

This Diversion I had the pleasure of one Day, when we Sailed Several Miles up, and had a pleasant walk into the Country, where I observ'd in many Places the Land well cultivated, and prettily laid out in Divisions and enclosures, in which I Saw Severals at

---

[1] The *Britannia* took on board 15 leaguers, or 250-gallon casks, of Batavia arrack at Cochin (BL: IOR L/MAR/B/285BB, entry for 20 October 1736). Here Fergusson uses 'venting' as an archaic form of vending.

[2] This is a form of elephantiasis that became so common in Dutch Malabar, that it became known as Malabar- or Cochin-leg. The disease is carried by microscopic worms spread by mosquito bites. The adult worms attack the lymph system causing the chronic pooling of fluids.

[3] 24 October 1736. The water was collected the following day (BL: IOR L/MAR/B/285BB, entries for 24–25 October 1736).

[4] Now Anchuthengu, the EIC established their first permanent fort along the Malabar Coast there in 1694–8. It never became more than a minor trade settlement and convenient stopover for ships sailing along the coast.

[5] This is the Vamanapuram River. The region's riverine landscape was altered during the early 19th-century building of the Parvathy Puthanaar canal, which runs behind the fort.

[6] The chief of the factory was William Wake, who was appointed in 1732 and would stay till 1742, when appointed governor of Tellicherry. Wake was well known for enriching himself through private-trading activities, leading one scholar to recently refer to him as 'undoubtedly a rather slippery character' (Subrahmanyam, *Europe's India*, p. 182).

work in ploughing & the Like. Tho' I'm told this Country in general is not So well Manur'd.

From Anjango They principally have Pepper and White Cloth which is reckoned much the best of its kind in India.[1]

[fasc. 13, f. 6v] **Sunday October 31st.** We Sail'd from Anjango saluting the Fort with 21 Guns, as a Mark of Gratitude for the kind & friendly Entertainment we had mett with from the Chief Mr Wake and Lady, whose Civility and generous Hospitality were as great as ever I have mett with any where; nor can I well forgett it, but must ever remember it with pleasure and gratitude.

From Anjango to St Helena we had a very quick and pleasant passage.[2] On the evening of [Saturday] the [27th November] we discovered the Island of Don Rodrigues[3] unexpectedly, not thinking ourselves so far to the Westward by five or six Degrees and the first of January 1736/7[4] we saw the Land of the Cape of Good Hope, and the table Land[5] bearing at Noon North East from Us.

[fasc. 13, f. 7r] From thence having pleasant Gales we arriv'd at St Helena the 17th of the same Month.

This Island has a very barren aspect from Sea appearing intirely one heap of high rugged Rocks & precipices. It is reckoned about 25 or 30 Miles in Circumference, It is every where of a Considerable heighth [sic] from the Sea being Steep and inaccessible; except in a very few places where there are very Narrow and deep valleys where Small rivulets run down. In all these valleys to the Leeward of the Island where there is any danger from an Enemys Landing there are built some batteries with Guns Mounted. And on the projecting Corners of two different Rocks Near which the Ships must pass that go into the road before the Town and Fort, are two Strong batteries with 12 or 16 Large Guns each cutt out of the Rock 30 or 40 yards above the Surface of the Sea.[6] [fasc. 13, f. 7v] Before a Ship can pass any of these batteries, she is oblig'd to Send her boat ashore with authentick accounts of what She is.

The Town, Fort, and principal Battery are Situated in James's Valley, where there are mounted about 80 Guns 12 or 14 of which are 32 pounders, and the rest of an intermediate kind to 3 pounders. The walls of the Battery are extended betwixt the two Rocks that form the Sides of the valley So that there is no passing but by the Gates, and the Lower battery wall is So nigh the beach, that in Large Seas Sometimes the spray flies over it.[7] The Upper or Inner wall is much higher than the other, and closs to the Inside of it at one Corner is the Small fort, where are the Governors House, with the Companys

---

[1] Plain cotton cloth, the base material for the famed printed Indian calicos.

[2] The *Britannia*'s passage from Angenjo to St Helena took 78 days.

[3] Fergusson leaves blank spaces where the square brackets have been included with the relevant information, which he forgot to fill in later. This is Rodrigues Island, the furthest eastern island territory in what is today Mauritius. The ship's log recorded it as 'Diego Raias', also spelled Rays or more properly Ruiz (BL: IOR L/MAR/B/285BB, entry for 27 November 1736).

[4] January 1737.

[5] Meaning Table Mountain, Cape Town.

[6] These are Banks Battery and Mundens Battery, known collectively as the Banks' Lines. They protected the main settlement at James Bay, since the trade winds forced ships within range of the guns as they rounded the island coming into land. The portions that Fergusson saw were constructed 1673–1710.

[7] Indeed in 2010, this lower wall of Banks Battery collapsed into the sea due to erosion.

Storehouses, and other offices.[1] And from Hence on each Side alitle way up the valley is a row of Houses which [fasc. 13, f. 8r] makes up the Town, where the Planters and other Inhabitants live in time of Shipping, consisting of about 40 or 50 Small houses with Neat Rooms to lodge in, at the opposite Side of the valley over against the fort Gate is the Barracks for the Soldiers. And betwixt the fort and the Town is the Government Gardens, which are but Small tho' pretty well laid out into pleasant Walks.

The Garrison consists of about 140 or 150 Soldiers; But upon every alarm all the Male Inhabitants betwixt 16 and 60 [years old] are oblig'd to repair to their respective Quarters, on the different Batteries. And upon a double alarm each Inhabitant is oblig'd to bring with him all his Male Slaves of that age. The Single alarm is Constantly given upon Sight of every Single ship; and the double alarm upon more Suspicious occasions, as upon the Sight of Several Ships, in [fasc. 13, f. 8v] time of War or the like.[2]

The Companys affairs here are Managed by a Governor, and 3 counsellors, who however are oblig'd to be allwise at the Governors Nod, or to think and act at his discretion. The present Governor Pike, and his predecessors for several Years by past I'm told have acted in a very arbitrary Capricicious [sic] Manner, of which in his two predecessors Byfield & Johnson[3] I am told of Some of the Most Strange Instances that can well be imagined; But as Yet He himself has not proceeded So far, tho' I find he daily creeps in that selfish peevish, obscure, Tyrannical way.[4] [A]s a true picture of the despicable Dispositions of Some of those vile mean wretched Scoundrels, whom nature Seems to have design'd for the most abject offices among men; but by Some Sneaking artifices being exalted into a small measure of pow'r, their litle Circumscribe'd Souls know not [fasc. 14, f. 1r] Not [sic] how to Show or exercise it, but by the most petulant & inhuman actions, I Must take notice of two late Instances of the most barefac'd capricious and unjust kind that ever I have heard of. The one happened to an Ensign who using to be pretty familiar with the Governor (Byfield), and being over a botle [sic] together, the Governor propos'd Some particular health which being contrary to the Laws, the Ensign modestly begg'd to be excus'd, But the other turning More importunate, the Ensign atlast positively refus'd to do it; Upon which the Governor calling in his Guards ordered the Ensign into closs confinement, as one who had dar'd to propose that very Health which he had refus'd; and was afterwards commanded by the Governor to be ty'd to the flag Staff, where he recieved a thousand lashes in the most violent manner; the flesh being all tore off his back, and the Spectators

---

[1] Rising above the town of James Bay, the small original defensive fortification was built in 1659 as the Fort of St John, before being demolished and rebuilt as The Castle in the 1710s.

[2] This nervous preparation is likely due to the fact that the Dutch invaded and occupied St Helena for six months from December 1672.

[3] Fergusson is referring to governors Edward Byfield (in office 1727–31) and Edward Johnson (in office 1719–23). However, he failed to mention John Smith who was governor from 1723 to 1727. While both Byfield and Johnson had their detractors, Smith in particular was deeply unpopular for his harsh punishments against vice. An early 19th-century history of St Helena described him as a 'tyrant who had thus turned the pure stream of justice into a course of oppression' (Brooke, *A History of the Island of St Helena*, p. 210).

[4] Governor Isaac Pyke (d. 1738) had served as governor 1714–19, before beginning his second term in 1731. Fergusson was proven correct in his prediction of his style of governance. Pyke's tenure was summarized several decades later in the following manner: 'he fully justified the charge of arbitrary conduct, of which he was accused. The white inhabitants were ignominiously whipped and imprisoned for trivial offences. The military officers fined and suspended without courts martial [...] he gave full scope to his own tyranny; a detail of which would be improper and indelicate' (see ibid., pp. 225–6).

imagining him dead, he fainting with [fasc. 14, f. 1v] the violence of the pain and the loss of blood. And Still all this not being able to Satiate the despicable Monster, The poor Ensign was again ordered to be convey'd to prison where Not a Soul was permitted to See him, but One of the Brutes Slaves who brought him a litle rice and water once a Day. And in this condition the unfortunate Man continued for the Space of two months, (tho' his Back was mortified and Slogh'd off in Several parts) without being allow'd one thread of cloths wherewith to Shift himself; insomuch that all the inhabitants imagined that it was impossible almost for one to Survive So much barbarity.[1]

Immediately after he was Sent off in a Ship to Bencoolen;[2] the wretch I Suppose, fearing the Desperate & just vengeance of the highly injur'd Man. After a Year or two this Miserable wretch of a Governor was call'd home, and not being long afterwards, the Ensign found means to gett to England. But the Scoundrel fearing his resent= [fasc. 14, f. 2r] =ment, found means upon some pretence of a Debt, to gett the poor Ensign taken up by a writt and clap'd into Prison. But his Case being made known, he was Soon releas'd; and the wretch clapp'd up in his place, where he must needs have remain'd for Sometime, and been Strip'd of all his ill gotten wealth, by the just Severity of the Law, had not the Unhappy Ensign been So weak as to give up the prosecution, for a few hundred pounds, and the Security of being Sent out a Captain of the Soldiers at Bombay, where he died 2 or 3 Months before my being there. His name was Slaughter.[3]

The Other Instance remarkable of this kind happened before in the government of Johnston, [sic] which I think Shows the petulancy of A low tyrannical Soul in a very extrordinary [sic] manner. It is this.

A tradesmans wife happening one night to dream that there was a new Governor and Council come to the [fasc. 14, f. 2v] Island, and relating her dream in the morning to one of her neighbours, he happened to talk of it in Some company, where there happened to be one who told it to the Governor. He Sending for the Man and Woman, ordered them both to be ty'd up Naked and Whip'd, Her for Dreaming (as he express'd it in his laudable sentence) and Him for telling the Dream to others. The poor Man Suffered according to the Sentence, and the Woman was strip'd Naked and ty'd up, but by the Sollicitation [sic] of Some Friends gott off without Whiping.[4]

[1] This is the case of Ensign William Slaughter, who was accused of slandering Governor Byfield in November 1728. Slaughter claimed the governor had 'spoken treason' by stating that King George 'was a scrubb fellow' (Janisch, *Extracts from the St Helena Records*, p. 172). There is no record of how many lashes Slaughter received, however, it was carried out with 'wire whips and fish hooks tied to a cane' (Jackson, *St Helena*, p. 175).

[2] Now Bengkulu. It is the second largest city on the Indonesian island of Sumatra. The EIC founded it in 1685, before ceding it to the Dutch in 1824 to focus on Malaysian possessions.

[3] According to contemporary sources, Slaughter, by then promoted to sergeant, and his wife were sailing to Bombay as passengers aboard the *Derby* when it was taken by Angria in December 1735. They were both taken prisoner along with all crew, some of whom did not outlive their captivity. See Downing, *A Compendious History*, p. 69.

[4] There is no case in the records matching these details. However, under Johnson's term on 8 August 1721, a soldier and a widow were married by a doctor aboard a ship at harbour. The couple failed to seek the approval of the governor, which brought a severe rebuke. Governor Johnson ordered the groom to receive 50 lashes on his bare back whilst tied to the flagstaff and then imprisoned till the next store-ship arrived. The bride, meanwhile, was to be publicly whipped upon her naked back with 20 lashes. When she was tied to the flagstaff and stripped, the governor apparently relented 'hoping the shame of being so publicly exposed would have the same effect on her, as the smart had on some'. See Jackson, *St Helena*, pp. 191–2; Janisch, *Extracts from the St Helena Records*, pp. 161–2.

It would be almost impossible to believe that there could be such horrid monsters in the human Shape, did not a cloud of witnesses testify the Same.

The Number of white people upon this Island as I'm informed, is betwixt 4 & 500 Men[,] Women & Children besides Soldiers. And of Blacks about 700. Almost all [fasc. 14, f. 3r] the White Familys [sic] have gott Farms or Plantations in the Country. Some of the Poorer's [sic] are indeed but very Small. But the better Sort or Planters as they are called, have a considerable extent of ground, the most fertile or wattery parts of which is us'd for the planting of Yams which is a large bulbous root which all of them use for bread; and on which Some of the poorest people & all the Slaves almost entirely live, ~~upon~~ they being reckoned very good Nourishment When Well boil'd or bak'd. The rest of the ground is us'd for Pasturage, Some parts of which is covered with plenty of fine grass, tho' the greatest half of the Island is intirely barren, by reason of its being almost every where furow'd into very deep & Steep valleys, So that the Sides of Many of them have the Mould[1] quite wash'd of, Neither can the rain or moisture rest upon them for the Same reason of their excessive Steepness. It is indeed not alitle wonderful [fasc. 14, f. 3v] to observe the pains and Labour it must have cost to bring this Island into the Condition it is now in.

It would appear at first Sight utterly impossible to pass from one valley to another, the Sides of the Rocks are So Steep and rugged; and yet there are Many fine broad roads to all the habitable places of the Island, made with inexpressible Trouble along the brows of these frightful precipices. In Short I cannot think that in any part of the world are to be Seen more visible traces of indefatigable Industry in a Small spot.

They have here exceeding good Black Cattle and in plenty, as also Sheep, Turkeys, Goose, Ducks & Fowls. Here are also Wild a great Many Doves and Patridges [sic].

There grows here no kind of Corns the Yams Serving in the Stead of Bread. And for those who can afford it they May buy flour or biskett out of the Companys Stores & alitle Rice is gott from the Ships.

[fasc. 14, f. 4r] Upon this Island they have no kind of Manufactory, all their clothing comes from England or India; and of their wool which is for the most part Coarse they Make Scarcely any use, So that the greatest part of it is thrown away.

They have here no Shipping of their own; Neither does the Island produce any thing fitt for exportation by way of merchandize. Formerly I'm told they had a few Small Ships that traded betwixt the coast of Guinea and the West Indies, but that is now quite Sett aside.

The Islanders are esteemed a very healthy people. Their looks are exceedingly fresh. And their Women are of as fair and lively complexions as are to be Seen in any part of the World. The Small pox yet has never been known upon the Island. The People generally marry Young, and are commonly very prolifick. I was told that for Sometime by past there has been known [fasc. 14, f. 4v] but one childless Married Couple.

One however cannot help regretting the Case of the poor Girls, who Scarcely above one of 5 or 6 have a chance for a husband upon the Island, for it being so very Small cannot maintain above a certain Number; upon which account most of the Young Men gett abroad in the Shipping; where as but a very few of the Young Women can gett off the Island, where there are reckoned 5 or 6 Women to every Man. A case not alitle hard,

---

[1] Fergusson means mould in the sense of earth, or the topsoil suitable for plant growth.

it must be own'd, and especially when one considers that the generality of them are exceeding well looked, and every Way fitt for being mothers.

When any of the East India Ships arrive, all the Principal Planters come from their Farms in the Country into their Town Hous's in the Valley, bringing with them their wives and Daughters that are grown up, who [fasc. 14, f. 5r] on those occasions putt on their best Looks & best cloths; in hopes no doubt of engaging the attention of the Captain or Some of the unmarried officers & Young Gentlemen in of the Ships. All of whom when they are ashore lodge and board with one or other of the Planters. Some of Them Young Ladys now & then pick up a Young Captain[,] Supracargo or officer of the Ships; but this happens Seldom, Which is Somewhat Surprising considering their good Looks, and the Frankness with which they behave together with the known Temper & Passions of Young Seafaring Gentlemen So long coup'd up from all Commerce with the fair Sex, in their passage to this Island.

But what is Still more Surprises me is, That So few of Them Suffer in their Characters, by the great libertys they Seem & opportunitys they Seem to give the Young Gentlemen at which No doubt their Parents Wink, from the hopes of a Marriage, be= [fasc. 14, f. 5v] [=]ing the Consequence of Such Familiarity; whereas a very different Consequence might be justly apprehended from a Young Man and pretty Young Girl being left alone in a Room by themselves with every favourable opportunity of indulging their Passions to the utmost. But in spite of all these appearances, the Ladys remain Virtuous; there being very few Instances of the contrary apparent by pregnancy. For I am well inform'd that tho' they will at times after alitle Intimacy and profession of admiration Love &.C. as is usual; allow Such libertys as makes a Man believe The Lady ready to Submitt to his pleasure, Yet when the attempt is made they resolutely refuse & preserve themselves on the Brink of Ruin.

To the fear of Shame we must in a good measure impute this extrordinary [sic] Fortitude; For when a Pregnancy happens, there is no [fasc. 14, f. 6r] possibility of concealing it in a Small Island where every one is known & observ'd, & from whence there is no possibility of escaping, or avoiding the Shame & Infamy that attend their weakness.

This alarming Consideration to Young Ladys, assisted by a Sense of virtue & of their Duty, preserves them from the precipice to which their Desire of engaging the affections of the Young Gentlemen in the Matrimonial Way, had led Them.

The Planters support their Familys & Slaves by the Produce of their Farms in Yams, Catle &.C. and by Selling their black Catle[,] Sheep, Turkeys, Geese &.C. to the Ships they procure money to purchase clothing, Flour, Rice[,] Liquor[1] &.C. which their Island dont produce.

Many of their Sons gett into the East India ships & Some of them become Captains. Others of Them, go in the Store Ship to Bencoolen, where and in other Parts of India[2] they gett into the Civil or military Service of the Company as they have Interest. A Few of their Daughters gett also their passage to India in that Ship; but as I have heard dont retain the Same Fortitude against Temptation, as they do on their Native Island, So that Few of Them Succeed So well in making good marriages in India, as those do who come

---

[1] It is presumed that Fergusson meant the staples of rice and liquor, rather than rice liquor.
[2] Fergusson means the Indies rather than India, since Bencoolen is in what is today Indonesia.

from England with the Same views, tho' often their Looks are not So good as the Ladys of St Helena, tho' their Education & behaviour is preferable.

The 27th of January we left St Helena[1] and gott into Soundings in the Chops of the [English] Channel in 130 Fathom the 8th of April. On the 13th we had gott as far [fasc. 14, f. 6v] up as Portsmouth when we were check'd by a Strong Easterly wind at night, and next morning finding we could not reach Portsmouth after attempting it for Sometime We bore away for Plymouth Where we arriv'd & got into Hamoze[2] the 16th.

We waited there for a Fair wind 10 Days; and then Sail'd for the River [Thames] where we arriv'd at our moorings the 30th.[3]

---

[1] According to the ship's logbook, the *Britannia* left the island on Friday the 28th of January (BL: IOR L/MAR/B/285BB, entry for 28 January 1737).

[2] The Hamoaze is part of the estuary of the River Tamar that flows past the Devonport Dockyard, one of the main bases for the Royal Navy.

[3] The *Britannia* moored in Deptford from 30 April to 19 May to unload the ship (BL: IOR L/MAR/B/285BB, entries for those dates in 1737).

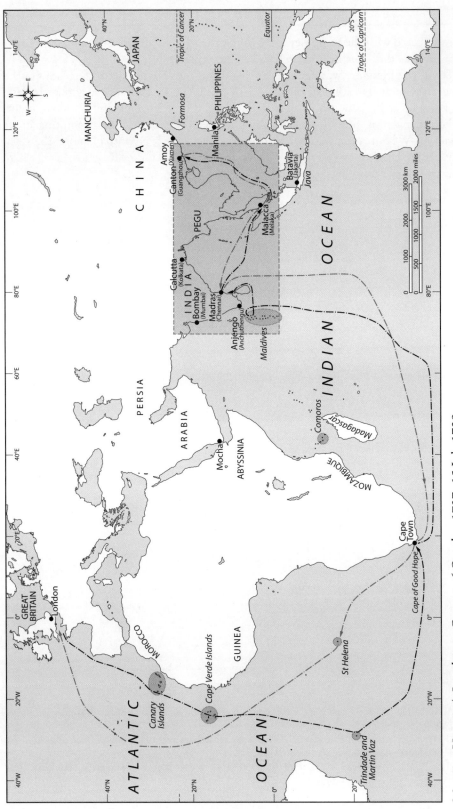

Map 7. Voyage 4: London to Canton, 6 October 1737–15 July 1739.

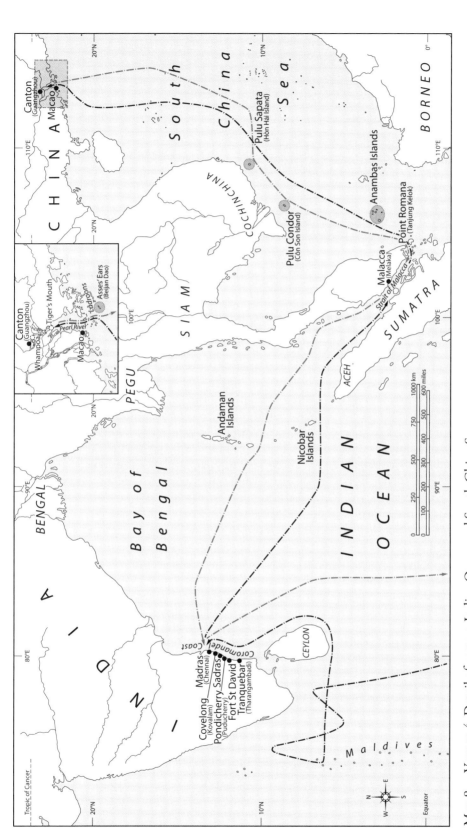

Map 8. Voyage 4: Detail of eastern Indian Ocean and South China Sea.

VOYAGE 4: FROM LONDON TO CANTON
6 OCTOBER 1737–15 JULY 1739

[fasc. 15, f. 1r] **October 6th 1737.** We Sailed from Gravesend and gott into the Downs the 9th, Where we staid [*sic*] three Days.[1]

Wednesday October 12th. Having a fair wind we weighed anchor and the 14th took our Departure from the Lizard,[2] which was the last part of Europe we Saw.

Thursday the 27th [October]. We made the Island Porto Santo[3] which is one of the Madera's. And two Days following we Saw another of these Islands called Palma.[4] It is a pretty Large Island that Shows at a great Distance, being very high land. From this Island the Palm Wine has its Name, it being its place of growth.

Thursday November 11th. We saw Land one of the Cape de Verd Islands which by our Meridian Distance we took to be the Isle of Sal; But next morning Seeing St Jago to the Eastward & a head we found ourselves out in our accountts being to [*sic*] Westward; and that the Island [fasc. 15, f. 1v] we had Seen the Night before must be St Nicholas. We design'd to have gone into St Jago, but by this mistake which could not be foreseen, having gott to the Leeward of the Harbour we could not gett in. Here we Saw the Island Fogo, which emitted much Smoak [*sic*] from its Summit, but this time I Saw no fire as I had done last voyage. This is a very remarkable volcano, the place of Eruption being the Highest Peak of the mountain which is of a very great Heigth.

   Having fair Winds cross the Line without any calms as is usual, we gott into the Southeast trade wind and the 5th of December in the morning we Saw the Small Islands called Martin Vaz, being about 15 miles Distant. Here we were visited by great flocks of Fowls, who attended us for many miles, admiring I suppose our unusual and Strange appearance. Besides the Sea was covered with others who were flying about upon its Surface Seeking their prey.

---

[1] Fergusson's last voyage was serving as surgeon aboard the *Godolphin*, a regular, 32-gun ship of 480 tons, and a crew of 98. This was the *Godolphin*'s second voyage for the EIC under the command of Francis Steward, since being built and commissioned in 1734.

[2] The Lizard is a peninsula in Cornwall forming the most southerly point of mainland Britain.

[3] This island lies just 27 miles to the north-east of Madeira.

[4] La Palma is actually the north-westernmost of the Canary Islands. What Fergusson calls Palm wine, had many different appellations, including Canary wine, Canary sack, or just sack, and malmsey, the latter derived from the best-known grape variety of the island, malvasia. The island is volcanic and is dominated by the almost 2,000-metre summit of Cumbre Vieja.

[fasc. 15, f. 2r] **Friday January 6th 1737/8.** We arrived at the Cape of Good Hope, where we Stay'd 10 Days in order to water, and to refresh our men. The Situation, Extent &.C. of the Town are taken notice of in the notes of my last voyage.

One Day during our stay here, I went up into the Country to a place 12 Miles distant called Constantia, remarkable for its being the only Spott in the whole Country where the richest wine is made, which has its Name from this place.[1] It in comparatively excells [sic] all the wine in these parts, and is, I think, the most generous Cordial of any wine in the world. It is Somewhat Sweet to the taste, but of a most exquisite relish and agreable [sic] flavour. It is of two Sorts Red & White, The red is most valued, as the richer & finer Wine. The Spott where this wine is produc'd is but of [fasc. 15, f. 2v] Small extent, There being only 3 or 4 vineyards of about 2 acres each. These vines have been transplanted into all parts of the Neighbourhood, but to no purpose; for they lose their generous nature in any other Soil; Yea in the parts that are immediatly [sic] contiguous to this plantation, they degenerate after the Same Manner as elsewhere. This is a Phenomenon Somewhat Surprising in my opinion; Nor do I See how it can any how be accounted for, but by Supposing that the Soil in this particular Spot, to be inspired by Some Subterraneous effluvia,[2] which occasions a more kindly warmth and exalts the Vegetative juices in a peculiar manner into a more generous Spirit.

This Wine bears commonly double the price of the other Cape wines, tho' it is very oft adulterated, with mixture of the others, to which alitle [fasc. 15, f. 3r] of it, will give the flavour and taste in Some measure of the Constantian.

In this Country grows almost evry [sic] kind of fruit that is to be found in Europe, and many of those that usually are prouduc'd betwixt the Tropicks. For here are aples [sic], Pears, Plumbs [sic], Peaches, Figs, Almonds &.C. in the greatest Plenty; as also Guava's Pineaples and others. Besides all kinds of Roots, Sallading[3] & Pott Herbs. In short the Cape of Good Hope, appears to be in a true Medir[4] betwixt the Extremes of Heat & Cold, it lying in 34° & 30′ ~~South Lattitude~~ its farthest South Lattitude. The Country is beautifully diversified, with Spacious plains, gently rising grounds, & Some high Mountains. And the Natural Innocent Simplicity and Humanity of the Natives, I mean the Hottentots, correspond to the Clime. It is not alitle Surprising, & much to [fasc. 15, f. 3v] be regretted, that this People by general report, Should have been So much misrepresented, as Creatures that had no more title to Humanity than what proceed ~~from~~ their Shapes; Yea I have read & heard it asserted, that they had Scarcely an articulate voice. These So unaccountable & evident falsehoods, must have had Some common and general Sources. One plainly I have been able to discover, which I in My accountt of them last Voyage took notice of, Viz the inhumanity and tyrannical oppression of their Bowerish Neighbours the Dutch, who because, in Habit manners & language, the Hottentots are So different, Observing almost the Simplicity of nature, are therefore Stiled [sic] Savages, and used in the most inhuman Manner by the generality of the Dutch, who rob them of their Catle, expell them from their Pasturages, and knock them in the

---

[1] Now a suburb 15 miles to the south of Cape Town. It has been a major wine-producing centre since 1682, when the first vineyard was established, pre-dating the town by 3 years. Its most famous product was *Vin de Constance*, a dessert wine to which Fergusson is likely referring.

[2] Meaning the discharge of minute and unperceivable particles.

[3] This refers to salads or leafy greens.

[4] From the Latin *metior* via Old Portuguese *medir*, meaning measure.

head with pleasure; and in order to justify their Tyranny or palliate it to [fasc. 15, f. 4r] themselves and others, represent the Hottentots as a kind of wild Savages or Brutes who have no claim to compassion or justice. Besides, there are very few of the Dutch who have any Curiosity which may prompt them to inquire or examine into the Natural Disposition or Customs of the Hottentots. The Dutch in general are known to be industrious only in what they deem gainfull; and especially those who go abroad, who have no more learning than is Sufficient to keep accountts, and who have been early taught to think, that money alone is the Summum bonum[1] of Life. From Such People we cannot expect any rational Satisfactory accounts of any things that require impartial consideration and Curious inquiry. And 'tis the misfortune of the Poor Hottentots that their Characters have been Spread abroad, by Such alone Whose interest it is to misrepresent them, & who have neither Capacity nor humanity Sufficient to make them [fasc. 15, f. 4v] do justice to Characters much preferable to their own.

These are the opinions which upon good grounds I had embrac'd when I was before at this place.[2] And was much pleas'd to find them indubitably confirm'd this voyage, by the conversation of a Gentleman, who Seem'd every way well qualified to give a just Character of this People.

He was a minister who being by birth a French man, had been Sent over by the Dutch, in order to assist the French Refugees who in great Numbers at that time had transported themselves to the Cape from the religious Persecution in France.[3] This Gentleman being bred at the Universities in Holland was judg'd a proper person to officiate as minister in the Country, where it was necessary to understand both Languages, the Refugees at first not understanding Dutch. He came over from Europe in the Year 1700, having been [fasc. 15, f. 5r] at this time 37 Years in this Country, 25 Years of which he acted as Minister to the Bowers & others who liv'd up in the Country and by that means, had the best opportunitys of examining into the Manners &.C. of the Hottentots.

His accountt of their Natural disposition agreed intirely with that of one of his Brotherhood, I had convers'd with the former voyage. He added that he thought their Capacity or Understanding was rather Superior to that of Europeans; and that for Honesty fidelity & kindness, they much exceeded any People he has ever known or heard of; That they are a Constant reproach to Christians; and that he doubted not but at the great Day of accounts they would appear as a reproach to the generality of Christians, and be admitted to Happiness preferable to them. These were the very words he express'd with that dissinterested [sic] Regard to Truth, and with that Impartiality & Sincerity for which [fasc. 15, f. 5v] his Character is distinguish'd by all that know him.

I ask'd this gentleman (whose name was Beck) if he ever had been at any pains in order to instruct any of the Hottentots, in the Knowledge of God or of the Christian faith, and if he thought they had any Notions of a Supreme being. He answered as to the last

---

[1] Latin, meaning 'the highest good'.

[2] See above, pp. 71–2, 75.

[3] This is Henricus Beck (d. 1755) who arrived in Cape Town in 1702 to minister to Huguenots. He served in Stellenbosch and Drakenstein before retiring in 1731 to a farm outside Cape Town where Fergusson met him. Beck and his wife Aletta are the subjects of a study in Afrikaans on early 18th-century Cape life, Schoeman, *Twee Kaapse lewens* [*Two Cape Lives*]. For an English reference, Beck is one of many recurring figures situated within the religious ecumene of Cape Town in Gerstner, *The Thousand Generation Covenant*, pp. 67, 83–98, 249.

question, that they certainly bore a veneration for Some Superior in visible Being; for in Cases of trouble or Disaster, they fold their hands compose their looks, and behave in Such a Manner as one addressing the Deity; but without words; And that all of them with whom he convers'd upon the Subject of a God, immediatly [*sic*] putt on the Same devout Looks, with their Eyes fix'd in a kind of astonishment or admiration, but that Seldom or ever could he persuade any of them to give him an answer, which is the reason that he dispair'd of bringing them over to the Christian Faith. This compos'd [fasc. 15, f. 6r] taciturnity, he imputed to a kind of profound veneration, or incapacity to Suit words to their conceptions.

This account of their Behaviour in matters of Religion, makes me hope that the attempts Now making by a Romish Missionary will be fruitless.[1] He I'm told is lately come over by the Permission of the Dutch, and is gone far up into the Country where the Hottentots are most frequent, with whom he lives according to their manner, in order to procure the more Respect and Confidence to be place'd in him. He has already in a good Measure acquir'd their Language, and has begun his Harangues, So as to procure a Considerable Audience. One of the Hottentots, a young man Who is at Service in a Dutch family, and who had lately been one of his Hearers, gave this account of the Missionary; that he was much esteem'd with the Hottentots, who Seem persuaded that he must be an exceeding good man, who [fasc. 15, f. 6v] has left his Friends and Country, & come to live among them for no other view, but from a Desire of teaching them what he thinks necessary for their happiness. How easiely [*sic*] are Innocent honest People impos'd upon by the affected Sincerity of these crafty Wolfs in Lambs clothing. It would be a Subject to me of the greatest regrett [*sic*], to hear that the Missionary had any Success in his Labours; For I cannot concieve [*sic*] what these People could possibly gain by such a Conversion. What might be los'd is too evident, if we may judge by the common & necessary effects of Such a religion. Confus'd Notions of the Deity, perplex'd & multifarious objects of adoration, absurd and Childish Mumpings & Grimace with all the Shim Sham train of the most whimsical Ceremonys, Seem to have a quite contrary tendency to that of Making us Better or Wiser, which can be the only use or pretence of Religion.

Pure unbiass'd Nature teaches men Benevolence, Justice & Compassion to [fasc. 15, f. 7r] one another. But antipathys, rancour and the most cruel Hatred to those of a Different Faith, are Some few of the monstrous consequences of that hellish Religion. It is in my judgement much preferable to be one of the most ignorant Hottentots, with their Native humanity & innocence, even Supposing them to have no belief of God at all; rather than believe the Existence of the Deity, together with all the Absurd jargon of the Romish Religion.

There is a Story told by the abovementioned Hottentot which I think Shows the low falshoods [*sic*] & other mean artifices of these Missionarys. It is this, The missionary, he Says, gives this reason for the hinder parts of Bavians being bare or void of hair.[2]

---

[1] By Romish Fergusson is referring to the Catholic church. However, there is no record of Catholic missionaries in Cape Town at the time, and certainly none under Dutch government authorization. It is likely that Fergusson is referring to Georg Schmidt (1703–85), a Moravian missionary who evangelized amongst the Khoikhoi deep in the interior at Baviaanskloof (now the village of Genadendal) from 1737–43 (Rabie, 'The Legacy of Georg Schmidt', pp. 52–4).

[2] As explained above in Voyage 2, p. 75, n. 1, bavians are baboons, so here Fergusson is introducing a story for why these monkeys have bare bottoms.

When Christ was riding into Jerusalem upon the Colt, and the People Saluting him as he pass'd with acclamations, a Parcel of these Bavians or Baboons, being on a cliff by the way Side, Caught and threw dirt at Him; upon which Jesus turning to them curs'd [fasc. 15, f. 7v] them and Said from henceforth Shall Your hinderparts be bare So as You shall be expos'd to Shame & to the contempt of other Beasts; and from that Day all the Bavians have had their hinderparts uncovered.

Mr Beck the Gentleman I'm oblig'd to for the Most of the above accountts of the Hottentots, Seem'd to me to be passing the Evening of his Life, in the manner the most delightfull and rational of any Person I have ever known; in So much that tho' I view'd his Tranquillity & retirement without the least Envy, and was even transported to See One actually in the Enjoyment of a Life I had So much approv'd in Speculation; yet it fill'd me with a kind of melancholy & Despondency, that what I So much long'd for, Seem'd to be at So great a Distance, if not So far beyond my reach, that I Should never be able to See or find the accomplishment of My [fasc. 15, f. 8r] wishes. His way of Life in Short is this.

Being now 75 Years of age, he had given up his charge of the ministry about 6 or 7 Years ago; and having made a moderate Provision for his Retirement, he chose for the Place of it a Small Spott of Ground Sufficient for a House and pretty Large gardens its Situation is a large mile from the Town Near the root of the table Land,[1] by which and the contiguous hills it is Shelter'd intirely from the Cold South winds as also from the East & West. Its View is only open to the North, from which art [sic] is to be Seen the Town and the road where the Shipping ride. From the Town to His house there is a gradual ascent the whole way, So that He intirely commands the view of it with the Ships, and all the Private houses & Gardens which lye [sic] below Him which Make one of the Most beautiful Landskips[2] that is any Where to be Seen.

[fasc. 15, f. 8v] His House is Situated at the upper part of his gardens or vineyards, near to which Alitle higher is the Source of a fine Rivulett of water. This water he has convey'd So as to rise up in a fine fountain which Stands in the midle of a pretty Large Bason [sic] a few Yards from before the front of his house. It Spouts up in a continued Stream for some height, and with an agreable Noise falls into a Small Bason, of Lead from whence by Several Spouts it is poured into the Larger Bason or Reservoir, & from thence by diverse Canals it is carried through his Garden, So as to be lett in to any apartment thereof, to be watered with it at pleasure.

From this Bason is a Spacious walk Sett with oak Trees, and with in them on each Side is a row of aloe Plants quite to the End of the walk which is about ⅛ or 10th of a mile in Lenth. [fasc. 16, f. 1r] His Garden is finely laid out into an agreable variety of irregular walks, with high hedges of different kinds, that inclose different apartments which form So many distinct vineyards, and orchards or Kitchin [sic] Gardens. He is the layer out and overseer of his own garden in which he Spends much of his time, in the wholesome exercise of Planting & pruning his vines &.C. His vineyards Yearly afford him betwixt 30 & 40 Hogsheads of Wine;[3] in the making of which he is reckoned much the nicest of

[1] Table Mountain.

[2] Archaic usage meaning landscape.

[3] The volume of a hogshead has fluctuated since its first standardization by Parliament in 1423. The term refers to large casks of roughly 300 litres.

any person in these Parts; For with his Slaves he carefully picks out all the Spoil'd or unripe grapes, and is very particular in every other part, So that nothing but the purest juice is us'd for his wine. As indeed it appears by its rich taste and flavour which exceeds most of the Same kind of Grape. His vines are of Several kinds, So that he Makes 5 or [fasc. 16, f. 1v] 6 different Sorts of wine, which he keeps in a vault under his house, using part of it himself, and making presents to Some of his friends, and Selling what remains.

His house is not large but exceeding Neat, Shelter'd from the winds by the Neighbouring hills, and from the heat by Some large oak trees, which were planted there a long time ago, by Some gentleman who had a Small garden house there.

His bed Chamber which commands the Prospect of his Gardens and of the Whole Town & Shipping, is on one Side intirely lin'd with Shelfs full of Books in the learned languages with a mixture of French & German authors. It is at one end of the House, and in the midle is a pretty hall, and at the other End another Chamber. This made up the fore part of his first Story; But of the rest of his house I did not See the Rooms.

[fasc. 16, f. 2r] His Sister who is a widow Lady lives with Him; and I understand is much of his own Turn of Mind. He is Married but has no children. His wife parted from him Some Years ago and went to Holland; The reason of this I could not well learn; but heard it Surmis'd that She being considerably Younger than He, was not Such an admirer of Temperance Continence & retirement, which made her chuse [sic] to leave him and go to Europe where he allows her a very Sufficient Sustenance.

When last in Company I told him how much I admired his happy retirement. To which he answered, that He was perfectly Satisfied with the Situation Providence had assigned him, and that he had not So much as a wish to form for any other temporal Comforts than what he was possessed of; Only this, that his Slaves and other Servants, were very often [fasc. 16, f. 2v] vexing him with their Dishonesty and Carelessness, in Spite of the Best usage, for that he allow'd them better Sustenance and more indulgence than any others in these parts. Yet all in vain; they had been So us'd to Stripes in the Service of others, that they would not do their Duty without it in his Service; and as cruelty to Slaves was what he constantly abhorr'd in his Dutch Neighbours, he could by no means allow of it in himself and would rather Suffer many other inconveniences.

In Short the Person has Such a compos'd chearfullness [sic] in his Looks with So much health in his Countenance in Such an advanced age, that Seem the natural effects of his admirable manner of Life, which has been Celebrated and approv'd by the greatest Men in all ages, as the most Suitable to the Nature of Man and most productive of true happiness. For Hic secura quies, & nescia fallere vita, Dives opum variar.[1] ————————

[fasc. 16, f. 3r] **Tuesday January 17th 1737/8.** We sailed from the Cape of Good Hope having fair gales of wind till the fifth of February, when having a very hard Gale the preceeding [sic] night and next morning, about 4 of Clock our Bowspritt sprung close to the Bows and before they could succour it or the foremast, they Went away the last about 6 foot [sic] above the forecastle, and afterwards the Main topmast after it had considerably

---

[1] Fergusson is taking this from lines 467–8 of book 2 of Virgil's *Georgics* on the benefits of simple country life: '[this] quiet life – carefree and no deceit – and wealth untold', Virgil, *Georgics*, trans. Fallon, ed. Fantham, p. 43.

Wrung the head of our Mainmast.[1] The wind blowing very hard with a great Sea, with all possible expedition We cutt away the rigging to free ourselves of the masts, that hung closs along Side, and putt us under no Small apprehension that the Ships Sides or bows might be Stove in[2] by them. At the Same time by the falling of the foremast, Several of the Anchors were broke loose from the Bows and hung partly over, beating against the Sides. In Short the disaster was Very great and our Situation Seem'd Melancholy enough, nor were we free of the apprehensions of being foundered by the [fasc. 16, f. 3v] Seas breaking over us in a terrible manner, tearing the long boat loose from her lashings, and washing Casks, Men, and every light thing about upon Deck. But it pleas'd Providence that the Wind lull'd in alitle time, and that None of our men were either kill'd or considerably hurt by the fall of the masts and rigging or by the Sea's breaking So much over us. To our comfort also about 6 or 7 in the morning we discern'd a Ship pretty nigh us which we took for our Consort the *Princess Mary* Captain Martin, but when it clear'd up we found it to be the *Royal George* Captain Jobson who had Sail'd from the Cape the Day before us,[3] however alitle after we observ'd Captain Martin at a Considerable Distance, all which gave us hopes of being Supply'd with Some Necessarys and assistance to gett ourselves again putt in Some tolerable condition for Sailing; But we were at once Surpris'd and confounded, when we Saw Captain Jobson making Sail away from us Notwith= [fasc. 16, f. 4r] =standing of the apparent miserable condition we was in, without So much as coming So nigh as to ask us if we wanted help.[4] Although we Were So Near him as to Sea [*sic*] his people plainly go to and fro upon the Deck & Shrouds; nor was it any ways possible he could miss Seeing of us, or the Colours we hung out as Signals of Distress, besides those too Conspicuous Marks that our misfortune had occasion'd; But Such was the inexpressible Barbarity and Savage Stupidity of that inhuman Monster that we were left alone in this dismall Condition, tho', for ought he knew to the Contrary, we might have

[1] The bowsprit is the spar which extends from the front, or bow, of a ship. This has rigging to the sails of the foremast. Thus, what Fergusson is describing is that in rough winds and seas the bowsprit snapped and caused it to break the foremast, which in turn pulled down the main topmast. This is an extension above the central main-mast, which was damaged by the swinging around of the other broken masts, which were all still attached to rigging. Thus, they were swinging around and hitting against the ship, threatening to damage the hull and forecastle, or upper deck, where sailors usually had their living quarters.

[2] Meaning smashed in.

[3] Indeed, the *Godolphin* was in company with several ships all of which left Cape Town within days of each other. They were frequently in company with the *King William*, the *Princess Mary*, the *Royal George* and others as they rounded the Cape of Good Hope (BL: IOR L/MAR/B/594M(1), entries for 15 January through 7 February 1738).

[4] The *Royal George* had good reasons for not coming to the *Godolphin*'s aid. In the ship's logbook, Captain Jobson recorded: 'at 5 AM the wind Came to N and Blew a violent Storm [...] about 6 AM saw a Ship on the Weather Bow in distress she having lost her Bowsprit and foremast & Maintopmast she lay rolling in a Dismall manner, we soon perceiv'd that it was the *Godolphin* Captain Steward upon which I Call'd a Consultation of Officers and propos'd laying by them 'till the Storm was over in order to assist them after ward which was agreed to. Soon after we saw the *Mary* Captain Martin Just to windward of him Seemingly in very good Order [...] The first part of These 24 hours it Continued to Blow hard we Still lying under Settl'd Mainsail the Ship pitching very much against a Head sea; upon Examining our Bowsprit found it was Shiver'd from the End to the Gamoning and sprung a Cross in Severall places fetching so much way that we fear'd loosing our foremast every minute which putt us under a necessity of Bearing away [...] Left the *Princess Mary* with the *Godalphin* [*sic*] She being her Company keeper from England' (BL: IOR L/MAR/B/17a, see transaction for 6–7 February 1738). Captain Jobson had no way of knowing that the *Princess Mary* could not see the *Godolphin* and would thus not come to her aid.

been bilg'd by our own masts, and then ready to Sink. Captain Martin was at So great a Distance (as we Suppos'd) that He could not discern us in that low deform'd State we were in, but Seeing the other ship under Sail and taking her for us, made Sail after her, So that we were at once rob'd of all our hopes of [fasc. 16, f. 4v] Supply or help;[1] However it proving easie weather next Day, we Sett all hands about getting Up a Jury foremast,[2] which by next afternoon we compleated, and in a few Days more we were putt into a tolerable condition, and Sail'd pretty well on our way.[3]

It would not have been a Small degree of Evidence that could have determin'd me to believe there was any of the race of Mankind So intirely destitute, of all Compassion or humanity, and So thoroughly monstrous and obdured[4] in his Soul, as to be capable of Such a barbarous piece of conduct as this of Captain Jobson. Yea I wonder his officers and Ships Company were not prompted by that humanity that is naturally implanted in every human breast to compell their Commander by force to Stay till he knew the State we were in. But this tyrannical Authority which he by Character exercises aboard & which oblig'd many of his Men to run away from his Ship at the Cape, has I Suppose, So much daunted the rest, that they durst Not venture to advise him on [fasc. 16, f. 5r] this occasion. I make No doubt but to have Seen us Sink, would have been a joyfull Sight to the wretch; for he being bound to the Same port, might thereby hope for a greater price for his Goods, which I Suppose was the prevalent Motive in his base Mercenary breast for leaving us without affording us help.

On **Sunday the 22nd of April** we gott in Sight of the Eastern Side of the Maldivee Islands[5] in the Lattitude of 6 Degrees North, having miss'd Seeing of Zeilon,[6] before, which made us imagine ourselves to the Eastward So that fearing to fall to the leeward of Madarass, we beat up to the westward for twenty Days, till the Seeing the Maldivees discover'd our mistakes upon which we bore away for Zeilon, which we discovere'd on thursday [sic] following,[7] and by Night came in with the Southwest part of the Island Sailing within a few Leagues of the Shore for Several Days.[8] Here when the breezes came off the Land, they brought with them the Most agreable Smell that ever I have felt. It was Such as proceeds from a fine Garden when Walking in it in a Morning, that is full of

---

[1] Captain Steward was naturally upset at the incident but had no idea why Jobson of the *Royal George* did not come to their aid. As Steward recorded in the *Godolphin*'s logbook: 'the Ship we first saw was the *Royal George* & was about a mile from us at 2 afternoon and not with standing the Distress we was in, he made Sail & left us; the *Princess Mary* was about A league off and [I] am willing to believe did not see us; if he had I thing [sic think] Captain Martin would not have [...] left us in that condition as Captain Jobson did' (BL: IOR L/MAR/B/594M(1), entry for 7 February 1738).

[2] Jury refers to jury rigging or completing makeshift repairs.

[3] It took 10 full days of work to repair the damage to the ship (BL: IOR L/MAR/B/594M(1), entry for 18 February 1738).

[4] Meaning hardened.

[5] The Maldives are a chain of 26 atolls spanning some 115 square miles off the south-west tip of India. There is no way of knowing which island Fergusson saw.

[6] Meaning Ceylon.

[7] Fergusson's dates are off slightly. According to the *Godolphin*'s logbook, Ceylon was sighted on 28 April 1738 (BL: IOR L/MAR/B/594M(1)).

[8] Captain Steward was indeed worried the *Godolphin* was too eastward and was trying to make the Maldives. He was very concerned about getting to their main destination of Madras, particularly as the crew began 'to be sickly' (BL: IOR L/MAR/B/594M(1), entry for 20 April 1738).

odoriferous [fasc. 16, f. 5v] plants & flowers. I could not indeed Say that I felt distinctly the Smell of Cinnamon, which is produced in plenty on this Island; Yet the fragrance that the Goulle Gales[1] wafted from the Shore was more peculiarly delicious than I had before felt any where; This was no doubt more agreably relishing by reason of our having had So long a passage. Yet the agreable odour was So evidently Sensible, that even in our Cabbins or a Bed, we could as punctually tell the coming off of the Land wind, as if we had been up on Deck. So Strongly fragrant were the delicious Exhalations that it~~hey~~ conveyed along with it.

   This Island has to the Eye a very beautiful appearance, by the delightfull variety of Hills and Plains, that are diversify'd with woods, Groves of Trees & open green fields. And did not its Situation So near the Equinoctial Line,[2] necessarily occasion a very Great Heat of the clime, it might no doubt be one of the finest Islands in the world.

[fasc. 16, f. 6r] **May the 3d.** We gott Sight of the Cormandell [*sic*] Coast Near Trincumbar a Fortification & Factory belonging to the Danes,[3] and Sailing along in Sight of the Coast, we pass'd Fort St Davids a Settlement belonging to the English Company,[4] Ponticherry [*sic*] the greatest of the French settlements in India,[5] Sadrassapatan which belong to the Dutch,[6] Cabalong which belong'd to the Ostenders,[7] San*ta* May possess'd by the Moors,[8] and arriv'd in Madrass road the 5th, where were riding Many Country Ships with 3 More of Europe.

   I See not any thing particularly worth the remarking about this place to be added to the Notes I made my first voyage.

---

   [1] Goulle, as Fergusson wrote, means Galle, the primary spice port in Ceylon's south. Fergusson is referencing the perfumed winds that were fabled to waft off the coast of this 'spice island' famous for cinnamon, cardamom, nutmeg, and mace. Maybe these scented breezes existed in Fergusson's day. By the mid-19th century, however, they were the stuff of legend and shipboard pranks. As reported by one sailor in 1850s: 'There is no such thing as "spicy breezes" [...] This is purely a myth, and arises from a hoax sometimes played on "griffs" when first sailing in these seas. Perfume is put on the side of the Ship and the greenhorn is requested to come and scent the breeze'. (Anon., 'The Overland Route to India', *The Friend*, p. 68).
   [2] Meaning the equator.
   [3] Known also as Tranquebar, the town was a Danish colony from 1620 to 1845, when it came under British control. Now called Tharangambadi, it lies about 150 miles south of Chennai.
   [4] The EIC's Fort St David was built by the VOC in the small village of Devanampattinam (now a neighbourhood of Cuddalore), 100 miles south of Chennai. The Dutch received permission to establish a factory there from the ruling Nayacks of Gingee, who controlled much of Tamil Nadu in the 16th–18th centuries as provincial governors of the Vijayanagara Emperor. When the region was conquered by the Marathas in the late 17th century, they decided to auction the fort to European companies. The EIC offered the highest bid and in 1690, Madras governor Elihu Yale took possession and renamed the fort after a Welsh saint.
   [5] See above, Voyage 2, p. 47, n. 5.
   [6] Known more commonly as Sadras, and originally as Sadiravasagan Pattinam, the port was an important weaver's settlement, prompting the Dutch to establish a factory there in 1648. With the exception of the years 1796–1818, they controlled the settlement until 1854, making it the last remnant of Dutch rule along the Coromandel Coast.
   [7] By 1738 the Ostend Company was dissolved and the factory at Covelong was in the hands of the Carnatic Nawab Dost Ali Khan, along with the region around Madras.
   [8] Fergusson means Santhome, not Santa May. Now a southern suburb of Chennai, Santhome is named after St Thomas, an apostle of Jesus Christ, who is said to have travelled to India to spread Christianity until his martyrdom in AD 72. His tomb in Santhome, located in the eponymous St Thomas Basilica, is a site of pilgrimage, and even attracted Marco Polo in 1292.

It may not however be amiss to take Notice of a Nuptial Show the greatest, & most magnificant. [*sic*] [fasc. 16, f. 6v] of any thing in that way that ever I Saw. It was occasion'd by the marriage of the Son of a very rich Gentou to a Young girl of the Same Cast. The Young Man was about 18 or 20, but the girl appear'd to be Not above 8 or 9 Years of age.[1] It would be almost impossible to explain all the different ornaments and oeconomy[2] of this procession of the Married Couple through the black town. The number of attendants, Their peculiarly Splendid Dress, The Musicians, Dancers, Garland Bearers, and infinite Number of Lights dispos'd in a peculiarly grand manner. The fireworks [fasc. 16, f. 7r] playing in all parts of the Streets as they pass'd. The Rich & magnificent Equipage of the Bridegroom & Bride, with the Disposal of the whole Solemnity Struck me with uncommon Surprise, & afforded me a Sight the most remarkable that ever I Saw of that[3] kind.

The procession began after Sunset and ended about 10 at Night. The Bridegroom Sumptuously Dress'd was mounted on a Stately white horse, richly caparison'd[4] & adorn'd with the most Shining ornaments. He was Sorrounded [*sic*] or in closs'd by a frame of wood that was Supported by a Number of Servants and on this frame finely painted were fix'd an infinite number of green bushes, flower potts, fragrant plants & [fasc. 16, f. 7v] fruit, disposs'd in the most beautifull manner, & Sorrounded with a multitude of Lights.

This Splendid frame was open only before, where half a Dozen of dancing wenches finely dress'd and their hair plaited full of flowrs [*sic*] walk'd before the Bridegroom, and at proper intervals a Stop beeing [*sic*] made they turn'd about dancing before Him & Singing in their Country Manner. Several Men well dress'd & mounted on horses preceeded & follow'd the Bridegroom. The Bride Satt in a richly adorn'd Paranquin,[5] dress'd up as in their manner with many Sparkling Jewells. Her wrists being quite covered with rich braceletts which they call Joys,[6] [fasc. 16, f. 8r] as also her neck, Ears & the Pinnee[7] or Sides of her Nose[.] Her hair was plaited in a long plaite that hung down betwixt her Shoulders, Stuck full of flowrs [*sic*], and on her forehead Shone many Lucid ornaments of precious Stones Tinsell &.C.

At the lower End of the Paranquin Sate two Younger girls which I was told were her Sisters, they were also very finely dress'd. I could not help taking particular notice of this So Young a Bride, who Sate with all the Matrimonial gravity of a matron, & unconcernedly Seem'd to Neglect the Numerous Spectators that gaz'd upon her. Her

---

[1] Child marriages still take place in India today, despite being on the decline and made illegal first in 1929 and more stringently by the 2006 Prohibition of Child Marriage Act. It is thought that poverty and certain customary traditions, such as dowries, help sustain the practice.

[2] This has more meaning than simply an archaic spelling of the modern economy. The use of oeconomy in the 18th century generally refers to how private affairs were managed, particularly those concerning the household (Harvey, *The Little Republic*, pp. 24–6).

[3] Fergusson also has written 'any' under or on top of 'that'. Unable to tell which word Fergusson wanted to use, I have selected the word that flows best in the sentence.

[4] Referring to a horse being covered in rich decorations.

[5] Meaning palanquin, a litter carried by servants. This formed one of the principal modes of local transport for the better-off in 18th-century India.

[6] This was a common word for ornament, or jewellery in 18th- and early 19th-century South India. It did not just refer to bracelets, which are better known as bangles, as Fergusson states.

[7] More commonly pinna. This usually refers to the external ear, though can mean any projecting body part.

attendants were many, with all kinds of Musick playing around, & the Same Number of Dancing [fasc. 16, f. 8v] wenches before her as the Bridegroom, who went foremost with his attendants She following; There were Several of the Black People arm'd who attended them to prevent any abuse or disturbance from the mob. Thus far I have describ'd this Darling procession, as to what occurs of the Bride & Bridegroom. But the rest would require a volume if they were to be particularly ennumerated [sic].

It may be worth observing that these Dancing wenches are Girls bred up to this office of Dancing & Singing before their Idol Gods and other Solemnitys, for which they are hir'd & pay'd. They in general turn whores, being for the Most part likely Girls, and like our own Players,[1] probably thinking that there [sic] business allows them to gett a livelyhood by more than one kind of Dancing.

[fasc. 17, f. 1r] **Friday the 9th of June.** we Sailed from Madarass for China. The 17th we Saw the Nicobar Islands[2] and the Day following Achin Head.[3] As we Sail'd up the Straits of Malacca we kept pretty near the Malay Coast which had a very pleasant appearance, it being every where covered with Lofty Verdant Trees quite down to the Waters edge, as were almost every one of the Islands.

[**Friday the 7th of July.**] On the 7th of July we Arriv'd at Malacca.[4] This is a pretty Large Town and Strong Fortification belonging to the Dutch who took it from the Portugueze they being the founders of the Setlement.[5] The Fortification is the largest and Strongest that I have Seen any where in India,[6] and Seems capable of making a Strong defence, but requires a Numerous garrison for that purpose by reason of its Extent. The Dutch I understand found this the hardest of any of their undertakings in India against the Portugueze; nor could they have carry'd their Point, tho' they attempted [fasc. 17, f. 1v] it oft with great bravery; if they had not found Means to bribe one of the principal commanding officers, who for a Stipulated Sum, had agreed to leave one bastion Naked, by which in the Night the Dutch made their Entrance, and carry'd all before them. They

---

[1] Meaning stage actors.

[2] The Nicobar Islands are an archipelago of 22 islands in the eastern Indian Ocean.

[3] Near the city of Banda Aceh, this is the northernmost point of Sumatra, modern Indonesia's largest island.

[4] Malacca rose to prominence as the capital of the Malacca Sultanate (c.1400–1513). From its strategic location midway along the Straits that connect the Indian Ocean and South China Sea, it became one of the principal trading entrepôts of the wider region and as a result, grew incredibly wealthy. When the Portuguese entered the Indian Ocean in the late 15th century, they learned of Malacca's importance, and in 1509 a Portuguese envoy arrived seeking to trade with the city. However, like elsewhere in the Indian Ocean, the religiously motivated violence of the Portuguese caused trading relationships with Muslim powers to suffer, leading to further conflict and the eventual Portuguese attack against Malacca a couple of years later.

[5] Fergusson is not quite correct here. Portuguese Viceroy Alfonso de Albuquerque captured independent Malacca from ruler Sultan Mahmud Shah (r. 1488–1511) in 1511. In 1641, the VOC and the Sultanate of Johor (descendants of Mahmud Shah) together captured Malacca, thus expelling Portuguese power from the region. As per their treaty of alliance, the Dutch took possession of the port, which they held until 1825, except for a brief period of British rule (1795–1818) during the Napoleonic Wars. The fortress referred to is best known by its original Portuguese name *A Famosa*, meaning 'the famous'. It was originally constructed immediately following the Portuguese capture of the city and was expanded several times under both the Portuguese and Dutch. The fortress was destroyed in 1806 during the British occupation of Malacca. Today only a small gate house, known as *Porta de Santiago*, is all that remains.

[6] Meaning the Indies.

rewarded the Betrayer by Death, which was Suitable enough to his Crime, as also to the Temper of the Dutch, Who thereby Sav'd their money.[1]

The walls of this Fort ~~are~~ appear exceeding Strong being built with Large Square hard Stones, and in Circuit they are about[2] ¾ of an English mile or more. They enclose a Small Hill which rises in the midle of the Fort on one Side of which is the Governor's house & gardens, and on the Top is the Church, which Suffers often by Thunder and lightning that are So very frequent here that no Night passes without them.[3] However the Superstitious remains of the Portugueze & other converts of that Religion in these parts, attribute this [fasc. 17, f. 2r] to the Judgements of Heav'n, upon the Treachery & Sacriledge of the Dutch, who it Seems riffled this church of its holy utensils, converting them to profane uses, and the Church itself to the Service of Hereticks. They with all affirm from their favourite Tradition, (for None are now alive that can assert this from their own knowledge) that nothing of this kind ever happen'd to the Church while it was in possession of these Pious Catholicks the Portugueze. And to confirm this their bigotted [sic] fancy, they observe that the Dutch Flagstaff has been So often beat down by the Thunder, that they became weary of Erecting another. This last is true Enough but the Causes of it are obvious and Natural; tho' I have heard Some of the Dutch themselves acknowledge that it was Somewhat Strange that their Flagstaff Should be beat down So often whilst other Places that are as high remain unhurt. But the reason must be that their Flagstaff is naturally more weak, and not So capable of being well fix'd. However the Dutch are building a new Steeple to their Church, the [fasc. 17, f. 2v] fate of which is eagerly expected by the, Poor Ignorant Biggotts of the Romish Religion. What has much of late carry'd them into this Strain more than usual, is an affair which maybe worth notice. There happened Some Years ago ~~in the~~ to be affix'd to the Fort gates and Some other publick places about the Town, a Paper affirming that against a Short period of Time all the Dutch would certainly be destroyed advising the other Inhabitants in Time to retire lest they Should Share their fate. After much Inquiry they Were not able to find out the Author of this; attlenth [sic] as it was Natural to Suspect that the Portugueze Priests knew Something of the matter, the Governor Sent for them, and by promises & threatnings in vain endeavour'd to extort the Secret. atlast [sic] he told them, that if by Such a Day they did not procure him proper Intelligence in that affair, he would destroy their church, which was a very fine one that they had gott liberty to build at alitle distance from the Town.

This menace however weighty was not able to produce a Discovery. For either they [fasc. 17, f. 3r] were innocent, or thought The Governor would not execute his threatning,

---

[1] Dutch barbarity and avarice in commercial matters was a common trope for early 18th-century Britons. Such sentiments were popularized by John Dryden's play *Amboyna* written in 1673 during the Third Anglo-Dutch War, and subsequently fuelled by Anglo-Dutch mercantile rivalry in the East. See Raman, *Framing 'India'*, pp. 189–236. The role of bribery that Fergusson mentions in the taking of Malacca was a common myth amongst sailors at the time and was also related in Hamilton, *A New Account of the East-Indies*, II, pp. 78–9. Those versions of events, however, are not supported by archival sources and have been debunked. See Leupe and Hacobian, 'The Siege and Capture of Malacca', pp. i–iii, 52.

[2] This word overlaps with betwixt. I have selected the word that best fits the sentence.

[3] On the top of what is now known as St Paul's Hill the Portuguese built a small chapel dedicated to the Virgin Mary in 1521. With Dutch conquest it was converted to the Dutch Reformed Church and dedicated to St Paul. After a larger church was built by the Dutch in 1753, it was deconsecrated and incorporated into the fortifications.

but in this last they Were decieved [*sic*], for after the Day fix'd was elaps'd, he order'd the Church to be pull'd down, which was effectually putt in Execution; It being Riffled by the Mob of Dutch, Malays & others. I Saw Some of its vases and Stone Cisterns that were for Holy water, plain as ornaments in a Dutchman's garden.[1]

The Dutch have here about three Hundr*ed* European Soldiers, besides the Townsmen; who all are oblig'd to Carry arms upon occasion. These Townsmen Consist of Dutch, Chinese & Malays, which two last are pretty Numerous, for as the Chinese have an Yearly Trade by Sending Several of their Ships called Junks hither, a great many of that People Setle here under the Protection of the Dutch, and are the Principal Shop keepers or Small Traders here. The Malays are also encourag'd to come and live peaceably in the Town which many of them do. Both Chinese and Malays have their Churches or Places of Worship with Schools &.C.[2] The Chinese bring no women from their [fasc. 17, f. 3v] Native Country, but many of them Marray [*sic*] Malay Women.

Over each of these People there is plac'd a Captain, who is to be their Leader or Commander under direction of the Dutch governor, Much in the Same manner as is the Regulation of the Militia in Great Britain.

The Malays appear to be of a more robust bodys than any of the other Eastern People that I have Seen. Their Complexion is not quite black. Their Stature midle Size, but in general they are brawny & full of Flesh. In their Gait or walking they are very Stately, which at first appears affected, tho' it is really natural or atleast Universal; for the Poorest of them have the Same deportment. They are thought not to want Courage; tho' their Cruelty and Treachery is most remarked by Europeans who trade to those Places upon the Coast where the Malays are masters; and are there fore oblig'd always to be upon their Guard, lest they should be cutt off, as has been frequently their fate.

[fasc. 17, f. 4r] The Malays profess the Mahometan Religion, which has Strangely Spread itself all over these Eastern Nations, China only excepted of those that I know.[3] For it has made its Way into Sumatra, Java, Borneo, Pegū[4] & Many other remote Places

[1] This story may also be more myth than reality. Religious persecution of Catholics did follow the Dutch capture of Malacca in 1641, which included the pulling down of churches and forbidding worship. However, in 1703 the Dutch proclaimed religious freedom in Malacca, after which the Portuguese descendants built the still-standing St Peter's Church in 1710.

[2] Fergusson means temples and mosques, not churches. The oldest of these is the Daoist/Buddhist/ Confucian Cheg Hoon Teng Temple, which was built in Malacca in 1645 by Tauy Kie Ki the Chinese kapitan (civic leader) of the Chinese community. Under the Dutch each ethnic group had their own kapitan leaders who exercised varying degrees of power. Fergusson addresses these roles in next paragraph. Fergusson would also have seen the nearby Kampung Hulu Mosque, which was fairly new when he visited having been finished in 1728, a decade before his arrival.

[3] Islam was first brought to China in the early 7th century by merchants who established small communities of Muslims in towns along the coast and in the interior. Eventually it became the dominant religion in much of what is today western China.

[4] Islam spread across the Indian Ocean via mercantile networks. The first group of Muslims recorded in Sumatra was in 647, and certainly by the time of Marco Polo's travels in the late 13th century, the region was already predominantly Muslim. Sumatra and Java are the largest islands of the modern state of Indonesia. Borneo is another large island now shared amongst Malaysia, Indonesia, and Brunei. Pegu (now Bago) is in modern Myanmar and was a prominent port city, which was often fought over by regional powers, Asian and European alike.

where it is generally observ'd. So that I have reason to think, considering its progress in Europe, in all the Dominions of the Emperor of Morocco in Africa, in these of the Grand Segnior,[1] Emperor of Persia, Grand Mogul & others in Asia, besides those above mentioned, that its adherents are by far more Numerous than the Professors of the Christian Religion.[2]

The Malays are much addicted to the eating of opium, which is a considerable branch of Trade to these Parts, and commonly Sells at a good Profit.[3] With this many of the Malays intoxicate themselves as effectually as Europeans do with wine, altho' the Effects of opium are more lasting & Pernicious, it commonly producing a Stupor of the Senses, & Sometimes a madness [fasc. 17, f. 4v] in those that have us'd it much. It is their Elegant Entertainment when they have a mind to be merry, and like our Spirituous Liquors, the usual resource of those whose ill conduct or misfortunes ~~makes~~ has made reflexion become a Burthen. In which Case Some of them that are weary of Life intoxicate themselves thoroughly, and with their drawn Cress or Dagger,[4] run furiously along killing all they meet, untill they are destroy'd themselves. This Strange & unaccountable Piece of Madness, is peculiar to this People, and which frequently they fall into, especially after matches at cockfighting, of which diversion they are So extravagantly fond, that they will Stake not only all their money, Goods & Catle, but after these, even their wives and Children; So that if they have the misfortune Still to lose; Some of them in Dispair [sic] with their Naked Cresses run a muck as above. This makes it Dangerous to be present at their Cockfightings when the Stakes run So high. And then the Prudent & Cautious Retire.

[fasc. 17, f. 5r] In these matches they arm the Spurs of their Cocks with Small crooked Lances or rather knives; So that the match is almost allways determin'd by the Death of one of the Cocks, for they are of Such a brood as never to run from their adversary. These Matches are often fought with Quails, which are here of a Large kind, and are keept & bred up for this purpose.[5] The Malay Country is divided into several distinct Kingdoms, which have Each their peculiar King;[6] Tho' the Boundarys of their Dominions are often altered by the Conquests of the most powerfull.

Some of these Kings, I find, dont think it below their majesty to merchandize with Strangers; and I'm told they are the only merchants of foreign Commodities in their Kingdoms.[7] This I'm inform'd of from Several Europeans who have had dealings with them.

---

[1] This is an old way of referring to the Caliph of the Ottoman Empire.

[2] Demographic information is too incomplete for the 18th century to have any way of knowing if Fergusson's assertion is correct. However, data for modern times shows that there are more Christians (2.2 billion) than Muslims (1.8 billion) worldwide.

[3] It should be remembered that this was before the British took control of most of India and with it the global opium production, culminating in the infamous 19th-century Opium Wars against Qing China.

[4] *Kris* or *keris*, is a type of dagger common in South East Asia. Its blade is characteristically wavy from the hilt to point and is forged from many layers of folded iron.

[5] Quail fighting is still a popular activity in South East Asia and parts of Central Asia.

[6] Even today nine of the states of federal Malaysia are headed by traditional monarchies who use the title of sultan or raja.

[7] Fergusson's assertions ought to be qualified according to the sultanate and era. However, generally speaking, the rulers across the Malay peninsula and neighbouring islands, controlled trade through royal monopolies.

The Country is Sufficiently fruitfull, for they have plenty of Rain, a blessing much wanted in many parts of India; But here I'm told there Seldom [fasc. 17, f. 5v] passes a Day without it more or less; and this I observ'd to be so while I stay'd there. Here is Rice in Plenty, and Sago of the best kind in such Quantity and so cheap, that the Poorer Sort often eat it instead of Rice.[1] The Best Sago comes from the Coast of Sumatra; It is a factitious[2] Grain Made of the Pith of a Tree, and by a peculiar management run into this round Shape, which resembles the other farinaceous[3] Seeds So much that it is generally taken to be of that Kind. All kinds of Fruits that are produc'd betwixt the Tropicks, grow here in Plenty, Such as Pine=aples, Plantains, Pumle Noses &.C.[4] But the Fruit which is most valued by Strangers here, because it grows but in few other Eastern Countrys, & upon accountt of its Taste is the Mangustine.[5] This Fruit is inclos'd like a Kernell in a thick Coat rough & Prickly, Somewhat like that of the Horse walnutt in England. You cutt this thick Coat round, and Separate it easily from [fasc. 17, f. 6r] the Pulpy fruit, which Surrounds a Hard Stone that lies in the Centre, Somewhat like that of a Plumb. The bigness of this fruit when Separated from its rough external Coat is not more than that of an olive, which it also resembles in Shape. Its Taste is peculiarly Soft and delicious, exceeding all the other Eastern Fruit the Pine aple [sic] excepted. There are a great many other fruits of this Species, but none that are comparable to the Mangustine.

Here also is another very peculiar Fruit, remarkable for its being as much lik'd by some, as detested and abhorr'd by others. They call it a Durrian. It is about the Largeness of a Mans Fist, Some are larger, and has a thick coat which covers its Pulp. Its flavour is the Strongest most diffusive, and peculiar of any thing I have mett with. The nearest of any thing I know to resemble them is to the Smell of Garlick, assafoetida and aples Mix'd.[6] The Europeans that like them are the few= [fasc. 17, f. 6v] =est number; Nor do I wonder it, considering their forbidding Smell or rather Stink. But those who eat them affirm that their taste is exceeding rich and Delicious; and that their first dislike of their Smell was Soon remov'd by the agreableness [sic] of the Taste. But this I could not persuade myself to try; being assur'd that I must very much Shock one Sense; but was Not certain to have that compensated by the pleasure of the other; for I found Sev'rals after Trial were Still confirmed in their aversion.

[1] Sago is a starch made from the centre of the palm species *Metroxylon sagu*. It is a staple across South East Asia and is often produced in round pearls similar to tapioca, to which Fergusson makes reference.

[2] Meaning artificially created. For example, couscous is also a factitious grain as it is flour that is preserved by processing it into small pellets.

[3] Meaning starchy.

[4] Fergusson is inconsistent with hyphenating his spelling of pineapples. Pumlenoses, more commonly called pomelos (*Citrus maxima* or *C. grandis*), are a variety of citrus fruit native to South East Asia.

[5] Fergusson is confused over the types of fruit. He mentions mangosteen (*Garcinia mangostana*) but goes on to describe the rambutan (*Nephelium lappaceum*), which is a white pulpy fruit surrounding a small stone, covered in a red skin with soft hairy spines, resembling, as Fergusson states, something like a chestnut. Furthermore, mangosteens have several seeds within one fruit whereas the rambutan has only one, like a lychee or longan, to which it is closely related.

[6] Fergusson's description of the scent of durian fruit is likely to be familiar to the modern reader. Some find its aroma so offensive that it is banned from some forms of public transport in South East Asia. Asafoetida, also known as stinking gum, is a dried latex derived from plants of the genus *Ferula*. It is usually used as a condiment, or as a digestive aid, in some South Asian cuisines. Fergusson probably knew it as a medicinal ingredient used internally to treat ulcers or inhaled for various throat and sinus ailments.

The Produce of this Country for Merchandice is chiefly Tin, and beetlenut;[1] They have also gold, of which a good Deal is exported. The Dutch Company however I'm told dont gain near So much by the Trade of Malacca as is Sufficient to Support the Setlement. The greatest advantage by it is their being able to procure a good Deal of Tin, which Sells at a considerable Price over India, but especially in China. They likewise by this Setlement vent a great quantity [fasc. 17, f. 7r] of their Spices. And these two are their greatest if not only returns, I mean for the Company, who give no allowance for Europeans to trade here nor to any other of their Setlements. But their Governors &.C. find their account in Indulging a Clandestine Trade with the English, French, Moors & others, who bring opium, Some piece goods &.C., and carry with them Sugar (which comes from Java & Sumatra) Damar[2] (a kind of Gum which us'd for Ships instead of Pitch) Canes, rattans &.C. But they are So Just to the Company in this that they Seldom lett these Strangers purchase any tin there. Tho' the true reason I'm told is that it is Seldom worth their while to Give Such a gratuity for the Liberty as is expected by the Governor &.C., Seeing they can Meet with it cheaper at other parts on the Coast.

The Principal Men who reap advantage by this Private Trade are The Governor, The Fiscal, The Shabunder. The first it supreme; The Fiscal [fasc. 17, f. 7v] is Judge in all Criminal Matters, and in many things has a Power independant [sic] of the Governor.[3] The Shabunders Province, is to look after affairs of Trade; and is the Person to be applied to in Landing & Shipping of Goods.[4] However these three have Each their Quota in all Presents & other Perquisites gain'd by the Private Trade, Nor can their Interests be Separate in this without destroying the advantages of one another. As for the rest of the Council they are litle considered, they Seeming to be intirely at the Devotion of the Governor and other two.

It is not Safe for Europeans to travell into the Country at any great Distance from the Town. For the Malays are a People who Spare no Strangers, if they can gett any thing by Murdering them. And one's cloths however mean are a Sufficient Incitement to the avaritious[5] Inhumanity of these wretches. This has been fatally verified more than [fasc. 17, f. 8r] once upon this Coast, when Ships have Sent their boats unwarily ashore on purpose to gett Some wood or water, they have been found dead near the place of Landing Strip'd of ev'ry thing that was about them. These Instances besides others that happened but a few miles from Malacca have of Late made People more Cautious in their Conduct. But tho' the Town of Malacca lies almost open having no walls of Consequence round it, The Malay's have not lately made any attempt upon it, fearing

---

[1] What is commonly called betel nut is actually an areca nut, the fruit of the palm *Areca catechu*. It is usually chewed together with the betel leaf (*Piper betle*) in which pieces of the nut are wrapped, along with various other ingredients, such as tobacco, lime (calcium hydroxide), and various spices. It is a mild stimulant and is popularly consumed primarily by men across South and South East Asia.

[2] Dammar gum is more commonly associated with making varnishes. It is a resin made from plants of the *Dipterocarpus* genus.

[3] For the role of fiscals under the VOC, see above, Voyage 3, p. 69, n. 1.

[4] *Shahbandar* is a title of Persian origin, usually translated as harbour-master, from shah meaning king or lord, and *bandar* meaning harbour or waterside emporium. It was a position of importance responsible for receiving of customs duties and regulating the affairs of country merchants.

[5] Meaning avaricious, with an extreme greed and desire for material gain.

the Resentment of the Dutch of whom they Stand in much awe, being experimentally convinc'd of their Danger. Besides as the Dutch have Scouts posted at convenient Distances from the Town to give Notice timeously of any approaching Danger, they have no fear of being Surpris'd.

[fasc. 17, f. 8v] **Thursday July 20th.** We Sailed from Malacca. As we pass'd through the Narrow Straits among the Islands we Saw great Numbers of Small fishing boats call'd Proes,[1] of which Some Came aboard & brought us fish, for which they were paid.

Having a very quick passage through the Straits we took our Departure from Point Romana[2] the Extremity of the Land on the North Side, the 24th & the 29th we Saw Pouly Condore[3] an Island where our Company had once a Setlement but left it, not finding, it Seems the advantages answerable to the Expence. August 1st. We had Sight of P. Sapata,[4] and Thursday the 10th we made the North most of the Ladroons called the asses=Ears,[5] and the 11th we came to an anchor not far from Macao, having taken aboard a Chinese Pilot who came off to us in the Morning.[6]

[fasc. 17, inside back cover][7]
Sailed from Wampo Nov*embe*r 2d.
Pass'd the Tygers Mouth 5th
and that Night left our Pilot.
The 6th Shipp'd the great Sea
The 13 Saw Sapata, &
the 14th Poly Candore
the 17th Saw the Anamba's
the 18 saw P. Tinge & Barbucett Hill
The 19th pass'd Pedro Branco
Friday 24th arriv'd at Malacc [*sic*]
Thursday 30th Sail'd from Mal.

---

[1] A proa is a broad term for a classification of Asian and Pacific sailing vessels. In the waters of South East Asia it typically refers to a traditional vessel with outriggers used for fishing and transport.

[2] More commonly Romania Point in English and more properly Tanjung Penyusop in Malay, this is a point of land in Johor, Malaysia, where the Singapore Strait meets the South China Sea.

[3] Poulay, or rather *pulo* means island in several South East Asian languages. Condore Island is now known by its Vietnamese name Côn Sơn Island. The EIC founded a factory there in 1702, abandoning it just three years later in 1705.

[4] Pulo Sapata, or Shoe Island, is the easternmost of the three small Catwick Islands. It is today part of Vietnam and is known as Hòn Hải.

[5] The Ladrones (robbers in Spanish) Islands, are now the 104-island Wanshan Archipelago off the coast of Macao. The Asses' Ears are two peaks rising almost 900 feet above the island now called Beijian Dao. It was a prominent landmark that was featured in nearly all European sailing manuals to China in the 18th and 19th centuries.

[6] The shoals of the Pearl River were notoriously dangerous. Foreign ships like the *Godolphin* were required to hire registered Chinese pilots to guide them safely up the ever-changing river to the anchorage outside Canton.

[7] On the inside back cover of fasc. 17 Fergusson left a list of notes, likely to aid his memory in compiling the next sections of his voyage. They have been reproduced here as they appear.

[fasc. 18, f. 1r] Macao or Maccow[1] is a Town & Fortification Situated on a Peninsula or rather Island (it being Separated from the Continent by A River) of the Same Name near the Mouth of Canton River.[2] The Portugueze have had Liberty to Setle themselves here, with full privilidge & immunitys, granted them by a former Emperor about 100 Years ago, for their assisting to expell a Chinese Pirate who had possess'd himself of this Place.[3] Yet altho they have a Governor of their own with Soldiers &.C. they are notwithstanding under the Direction of the Chinese Mandarin[4] who resides here; and the Chinese Inhabitants are More Numerous than the Portugueze who however are many, allmost all Europeans of the Romish Religion who have a Mind, Setting themselves there. So that they have churches, Monasterys &.C. with considerable Revenues annex'd.

[fasc. 18, f. 1v] The Trade of this place is considerable; for the Portugueze & others Send Small Ships with the Commodities of China[5] Yearly to Several Parts of India, of which they make good Returns; Besides the Spaniards send some ships here from Manilla, one of the Philippine Islands,[6] to which all the commodities of India are carried from Bengal, Madrass [sic], Surrat, China &.C. tho' they Spaniards dare Send No Ships of their own to any Parts in India. The only Trade they carry on from that [p]art on their own Bottoms[7] is to China by means of Macow. However the English French & other Country Ships Supply them at Manilla with all kinds of Indian Goods, which being Sent thence by way of the South Sea[8] Supply the Spaniards in Europe.

---

[1] Macao developed under the later Ming Dynasty (1368–1644) as a commercial port in the early 16th century. Portuguese traders were attracted to the port and were eventually given the right to settle there in the 1550s. Eventually the Portuguese became self-governing through what became known as the *Leal Senato* or Loyal Senate, which regulated affairs relating to the Portuguese on behalf of the Chinese state. During the period of Fergusson's voyages, the Qing Emperor appointed an assistant magistrate to assist in governance and maintain some official presence of Chinese sovereignty over the territory.

[2] The Canton River is also commonly referred to as the Pearl River and sometimes as Chu Kiang but a more proper transliteration from Chinese is Zhujiang.

[3] This story of the Portuguese being granted the right to settle at Macao in 1557 for helping to eradicate piracy in the region is one that recent research has called into question. It seems that the narrative has its origins in the story of a soldier named Tristam Vaz da Viega, who told about his time in 1568 fighting pirates in China to an historian-chronicler in Madeira in the late 1580s. By the 1620s this had become the standard narrative of Portuguese possession of Macao and it is not surprising that Fergusson was told this story, however, it is not supported by archival evidence. Instead it seems that the Portuguese began stationing themselves at various locations around the Pearl River delta a few years earlier and secured the right to trade as long as they paid tribute to the local governor at Canton (today's Guangzhou). This occurred at a time when the *haijin*, the Ming ban of foreign private trade, was opening up. Gradually the Portuguese concentrated their ventures at Canton and had their presence there formalized in the 1580s with the recognition of the Portuguese Crown representative as the 'supervisor of foreigners' by the Chinese Governor-General Chen Rui (Wills, 'Maritime Europe and the Ming', pp. 32–42).

[4] Mandarin was the term Europeans used to refer to all the scholar bureaucrats of the Chinese state. In order to become Chinese officials aspiring candidates had to pass a series of competitive examinations. Under the Qing there were 9 ranks with multiple sub-ranks of officials, from the first who served the emperor directly, to the lowest, regional post such as local jail warden or tax collector. Fergusson also refers to them later as 'viceroys'. See below, p. 152.

[5] Principal Chinese goods for export will be described by Fergusson below.

[6] Founded by the Spanish in 1571, Manila was the primary conduit for American silver from mines in what are today Mexico and Bolivia. Along with other American goods, the precious metal was brought annually by the Manila Galleon sailing from Acapulco for trade with East Asian empires.

[7] Meaning ships.

[8] Referring to the South Pacific. Asian goods bound for Spain would usually be shipped via Panama.

To Moccow[1] the Portugueze Send yearly a Large Ship from Europe, or from Goa bound for Europe.

[fasc. 18, f. 2r] **[Saturday, August] The 12th.** in the Morning early we weigh'd from before Maccow, and next Day in the Morning we pass'd the Narrowest Part of the River called the Tygers Mouth. At each Side of this Entry is built a Small Fort, which if well provided with Cannon are Capable of commanding the passage effectually.[2] From each of these Forts came off to us a Boat with Chinese officers demanding Our Ship's & commanders Name, from whence we came, & what was our Cargo, in which being answered they in a very Civil manner left us. The Next Day we gott to our Proper Station at Ouampo[3] where we found two French Ships, two Dutch, two Swedes and three English all from Europe;[4] and in a few Days after Came in a Dane, another English Ship from Borneo,[5] a French Country Ship from Ponticherry & a Large Surrat Ship belonging to the Moors, who had lost all her masts off the Ladroon Islands.

[fasc. 18, f. 2v] In passing up this River One is entertain'd with as fine a Prospect of Beautiful Landskips as is well possible to be imagined. The Country every where appears exceeding fruitfull and Populous, as one may at first Sight conclude from the view of the Spacious plains on which their Rice and other Grain grows in abundance, the frequent Towns & Villages to be Seen, the Rising grounds nobly beautiful with Lofty Pines & other Trees; And all those other improvements of Gardens & orange orchards which add to the Natural Beauties of this happy Country. The Delightfullest & Most peculiar view is that of all the small Hills, which are cutt in Such a manner as to resemble the Gradations of an Amphitheatre.[6] From the Bottom to the Top the ascent appears like the Steps of Stairs. This they do for the Convenience of Culture; [fasc. 18, f. 3r] for by this means, these Small rising grounds turn to the Same account as if they were naturally Levell [*sic*]. And upon the Horizontal Beds they plant all manner of Garden Herbs, &.C. with Bushes and Trees at convenient Distances So that the Prospect of these Hills at a Small Distance entertains the Eye in a very peculiar manner.

From the Tygers Mouth to Ouampo is about 40 miles Distance, and from Ouampo to the City of Canton is about 12 miles by Water; And all along one is Surpris'd to See the Number of Towns & Villages that are plac'd So Near one another. But one thing particular I could not but observe, that there were no Separate farm Houses or very Small villages, as is common in Britain. The Country is So fruitfull they oft having 2 Crops a Year, that it affords Maintenance for a great Number of People in Small extent, which it Seems determines [fasc. 18, f. 3v] them rather to live together than Separate, Seeing it may be done conveniently enough, and Contributes to their mutual Security from Robbers &.C. from which this part of the Country is not free especially the River where

---

[1] Fergusson could not decide how to spell this city's name.

[2] The Tiger's Mouth, also known by its Portuguese name *Bocca Tigris*, is a narrow strait roughly 40 miles upstream where the Pearl River shrinks down from an average width of 15 miles across to just 2 miles. It was here that foreign ships would stop to receive the official *chop*, or seal, permitting them to continue up to Canton.

[3] More commonly Whampoa, this was the main anchorage for ships trading at Canton. It is now the Huangpu District of modern Guangzhou.

[4] These were the *London*, Captain Bootle; the *Prince of Orange*, Captain Hudson; the *Princess Royall*, Captain Backwell (BL: IOR L/MAR/B/594M(1), entry for 14 August 1738).

[5] This was the *Prince of Wales*, under the command of Captain Pelly (ibid., entry for 15 August 1738).

[6] Fergusson is referring to the terraced cultivation.

these Rogues have Boats with which they often Rob upon the River, and Sometimes the adjacent villages where they dare venture.[1] However the Government takes all possible Care to prevent these Robberies; for the Emperor has many very Convenient Boats well mann'd & arm'd, and plac'd in Such Stations as are most convenient to look after these Robbers, and to prevent any other Disorders upon the River, which they perform to very good Purpose.[2]

This River of Canton divides into So many branches, forming Numbers of Islands, that it contributes Much to the fruitfullness, Beauty & Advantage of the neighbouring Country, A view of which from a rising [fasc. 18, f. 4r] ground ravishes the Eye with the most Exquisitely beautifull rural view that the Earth is capable to afford. The Numerous Boats that pass the many branches of this Expanded river adds to the Beauty of the Prospect; And the wonderfull marks of Industry that are perciev'd on every Portion of ground, where many of the People are to be Seen constantly employ'd on one or other kind of rural labour convince us of the Indefatigable Diligence & Industry of the Chinese in the Culture of their Land.

And from this I began to give more Credit to what I had read in *Pere* Du Haldes History of China[3] which before appear'd to me almost impossible Viz. That in China it is Suppos'd there are as many Souls as in all Europe. A Supposition that cannot but appear incredible to those who have not been Spectators of the fruitfullness of the Country & Number of cities Towns and Villages [fasc. 18, f. 4v] besides the Multitudes that live constantly upon the water with their wives & children.

All over the Country at proper Distances upon Convenient Eminencys are built Stately & beautifull watch Towers of a Pyramidal figure.[4] On the Top of which is a contrivance Lanthern=like, by illuminating of which, the alarm in an incredible Small time is carried through every part of this vast Empire. These Towers are of ancient Standing, being design'd to alarm the Country in case of any Sudden Invasion. But for many Years or rather Centuries last past I'm told they have had no occasion to use them: Tho' they are Still Sustain'd and keept in repair. These contribute not alitle to the august appearance of this fine Country.

Thro' the levell grounds by the rivers Side, they have cutt out many canals of different bigness, which Serve not only to Water their Paddy grounds [fasc. 18, f. 5r] but also for

---

[1] Piracy was a major issue in the South China Sea, particularly in the Pearl River Delta, where the myriad of islets, inlets, and hideouts made patrolling by Chinese authorities difficult. In China's south-east coastal provinces of Fujian and Guangdong, the transition from Ming to Qing rule (1618–83) was chaotic and led to the rise of well-organized merchant pirates many of whom claimed political legitimacy under the banner of Ming loyalty. The best-known example of these was Koxinga (1624–62), who even established his own dynasty and short-lived kingdom (1661–83) on the island of Formosa (now Taiwan). By Fergusson's time, coastal piracy had become small-scale and opportunistic, usually undertaken by those seeking extra income in difficult times (Calanca, 'Piracy and Coastal Security', pp. 91–7). It is clear through the stories Fergusson heard that the effects of the earlier period of maritime depredation were still very much in the memories of the local inhabitants.

[2] With the consolidation of Qing control came the improvements of coastal defences and regular maritime patrols.

[3] French Jesuit Jean-Baptiste Du Halde's *Description de la Chine* first appeared in Paris in 1735 and was quickly translated and printed across Europe. The first English edition was published in London in 1736, which Fergusson may have purchased between voyages. Du Halde described China's population as 'infinitely numerous' (Du Halde, *The General History of China*, II, p. 32).

[4] These are the earlier versions of the *diaolou* or watchtowers, that were first built under the Ming in the 16th century.

the Convenience of Carrying more readily & Cheaply any things from the river in their boats. In Sailing up the Small Creeks it is a fine view to See the Numerous orange Gardens, the Trees loaden with delicious fruit hanging with their branches into the Waters edge. These oranges which are Sweet to eat, of a fine flavour, and very wholesome and refreshing in these hott climates, are in the greatest plenty and to be purchas'd at a very low Rate. Besides there grows here all kinds of Fruits almost of every climate Such as Pineaples, PumleNoses[,] pears[,] Chestnuts & many others that I have not mett with in other Countrys. Tho' I was Surpris'd to find no grapes; Nor do I know if there are any in this Country, which seems fitted to produce any thing. For altho they have Several kinds of Spirituous Liquors which to us they call Wines;[1] Yet these are all made of wheat, Rice & other grain, & Some with [fasc. 18, f. 5v] the assistance of Sugar, of which in this Country there is produc'd a very great Plenty, which is Sold at an Easy Rate; especially their Sugar Candy that is the whitest & finest I have ever Seen.

In Short there is not a Country in the world, (as it is generally believ'd) that has Such a variety and Such Plenty of all the necessary, conveniences & Delights of Life within itself, as China hath. For besides what the Surface of the Earth affords in Such abundance, they have from its bowells Gold, Quicksilver, Pewter, Iron, Brass, Pearls[,] Salt Petre &.C. However if they have Silver it is not So plenty as Gold; for, Some Years before this, there have been great Profits gott by carrying Silver from Europe & purchasing Gold with it;[2] tho' it's Exportation is prohibited by the Emperors order, as is likewise that of Iron & Brass. The only mettal I know that is allow'd to be exported in any quantity is Tutenague a whitish metall hard as copper, of [fasc. 18, f. 6r] which large Quantitys is carried to all Parts in India as also to Europe.[3] There is here a Very peculiar Metle that is Much in Esteem with Europeans which they call white Copper.[4] Utensils made of this & well polish'd look almost as well as Silver, which makes them be Sold at a dear rate.

Silk is here in the greatest plenty as is Cotton, of which they make many kinds of cloths; Besides they they [sic] have found out to make other Plants & trees part with their rinds for their clothing & furniture, the use of which is not known in other Countrys. It is

[1] There is a long tradition of various alcoholic drinks produced in China. Fergusson is probably referring to China's most popular clear spiritous grain liquor called *baijiu*. The less potent *huangjiu*, commonly referred to as yellow wine, brewed from various grains, and the sweeter rice wine, called *mijiu*, were and remain popular beverages.

[2] There is little historical evidence to support Fergusson's claim that silver was used to purchase gold from China. However, it is true that China's appetite for silver during the early modern period was nearly insatiable. This demand was driven by Ming China's monetary reforms that reintroduced coinage after abandoning an experiment with paper currency. Furthermore, the Ming also began demanding the payment of taxes in silver currency. China's own paltry silver deposits were not enough to meet the demands of the new economy and as a result, Japanese silver was imported by Dutch traders and, more importantly, American silver was brought in by the Spanish via Manila and other European middlemen. In Fergusson's day, silver was still the primary European export to China, though by the early 19th century it would eventually be replaced by opium (Pomeranz, *The Great Divergence*, p. 32).

[3] Also tutenag, from the Tamil *thuthanaagam*. It is an alloy of zinc, copper and nickel, also called raw zinc. Its export was also eventually banned by China in January 1833, probably because it was by then an important ingredient used in producing low-value Chinese coinage. While at Whampoa, the *Godolphin* loaded only 'Tutenague and Tea of the Honourable Company', which was destined for sale in Madras, where saltpetre was then taken on board for European markets (BL: IOR L/MAR/B/594M(1), entries for 15 August–2 November 1738, and 29 December 1738–20 January 1739).

[4] This is cupronickel, an alloy of nickel-containing copper, strengthened with other elements like iron.

needless to mention their Tea, or their utensils of Porcelane [*sic*] or china, which are the neatest and finest, and so generally admire'd over the world, besides many other things that would require more time & leisure than I can Spare; or is Suitable to the Design of these Short Notes, wrote to Serve as private memoranda of these occurrenceys [*sic*] that I thought worth being notic'd, & remembred [*sic*].

[fasc. 18, f. 6v] Canton City[1] which is the Capital of the Province of the same Name,[2] is of very great extent & Sorrounded [*sic*] with a Strong high wall The lower half of which is built with Square Stone, & the upper half with Bricks. The walls in Circuit are about 7 English Miles, and the City is reckoned to be about the Largeness of Paris in France. Besides this the Suburbs are very large, & would of themselves make no inconsiderable City. It is in the Suburbs where the Europeans who trade here reside, as do all the merchants of the Chinese who have dealings with them besides Multitudes of artificers[3] of all kinds Shopkeepers & others. These Suburbs Surround that half of the City walls that lie next the river. The other half of the walls is open to the adjacent Country, and afford a magnificent appearance. But as to their Strenth I can affirm nothing positive having never had an opportunity of examin= [fasc. 18, f. 7r] =ing their thickness, more than by looking in at the Gates, where the guard rooms and other conveniences built there prevents ones being able to Judge. For the Chinese will admitt no Europeans within the walls of their City, except on very particular occasions; tho' Some venture to go in a chair,[4] in a Chinese Dress, to prevent a Discovery which might be of Dangerous Consequence: This risque I car'd not to run, having had a Prospect of the City Several times from an Eminence not far from the walls, where we could See the Buildings Streets &.C. which did not differ from these of the Suburbs.

Near that Part of the walls which is most distant from the River are Several Small Hills, on which are built Forts with Small Garrisons in them; which are a great Security to the

---

[1] Canton was the official port for international trade with the Qing Empire, which was ruled at the time by the Qianlong Emperor (r. 1735–96). Foreign trade was heavily regulated under what was called the Canton System. As Fergusson will describe, foreigners were only permitted to arrive and stay in Canton, and then only in their own quarter where the foreign trading houses were built, known as the 13 Factories. The rest of the city lay beyond a wall and gateway that was closed at dark. Foreigners were never officially permitted beyond the wall. All trade was conducted through an officially licensed Chinese merchant known as a *hong*, or collectively as *cohong*. Any other trade between Chinese and foreigners was strictly banned, which gave the *cohong* quite a lot of wealth and status. The role of the *cohong* went far beyond mere business transactions. They acted as guarantors for the conduct of foreigners, collected customs dues and taxes for the government, and also served in an unofficial capacity as cultural interlocutors. All this was overseen by the Administrator of the Canton Customs, known in Chinese as *hubu*, which was mispronounced in English as hoppo. In the early 18th century, hoppos were appointed by the Emperor and with few exceptions only served for about a year. At the time of Fergusson's visit the hoppo was an official named Zheng Wusai (Schottenhammer, 'Characteristics of Qing China's Maritime Trade Politics', pp. 134–6). Each ship arriving at the Whampoa Roads was boarded by a hoppo who measured the ship to determine its carrying capacity and assess payments based on volume. This official activity took place under ceremony and accordingly the foreign ship would give the hoppo a gun salute, as did the *Godolphin* when their ship was measured at Whampoa (BL: IOR L/MAR/B/594M(1), entry for 18 August 1738).

[2] Not quite. In Chinese there has always been a distinction between Guangdong the province and Guangzhou the city. This was likely lost on foreign ears.

[3] Meaning artisans or tradespersons.

[4] Meaning a sedan chair, which was carried like a palanquin.

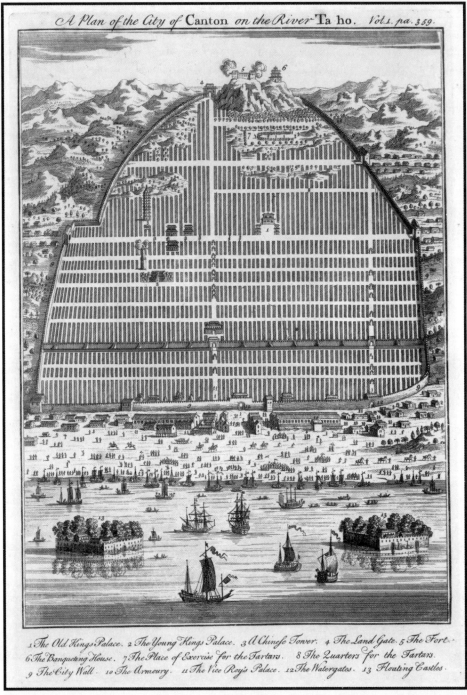

A Plan of the City of Canton on the River Ta ho. Vol.1. pa. 359.

1. The Old Kings Palace. 2 The Young Kings Palace. 3 A Chinese Tower. 4 The Land Gate. 5 The Fort. 6 The Banqueting House. 7 The Place of Exercise for the Tartars. 8 The Quarters for the Tartars. 9 The City Wall. 10 The Armoury. 11 The Vice Roy's Palace. 12 The Watergates. 13 Floating Castles.

Figure 9. 'A Plan of the City of Canton on the River Ta ho', 1744. Courtesy, The Barry Lawrence Ruderman Map Collection, David Rumsey Map Center, Stanford Libraries, Stanford University, California (http://purl.stanford.edu/dt252rx9323). A near contemporary map of Canton showing the walled divisions of the city, as well as its pagoda. What is not shown in this image are the thousands of boats clogging the waterfront that Fergusson described at length.

City in Case it Should be attack'd. For if these Hills were defenceless an Enemy by possessing them could annoy or Destroy a great part of the City, whose walls these Hills overlook.[1] [fasc. 18, f. 7v] The Plan of the City walls come near to the resemblance of a Square one Side of which runs along at alitle Distance from the Rivers Side. The Houses in the City are generally So low as none of them appear above the walls, excepting only the watch Tower, with a few other Publick buildings. Those of the Suburbs for the most part consist of one Story above the ground & one levell with it and those of the meaner Sort only of one. There is not much particular worth observing about the manner of their building, it not differing much from the European manner. The Materials are Stone or Brick, Some of which appear unburnt, and only hardened by the heat of the Sun; but those are only us'd for the meaner Sort of Houses. Their roofs are neatly built & covered with Tiles; and the shades that Jutt out from them Serve to keep off the Sun Beams and to keep the Houses cool. The Mer= [fasc. 18, f. 8r] =chants of Considerable Note, have Large Warehouses continuous to where they dwell. These are called Hongs, and in generall they have a Gate open to the river Side with stairs and proper conveniencys for taking in and shipping off Goods. These Hongs are very capacious and the apartments where the Merchants live and recieve Strangers are exceeding neat. These open at one end into a Small uncovered Square which is Separated from the other parts of the Hong by a Wall, built So in Several parts as to form Small lettice [sic] like openings for the admission of the air. In these Small Squares, they generally have Some curious flower potts, & Shrubs or other Plants, with Cisterns that contain many Small gold colour'd fish that Swim about & are pleasant to look at. Here also they have Some Curious pieces of rock work Sett up, of which they Seem very fond, as reckoning them a pretty piece of ornament. In Some of these [fasc. 18, f. 8v] Places they also have Bee hives and other Natural ornaments, in which their taste Seems generally to run. Their Rooms are very neat tho' plain. The furniture is Some Chairs generally two arm'd, a Table or marble Slab, a Large Couch at one End; and at the other a Cistern or Large Bason [sic] with water to cool their Hands, or for Other Such uses. The walls are Smoothly plaister'd & in Some have hangings. They are Sometimes adorn'd with Pictures & Looking glasses of the European make. Their Beds differ litle in Shape or furniture from ours in Britain. They have no glass in their Windows, but instead of it a transparent thin Shell, which being cutt into Small Squares of about 2 or 3 Inches, admitts the light tolerably well, but excludes the Sun beams.[2] Their rooms are lofty for the freer admission of the air. In the timber work of their buildings they Make litle or No use of Iron. The Hinges bolts &.C. of their windows being wood. [fasc. 19, f. 1r] And for the most part wooden Peggs Serve instead of Nails.[3] The apartments where they Sleep are Small and closs, generally without Light, or atleast if they have any it comes as it were at Second hand. In these Hongs they have commonly one & Sometimes two Large Halls above Stairs for their Entertainments. But in the Houses of the midling Sort, the Rooms are more calculated for necessary use, and therefore much Smaller.

[1] Fergusson was certainly correct. During the First Opium War in May 1841, the British took these fortresses in a matter of days, effectively encircling Canton and causing the city to surrender.

[2] These are again a form of nacre, likely from the shells of the windowpane oyster; see above, Voyage 3, p. 94, n. 1.

[3] This is a standard feature of traditional Chinese craftsmanship. Furniture and cabinetry joinery were achieved through the carving of intricate interlocking joints using a variety of techniques and styles.

The Streets both of City & Suburbs are very narrow, which they Say makes them much Cooler, Seeing the Sun can Scarcely Shine upon them except when vertical or on a Line with the Street. They are all pav'd with Square free Stones, which makes the walking along more easie; and they using no kind of Carriage for their goods, Porters alone being employ'd for that Purpose, the Pave ments [*sic*] are not So Subject to be broken or worn. But the [fasc. 19, f. 1v] narrowness of the Streets which are not in general above 10 or 12 feet broad, makes the passing very often troublesome, by reason of the Crowds of People, Porters &.C. that are constantly mett with.

From the river there are cutt 2 or 3 Canals that run into the midle of the City, by which Numbers of Boats are constantly to be Seen passing & repassing; The larger with Goods, and the Lesser with Passengers. These are exceeding convenient and Save much expence in Porterage to those who live in the City. Besides these there is a Canal or Ditch that goes almost round the City walls, from the river, in which Boats like wise can pass. This Adds to the Defence of the walls.

At the End of each Street there is a pair of gates, which are Shutt after 10 at night: There is a Porter that attends them, and keeps the Keys who at any time of the Night will open the Door to Europeans; But not to Chinese, unless [fasc. 19, f. 2r] he knows them well. These gates are to prevent Robberies & other Thefts or disturbances in the Night. For they Serve to coup up the Transgressors in So narrow a Space as easily to be found. In many Places are to be seen their Joss Houses or the Temples of their Idolatrous Worship;[1] These for the most part differ not much in External appearance from the larger kind of Houses; But Some of them are lofty Capacious buildings.

Upon the River all along before the City & Suburbs for 3 or 4 miles atleast, are to be Seen A most incredible number of Boats, most of them Large, and all covered with moveable Awnings Made of Bamboos, to defend them from the weather.[2] In each of these Boats lives a whole family, and in Some of the Largest two or three. Some of these Boats are employ'd as Lighters,[3] others in Fishing; but the most part I believe, are us'd pûrely as cheap Habitations, in which they live and work at their Small handicrafts, &.C. [fasc. 19, f. 2v] The number of these Boats at a modest calculation is Said to be about 60000. To each of which if we allow 5 Souls which is a moderate number considering the prolifickness [*sic*] of the People. The Number of these who live intirely upon the water in this place, will amount to 300000; a very great Number, tho' I have no reason to believe it less, but rather greater. Many of these people I'm told, especially the women, have liv'd to a great age, and never Sett foot ashore. It is an unusual Sight to behold, the women,

---

[1] Joss is believed to derive from *deus*, the Portuguese word for god. Canton has many ancient temples. Fergusson surely would have seen the rooftops of the recently expanded Dafo Temple, originally established in the 10th century, and the 3rd-century Guangxiao Temple, the oldest Buddhist place of worship in the city.

[2] If Fergusson is exaggerating, it is not by much. The floating boat-cities off the shores of Canton and at the Whampoa anchorage were famous sights. River dwellers provided all kinds of services off their vessels geared toward foreign sailors and local Chinese inhabitants. Restaurants, hotels, repair shops, bars and, of course, the so-called 'flower boats', or brothels, that served everyone at Whampoa but only Chinese at Canton, were popular destinations and diversions for sailors (Van Dyke, 'Floating Brothels', p. 112).

[3] Also called 'chop boats' by Europeans, lighters were generally smaller vessels used to ferry goods between ship and shore. Some that were used for bringing tea from the interior of China were huge, carrying as much as could fit in a 600-ton ocean-going junk (Van Dyke, *Merchants of Canton and Macao*, p. 15).

with their infants fastned [sic] on their Backs, assisting the Husbands in Sculling their boats along while the children that can walk, Scramble along from place to place upon the Sides of the Boat as Securely as if they were ashore. However those that are very young about 2 or 3 Years of age, have commonly fastened betwixt their Shoulders & round their Necks a Small Log of Light wood, or more Commonly the Shell of a Large [fasc. 19, f. 3r] calevansh,[1] in order to prevent their Sinking by buoying them up in case they Should chance to fall over board.

Without[2] these Boats in the middle of the River lye their Ships of Trade or Junks as they are called. ~~These~~ Some of these are very Large, of 7 or 800 Tons Burthen, But the generality are from 2 to 400 Tons. Their shape is very uncommon, and the whole contrivance appears very ill design'd, for resisting the violence of the weather at Sea, as is to [sic] well attested by the fate of many almost every year.[3] They for the most part have two masts, each consisting of one Stick, & carrying one Sail, which is made of rattans plett together, in Such a manner as upon lowering the Sail to Stow in folds. In fair weather they Sometimes hoist, a flying Small top Sail made of thick cloth. Their rigging is very Simple consisting of few ropes, the most of [fasc. 19, f. 3v] which are made of twisted rattans as are their Cables. Their Sails Stand abaft[4] the mast and press forwards upon it. Their anchors are made of wood, Somewhat resembling a grapling with three Flooks,[5] and in some these wooden flooks are tipt with, Iron. These Junks are built high afore & abaft, being like A Small Castle there while their middle or wast is very near the water. In Short the whole Machine to these that are judges, tho' it may appear well contriv'd in Some few respects, Yet in general is very unfitt for resisting the many accidents they are liable to; and in this the Chinese Seem to fall remarkably Short of the Ingenuity of other Nations.[6] Some to whom I express'd My Wonder that they did not take patterns of building more convenient Ships from the Europeans that come there Yearly, answered that their Carpenters told they could build after the European manner. But that tho' they had Ships of that kind [fasc. 19, f. 4r] none of their Sailors knew how to manage them, which was the only reason they did not imitate ours to whom they own'd their Junks could in no ways be compared. But I'm apt to believe the true reason is, a kind of Fondness for & Bigotry in favour of their own Customs. In these Junks ~~of these~~ there is one thing peculiar, Viz their Hold is divided into diverse apartments, which in freighting are lett out to various

---

[1] Meaning calabash, a large dried gourd that has been hollowed.

[2] Again, Fergusson means on the outside, not as we would understand the word without today.

[3] The Chinese junk as a class of ships is one of the more iconic and best-recognized in the world, largely due to their flat sails with full-length battens. First developed in the 2nd century, they have continuously evolved over the centuries. While it is clear that European ship-building technology had outstripped China's by Fergusson's era, there was debate amongst contemporaries on the seaworthiness of junks. Nonetheless, Fergusson is indeed correct that they were not designed for resisting violence at sea. This is because junks were designed, as many ship types in monsoonal areas were, to sail with the winds, not against them (Blussé, 'Chinese Trade to Batavia', p. 200).

[4] This is a preposition meaning toward or at the stern (rear) of a ship, or is to the rear of a location.

[5] An old word meaning the fluke, or hook-shaped protrusion, of an anchor.

[6] But in the early 15th century China led the world in maritime technology. Under the command of Zheng He (c.1371–1433) the Ming dispatched 7 'treasure fleets', each of over 300 ships and crew numbering in the tens of thousands. The size and sheer numbers of vessels involved made these the largest fleets in world history until the First World War (Levathes, *When China Ruled the Seas*, p. 20).

Merchants, unless one should hire the Whole. With these Junks, besides their Coasting Trade which is very great, they trade to Japan, Borneo, Batavia, Malacca, Siam, Cochinchina[1] &.C. whether[2] they carry their home commodities, and bring back the produce of these countrys. And a great Deal of their Gold is imported by these Junks. But what employs the most of them is the bringing of Goods from the Northern parts of China especially from Amoy[3] to Canton, whether [sic] are also [fasc. 19, f. 4v] Sent the manufactures of Canton.

Before I have done with an account of their Shipping & boats it may be worth while to take notice of a Custom they have of hatching Ducks Some Say in the oven & others in hott Dung, and afterwards putting them to the Number of 3, 4 or 500, in a boat they carry them to the river or Sea Side where they feed upon Small fish, worms &.C. These Ducks are So accustom'd that by a certain whistle of their keeper, they repair in an instant aboard without the least trouble; and by another Sound they are warn'd to go out in Search of their food which they as readily obey. Yet they keep allways within Such Bounds as to be ready to obey the Call.[4] This I have more than once been a witness of, with A mixture of pleasure & Surprize.

Provisions of all kinds at Canton are in great Plenty. Here is good Beef, Mutton, Veal, Fowls of all kinds tame & wild, as Ducks, Capons,[5] Snipes, Teel & Partridges, &.C. in plenty [fasc. 19, f. 5r] and at any ease rate. The Dearest of the Flesh kind is Mutton, which is Seldom to be mett with in their marketts, So that Europeans who want it are oblig'd to buy the live Sheep one of which costs betwixt 30 & 40 Shillings.[6] Pork is in the greatest Plenty, and is most of all other kind of Flesh eat [sic] by the Chinese. It is exceeding fatt, tho' very sweat;[7] But to eat quantitys thereof cannot be wholesome. Fish of many kinds and those very good, are to be had Cheap, being daily carry'd about in Plenty. Their Bread is good & Cheap, as are greens & fruits in abundance. Not to mention the Rice which is the bulk of the victuals of the Chinese especially of all the poorer Sort.

The Chinese in stature are of the middle Size, not So thin and Slender as the Indians, nor quite So brawny as the Europeans. The Complexion of those of the Province of Canton (which is one of the Southermost it lying in 22 & 23 Degrees of North Latittude) [fasc. 19, f. 5v] is somewhat upon the Dun or Olive, occasion'd by the Heat of the Climate which in Summer is exceeding great, tho' in winter they have very cold weather; But the colour of those in the more northern Provinces I'm told is as fair & florid as that of Europeans. The Hair of all that I Saw was black, except turn'd gray by age. However Since the Tartar Conquest they have been oblig'd to cutt their Hair all except a Small quantity

---

[1] Batavia is now Jakarta, the capital and largest city on the Indonesian island of Java. Siam is now Thailand and Cochinchina is the southern region of Vietnam.

[2] Fergusson means whither.

[3] Today's Xiamen in Fujian province.

[4] Now called rice-duck farming, this traditional East Asian agricultural technique is returning to regular practice for its ecological benefits. The ducks eat harmful weeds and insects while simultaneously fertilizing the paddy field with their droppings.

[5] A rooster that has been castrated to improve the quality of its meat.

[6] This is just over £200 in 2017 figures. See *TNA*, 'Currency Converter: 1270–2017', available at <https://www.nationalarchives.gov.uk/currency-converter/>.

[7] Likely meaning sweet.

that remains on that part where the turning of the Hair is.[1] This portion of Hair they lett grow to a great Lenth and wear it allwise Plaited and hanging down their backs, excepting when they are dress'd in their hatts &.C. which is Seldom.

To this the men only are oblig'd, for the women wear their hair which they bind up, and adorn in a very elegant Manner.[2] Those of the Better sort I mean the Men, who are Merchants or otherwise in good circumstances, commonly allow the [fasc. 19, f. 6r] Nails of one or mo[r]e of their fingers to grow to a great Lenth, as a token that they are not forc'd to labour with their hands for their Sustenance.[3] The Dress of this People differs much according to their Circumstances. The Boatmen or fishermen wear commonly a loose Jackett, Made of Brown coarse Stuff, and a pair of Draw'rs or trousers of the Same Stuff:[4] This is all their Dress, going barefooted and bare headed, excepting that Sometimes they wear a kind of broad brim'd hatt made of Bamboos.[5] The Porters and other common People wear much the Same habit, only that it is often of a different colour Such as blue black or white. The merchants and People of Fashion dress in a different manner when they go about their ordinary business near home, from that when they go a visiting or among Strangers. When at home & in ordinary they wear a loose thin garb generally whitish or of the colour of raw Silk, & Cotton. This is fasten'd with a few Small Buttons [fasc. 19, f. 6v] that being Sow'd [sic] to one edge of the Breast part overlaps the other and takes hold of the Same number of Small Catches that are fastened from the neck down to the thighs. This coat reaches to the middle of the Leg. Its Sleeves are long, turning narrower as they approach the wrist and cover all but the Hand.[6] Under this outer Garment they commonly wear another Shorter, that buttons closer round their Bodies, & Under this they have a kind of Shirt; Tho' Some for Coolness wear only the outer Coat & Shirt; besides those they have a pair of Drawers that are made very wide, & the Ends of them are fastened under the head of their Stockins [sic] or Socks. These drawers hang in an uncouth manner betwixt their thighs, and would

[1] By Tartar Conquest Fergusson is referring to the Qing invasion (1636) that ultimately led to the end of the Ming Dynasty. The Qing were also known as the Manchus due to their origin in Manchuria, in the north-eastern reaches of China, part of the historical territory of Tartary, which encompassed Manchuria, Mongolia, and the Central Asian steppe. During the late 17th-century consolidation of power the Qing issued the Queue Order that mandated that all Han Chinese cut and wear their hair in the Manchu style, under penalty of treason. This meant that male Qing subjects shaved their heads except for the back, which was kept long and braided down the back. The queue was worn until the last Qing Emperor, Pu Yi cut his off in 1921 (Rhoads, *Manchus and Han*, p. 246).

[2] Qing hairstyles for women, especially elite women, were famous for their elaborateness and elegance in what was known as *qitou*, or banner coiffure. They would wrap their hair around a fillet or crosspiece ornament (*bianfang*) made of ivory, wood or metal, creating a frame of hair extending over the sides of the head. Decorative tassels and flowers could be added for ornamentation and usually matched the pattern and colours of clothes worn. Fergusson will return to descriptions of female hair below.

[3] By the late Qing era long fingernails on the small fingers also became a fashion for women, leading to the wearing of incredibly ornamented nail guards.

[4] This 'stuff', as Fergusson calls it, was probably hemp.

[5] In China this is known as a *dǒulì*, the conical hat worn by agriculturalists across East and South East Asia.

[6] The Manchus introduced new forms of dress with their rule, often taken from the horse-riding culture of the northern steppe. It is difficult to say for sure which of the many Qing garments Fergusson is describing, however, he is likely referring to the *changshan*, which literally translates as 'long shirt'. These robe-like garments could be layered as described here or worn individually as warm weather or less formal occasions allowed. The *changshan* were usually worn under more formal outer jackets, which Fergusson describes in the following paragraph.

have a very ugly appearance did not their garb cover them. The Socks they wear on their Legs are made of cotton cloth double, Sowed together & Shap'd So as to cover the foot & [fasc. 19, f. 7r] Leg but So as to Spoil the Shape of it entirely, for they are wide enough in the Smallest part to fitt the thickest part of the Leg. And last of all they wear Slippers or Shoes, the Soles of which are very thick, being made of several plys of a coarse kind of paper Strong Sowed together. The upper part is for the most part thick Silk well lin'd, and adorn'd with embroidery of flowers &.C. in Silk & Sometimes in Silver & gold thread.

But when they go abroad upon more formal occasions to visit Strangers or their Superiors they dress in a more formal manner: for over their two former Coats they putt on a Large Garb made of thin flower'd Silk of a grave Colour, generally black or very dark purple, this is more wider & longer in all its parts than the above, it reaching to their ancles [sic]; and the Sleeves which are wide coming as far down as the midle of their fingers, So that it [fasc. 19, f. 7v] covers all the rest.[1] Besides these Socks above mentioned, they putt on more thick ones, the outside being Strong Silk betwixt which and the Lining is putt a great deal of cotton & So quilled, all except the foot-part which is allwise of a white Silk, where as the Leg part is of a Dark blue colour'd Silk or Some other grave colour with flowers; and the upper part which is Shap'd much like our boots has commonly A circle of embroidery in Gold.

Whereas in their Household or ordinary Dress they go bareheaded, with this garb they wear upon their heads a hatt of a particular kind. It is commonly made of a Small kind of tough rush or fine Straw neatly made and curiously Sowed together. In figure it resembles an inverted bowl; Its inside is lin'd with Silk, and its outside is covered with a bush of Long hair which being fastened to its Crown, hangs down So as to [fasc. 19, f. 8r] cover its outside entirely, and to reach about an inch beyond the brims of their hatt.[2] This hair is gott from their Cows, whose hair about their Dugs[3] in Some of them grows to a great lenth; and all of them have the hair dyed of a red colour, before it is putt upon their hatts. This last part of their Dress tho' it serves to shade their heads & face from the Sun, yet it to me has not So good an appearance as the rest. In the winter time or cold weather, they commonly wear a Small thick cap of quilled Silk, Velvett or Some particular Soft Skin. This is Shap'd much like the Small Caps that Some young boys in Britain Wear, & it covers only the crown of their Head leaving the Ears Bare. On the Crown of this Cap is fastened a thick Tuft or Tossell [sic] of red Silk thread, that Spreads itself all around. ~~In their address to one another they~~[4] In cold weather also their other Dress is much thicker.

[fasc. 19, f. 8v] The Habit of the better Sort of Chinese women I cannot describe, having never that I know of, Seen any of them So much as to be able to observe it Sufficiently. For the Chinese Ladies are Seldom Seen abroad, and all the merchants who reside in the Suburbs, keep their wives in the City where Europeans are not admitted. However In these Parts of the Suburbs that are remotest from the riverside, where the

---

[1] This is probably the *magua*, a riding coat often made of dark fabrics and used for formal occasions.

[2] This sounds like the Qing official headwear called *guanmao*, which had both a rattan-made summer and velvet-made winter versions. The colour, shape, and manner of tassels indicated the rank of the wearer.

[3] Meaning nipples, or in this context more properly udder.

[4] Line crossed out in original.

Europeans all Lodge,[1] I have Seen Several well drest women Sitting near the Doors, So as I could observe that their Dress in Shape did not much differ from the More common Sort, of whom multitudes are daily to be Seen upon the River.[2] Besides I have often Seen upon the Streets old women, who by the Smallness of their feet appear'd to have been of the Better Sort;[3] Yet [fasc. 20, f. 1r] their habit was Much of the same fashion. Their outer Garment resembles that which the men wear in ordinary, only it is longer, hanging as low almost as the ground. [O]f these they Seem to wear two atleast at the Same time, & under these all of them wear drawers.

The Boatwomen go barefoot, but those that live ashore wear Shoes, with high heels, & shap'd Much like these in Britain; Round their ancles especially of those who have Small feet is wrapp'd a piece of white cloth, So as to form a Considerable bulk, but has no agreable appearance. Their hair which is long & perfectly black, they fasten up rolling it round upon the crown of their heads in a very becoming manner where it is keept fast with a Bodkin either Silver, or Gold.[4] This they Sometimes adorn with flowers & other gay ornaments, which looks extremely well.

[fasc. 20, f. 1v] You can at any time know by observing a young womans Head, whither she has been married or not; For those who pass for virgins, leave a Small thin lock of their hair all around, hanging down upon their forehead cheeks & Neck, but cutt So as not to cover these parts too much. This may be called the coronet or apparent Badge of Virginity; for the marry'd women have all their hair compleatly ty'd up.[5] The features of the women in general are as agreable as these of Europeans, whom they resemble pretty much in the Shape of their face, only that for the most part the Chinese women have broader foreheads, Especially the lower parts towards the Eyes. These all are black and well made in general as are their mouths, which add much to the comeliness of their Faces. The Shape of their waste is intirely hid by the Coolness of their Garments, as is that of their breasts [fasc. 20, f. 2r] which are so compress'd by their Dress, as to Spoil in a great measure that agreable prominency of the chest, which we in Europe Consider as

---

[1] Fergusson has written live and lodge on top of each other. I have selected the word that most accurately reflects the lifestyles for the majority of Europeans at Canton at the time.

[2] The standard female garment under the Qing was the *qipao*. While today this is a form-fitting dress cut rather close to the body, this evolved from a looser robe-like garment that covered most of the body, excepting the head, hands, and toes. The fabric and cut could be different according to social rank of the wearer.

[3] Foot binding was a popular custom in China with origins going back to the early Song Dynasty (AD 960–1279). Originally an elite practice, by the 19th century it had spread to most social classes. Originally a Han Chinese tradition, it was banned by the Manchu Kangxi Emperor in 1664, but the ban failed. Foot binding thus became a marker of Han distinction under the Qing and became more common amongst the non-Manchu population throughout the 18th century. Nevertheless, the practice still carried with it significant cultural capital and Manchu women soon took to wearing a platform shoe called *mati xie*, or horse-hoof shoes, which had a small hoof-shaped platform in the centre sole, which served to hide the feet under the dress and inhibit walking so as to mimic the gait of foot-bound women.

[4] The Chinese hairpin, (also called *bianfang*), was highly ornamental and often made of precious metals. It was used to hold women's hair in a bun, which when worn on top of the head was the popular *liangbatou*, or swallowtail style, that was in fashion for decades under the Qing.

[5] Unmarried women were presumed virgins and wore their hair in a braid down their backs, often tied at the end with a red cord. The front would be cut into a fringe as a further marker of their unwed status. Styles varied according to class and ethnicity. It is unclear to which people Fergusson is referring. Married women wore their hair in a simple small bun (*gaoliangtou*) on the back of the head, or more elaborately, as described above, see p. 147, n. 2.

149

a very essential part of the Beauty of the fair Sex. But the most remarkable of all the Parts of the Women, except those of the meaner Sort, is the Surprising Smallness to which their feet is reduc'd. This is a Custom Universally pursued among the better Sort; they beginning to compress the feet of the Female Infants as Soon as they are born, which Succeeds So effectually, that I have Seen the Feet of Several women, One of which with the Shoe on it was not above 4 Inches long, and So Small as not to exceed 1 & ½ Inch below the Instep. This is no less true than Surprising. By this the women are very litle able to walk with any Steddiness, for they appear like one going upon Stumps, which obliges them to throw their arms to and fro, to keep them in poise, & prevent their falling.

The reason for this Strange Custom [fasc. 20, f. 2v] I could not learn, tho' I inquired at Several of the Chinese men, who Said they did not know from what reason it was first brought in use; But that it did the women no Harm, for their Business being intirely within Doors they had no occasion for walking abroad. From this one may guess that it atfirst had its Rise from the Jealousy of the men, & is Still Supported by the Same, in order to prevent their getting abroad, and engaging in unlawfull Intrigues. And this Seems confirmed by the closs confinement, their wives Suffer at Home, being keept in a remote apartment, where none visit them but their Husbands, Servants or nearest relations. But, as has been observ'd before, The Females of the better Sort Suffer only by this custom. For the Boat women, Servant maids, & others have feet as large as women naturally have. However a great many even of the ordinary Sort Use this method; It being a kind of mark of their not being of the lowest Sort; besides that it is esteemed, a great perfection in women, and what adds to their Beauty. For none of the richer Sort will marry a woman with= [fasc. 20, f. 3r] =out this distinguishing mark.

The Diet of the Chinese is different according to the different abilities of the People. The meaner Sort have boil'd rice for the Bulk of their victuals, with which they generally eat, alitle Stew'd fish, or Pork minc'd Small & fry'd with onions & Some other Sauce. But those in Better circumstances have a great variety of Dishes, of which I have eat Several times, they being exceeding rich & agreable to the Palate. Those for the greatest part consist of various kinds of Stews made of Flesh, Fowl, or Fish cutt Small, & So Stew'd up with rich Sauces. In which they Spare not cost; the Ingredients of Some of these being bought at a great price Such as Dear Sinews, Birds nests, &.C..[1] This last is truly the nest of a particular Bird, which is found in the Islands of the Straits of Malacca & else where, it resembles a kind of Jelly or Isinglass, but of a Hollow form, & often with mixture of Small Straws or fog,[2] which before Sale are carefully pick'd from it. A Pound of it Sometimes costs to the

[1] Duplicated full stop appears in the original. Both deer tendons and bird's nests are still expensive delicacies in Chinese cuisine. Deer tendons (*lù jīn*) are often transported and sold dried, taking several days of preparation to reconstitute them for use in dishes. They usually come from the sika (*Cervus nippon*) or red (*Cervus elaphus*) deer species. It is said they have medicinal benefits such as strengthening joints and bones, old strains, and can alleviate arthritis. Bird's nests (*yànwō*) are often served in savoury or sweet soups in which the nests become, as Fergusson goes on to describe, rather gelatinous. This is because they are not made primarily from straw, but from the saliva of certain species of swiftlets, most commonly the edible- or white-nest swiftlet (*Aerodramus fuciphagus*). Colonies of the birds breed high on cliffs or in caves, making the collection of their nests challenging, despite their widespread distribution across South East Asia. Although now produced commercially, they still remain incredibly expensive, with a pound of birds' nests costing around £900. Medicinally the bird's nest is said to be restorative and to aid in the recovery of various ailments.

[2] This is an old and unusual usage referring to the grass left growing in a pasture or remaining in a field after being cut.

[fasc. 20, f. 3v] Value of 3 or 4 £ Sterling;[1] And in one of their Stews I have Seen atleast the 3d [third] of a pound. It is reckoned a great Strenthner and provocative, to which the Chinese seem to have a particular regard in their Diet, being generally of a Lascivious Temper. Another favourite Dish is their Chow Chow[2] as they call it; It is made of a mixture of Pork, Beef &.C. especially of the first, cutt Small & fryed with Spices & other Ingredients. They likewise eat roasted Ducks, Pegs [sic] or Young Pork, Capons & other fowls. With all their Dishes they use much Sawie or Catch up; a kind of high Sauce kept in Jars & botles, & often carried to Europe, where it is much valued with Some in their Sauce for fish.[3] And rice is by them us'd with all their other victuals as we do bread.

They never cover their tables with a cloth, but place the victuals upon the Bare table. They ~~Dishes~~ are Serv'd up in A particular kind of Deep Small Dishes, much like ~~a~~ Bowls. The rice is keept in a Large wooden Plater or small Tub upon the Side board; And [fasc. 20, f. 4r] the Servants fill every ones Snaker[4] as often as it is called for. This Supplys the place of our Plates, and instead of Forks or Spoons, they use a Couple of long Streight Sticks, about the thickness of a goose quill & 8 Inches in lenth, which they are accustomed to manage So dextrously with one hand, that they lift the cutt bitts with them as well as we do with our Forks.[5] And with them they Shuft [sic] as it were, the rice out of their Snaker into their mouths, commonly great quantitys at a Time; For you may see them, after having eaten a bitt or two of the Stew or Fricassee lift up to their Mouths a pint Snaker full of boil'd rice, and with their chopsticks thrust one half of it in without Intermission. It is to the Quantity of Rice they eat with their other food, that I impute the preservation of their Health. For these High Season'd Sauces, & gross[6] food especially the Great quantity of Pork they eat must necessarily inflame & corrupt their blood, if this cooling [fasc. 20, f. 4v] wholesome grain did not very much contribute to prevent it.[7] Notwithstanding of this, the Chinese are very subject to a foulness of Blood, that appears in Many obstinate Cutaneous Eruptions to which they are Much Subject: And the Leprosy here is More frequent than in all the other Countrys of the known World.[8]

---

[1] £3–4 in 1740 is approximately £410 in 2017 figures. *TNA*, 'Currency Converter: 1270–2017', available at <https://www.nationalarchives.gov.uk/currency-converter/>.

[2] Due to its cosmopolitan nature, Canton developed a rather unique pidgin language to ease communication between the various Asian and European languages. It is believed that chow-chow meant food in general. This is a distinction Fergusson probably was not aware of, confusing the local phrase for the name of a particular dish.

[3] Originating in China in the 6th century, soy sauce was a readily available popular condiment across the Chinese world and its peripheries by the 1700s. Fish sauce, made from the brine of pickled fish, was also popular and called various versions of its original south-east Chinese, Amoy dialect name *kê-chiap*. It was only much later, in the mid-19th century that ketchup took on its now familiar tomato-based form. Here Fergusson is confusing the two sauces, as soy and ketchup often were in the early modern period. This was largely due to *ketjap/kecap* being the word for soy sauce in Indonesia, which was controlled by the VOC, then the world's largest exporter of the condiment.

[4] Fergusson presumably means 'snacker' for dish or bowl, as he just previously described. Archaically 'snack' meant a share or part, thus a snacker for Fergusson is a bowl into which one's portion is dished. He will use the word again below.

[5] These are of course chopsticks.

[6] Referring here to total amount.

[7] Fergusson is again making reference to the humoralist understanding of medical science predominate in early 18th-century Europe. See pp. 3–4.

[8] There needs to be significantly more research to determine if Fergusson's assertion is correct. China, the world's most populous country, probably had more cases of leprosy than any other country at the time, but it is unclear whether this is relative to population, or in absolute numbers.

People of all ranks drink Tea in great quantitys, it commonly concluding their meals, and being us'd at any time they are thirsty. They have Several kinds of Spirituous Liquors, made of Several kinds of Grains, & some with Sugar, of these they drink according to their particular Inclinations.[1]

The Government of the Chinese is absolute in the Person of their Emperor[2] who is Supreme master of the Lives and Fortunes of all his Subjects; Yet it is universally acknowledg'd, that there never was in the world an absolute Government, where the People Suffer So litle by it in all their Natural Rights & Liberties, as [fasc. 20, f. 5r] this of China. And this Happiness is chiefly owing to these admirable Principles, that are as it were the Foundamentals [sic] of their government, which intirely turn upon this, that The Emperor is considered, and must consider himself as the Father of his People: The Great Mandarins or Viceroys of Province, as the Father of their respective Provinces; and So of the other Subordinate Mandarins. This Great Maxim is the Source of the Emperors Authority, and of the Peoples obedience.[3] In order to preserve this in the minds of the People, the great respect & ready obedience that children are early taught to pay their Parents contributes much; for when advanc'd in Years the Same principle will teach them reverence & obedience to their Mandarins who are look'd upon as the Fathers of their respective Cities, &.C.. And that their Emperors may not forgett this great maxim, which the intoxicating Nature of Arbitrary power is apt to occasion, there are a few of the [fasc. 20, f. 5v] most experienc'd, wise and grave Mandarins, whose office it is to remonstrate to the Emperor when at any time he Seems by his actions or Orders to transgress or violate this Grand Principle; And this they continue to do untill he reforms his actions or revokes those orders that are found hurtfull or oppressive to the People. If the Emperor Should take this amiss, & Punish any of those for their freedom of advice, they are held in Such veneration by the People by reason of their Suffering for their Sakes, that their names are often immortiliz'd and the Emperors degraded & Vilifyed in the Heads of the People & in their publick annals.

The Mandarins likewise tho' they are Next to the Emperor, Supreme in their respective Districts, yet if they fall Short of their Paternal Duty or transgress it by unjust measures, there is an account of their proceedings Sent to the Emperor or those he delegates for that purposes, either by the chief People of the Province [fasc. 20, f. 6r] or by Inspectors who annually by the Emperors orders go into the Provinces and inquire into the conduct of the Mandarins; who upon Sufficient Causes are either degraded, deprived or putt to Death. Complaints of the Inferior Mandarins are Sent to the Chief of the Province, who is oblig'd every Year to Send an account thereof to Court.[4]

Thus this Numerous, active & rich People are keept in perfect Order & obedience by the authority of a few Mandarins in every Province to whose orders a ready obedience is constantly paid, as that of children to their Parents.[5]

---

[1] See above, p. 140, n. 1.

[2] Hongli the Qianlong Emperor (r. 1735–96) was the 6th Qing ruler of China when Fergusson visited. His long reign was marked by demographic and economic expansion resulting in one of the dynasty's most prosperous periods.

[3] The Mandate of Heaven (*Tiānmìng*) is the name typically given to the authority of a Chinese emperor's rule.

[4] Fergusson is again drawing upon Du Halde for the depth of his knowledge of China, which far surpasses that of what he tells us about India, in which he spent more time. See Du Halde, *The General History of China*, II, pp. 66–9.

[5] Fergusson must not be aware of the hard-fought consolidation of power the Qing had experienced in their conquest of the Ming.

As to their particulars Laws I could give no tolerable account. But from the order and quiet that prevails among them, one may be convinc'd that their Regulations are good.

They allow of Polygamy; For the People of Distinction have several Wives, tho' the Poor who are Not able to Maintain Many, have only one. Yet with those who have a plurality [fasc. 20, f. 6v] of Wives, there is allways one who is considered as mistress of the family, and has greater respect paid her than the rest. Whither this is the first married, or if it depends upon the humour of the Husband I cannot tell. Altho' their wives generally live under the Same roof, Yet each has their different apartments, to which they keep themselves and children Separate from the rest. This multiplicity of wives contributes much to the Increase of the People, as it is a means of preventing women from remaining unmarried.[1]

The ordinary Punishment inflicted for petty thefts & other misdemeanors [sic] is bambooing. The offender is keept prostrate upon his belly, and recieves the Strokes of a Split Bamboo (which is a kind of hollow Cane) upon his buttocks, thighs & Legs, mo[r]e or less according to his Crime; Some recieve so many that they expire Sometimes during the Stripes, but this must be on Some extrordinary [sic] account.[2]

[fasc. 20, f. 7r] By the Trade of Canton, the Emperor recieves a Considerable revenue. All foreign Goods imported pay 10 per cent, excepting that this last Emperor has taken that Duty off from Silver, which Saves the trouble of running it, which was for the Most part done.[3] The goods exported pays much Such a proportional Duty. All which must amount to a great revenue. This Duty is look'd after by proper officers, as in Britain, they are called Hoppo officers; and on the river Side betwixt the Ships & Canton, there are three Hoppo houses, where all boats that go to or come from the Ships are oblig'd to putt in, and recieve a pass before they can proceed further. But as a mark of Deference to the European Captains & Supracargos, they may pass & repass in their own pinnaces, with their colours flying as a Signal of their being aboard of them, and therefore need not putt in to any of these Houses. But all other [fasc. 20, f. 7v] Boats that carry European passengers must Stop to be Search'd at these houses, where it must be own'd the officers are abundantly more Civil than those of our own nation.

The Person at Canton who Superintends all the Customs, is one of great authority. He is called the Grand Hoppo, and is applied to in all Disputes of this kind. When any foreign Ship arrives in the river at her proper Station, he in a Day or two after, comes down the river in a lofty Barge; attended with many others, in order to See the Ship measur'd, in lenth & breadth upon Deck, by which the Anchorage She pays is determin'd. This amounts to a considerable Sum our Ship paying I think 600 Taels equal to 200 £

---

[1] It is unclear as to what Fergusson is actually reporting. Typically, Chinese marriages under the Qing were monogamous, though some groups, like the Hakka who are associated with the boat people of Canton, did practise polygynous marriages. Concubinage was also common, but it was considered shameful for concubines to live under the same roof with the wife.

[2] Dynastic China developed what was known as the Five Punishments. These remained relatively consistent, though with some alterations over the centuries. Beatings with a bamboo cane were part of all gradations of punishment, augmented by size of bamboo, number of strokes, with penal servitude, and exile also being used for the most serious of offences. Punishments could be remitted in lieu of fines paid in cash. The kinds of petty crimes that Fergusson describes probably earned punishments within *chî* (the lowest) or *zhàng* (second lowest) categories. These involved maximum penalties of 50 or 100 strokes with a light or large stick respectively.

[3] By 'running' Fergusson means smuggling, a common way to bring in high-taxed or illicit goods.

Sterling.[1] When he is to come aboard, there is Sent before him a Boat with a Table, Chairs[,] Carpetts & other utensils, as also Sweat [*sic*] Meats, Mandarin Wine & other refreshments.[2] These are putt in [fasc. 20, f. 8r] proper order and[3] he comes aboard, besides this boat brings, a wooden Ladder or rather Stairs, which being fastened to the Ships Side, at the usual place of entrance, Serves for his more Easy ascent. As Soon as he draws near to the Ship he is Saluted with Some Guns, and reciev'd along Side with much Ceremony & respect, the Supra Cargo's & Capt*ain* going first down into his Barge to pay their compliments & invite him aboard. When he comes upon the Quarter Deck, he walks up with much gravity & State to the chair & table of his own that is ready Situated & covered with a fine Carpett, all his attendants Standing at a Distance and when any of them Speak to him it is upon their knees.[4] The Capt*ain* & Supra cargo's stand at alitle Distance uncovered, till by his Interpreter he desires them to Sitt down after which the proper officers extend a Line from the Mizen Mast to the foremost, by which the Ships Lenth is determin'd, & in the waste under the Gangways, which is reckon'd [fasc. 20, f. 8v] her greatest breadth; These extended lines are measured, with a rule, at every lenth of which, the measurer calls out alloud [*sic*] which is mark'd down, and answered by two or three clerks. This being over, the Hoppo retires into the round house[5] where his repast of Sweatmeats is ready, after which he allows himself to be treated with a glass of Europe Wine, commonly Canary, the Chinese liking it most by reason of its Strenth & Sweetness.[6] [A]fter all the ceremony is over, he returns into his Barge, and is carried back to Town with his Numerous attendance, Colours flying & all kind of Musick playing.

The Chinese have been justly reckoned the Politest and most knowing of all the eastern nations; As their Government, or Kingdom is by all acknowledg'd the oldest in the world. For altho' Some of their Historians deduce their records from Times [fasc. 21, f. 1r] which according to the Christian and Jewish acc*ou*ntt, must be prior to the Creation, & therefore deem'd impossible. Nevertheless their most authentick Historians give particular acc*ou*ntts of Transactions, from the Second Century after the Flood.[7] And 'tis from this Period, they deduce their true History, reckoning previous Historys fabulous

---

[1] A *tael* is a Chinese weight and currency system based upon the value of silver. Under the Qing, the Canton *tael* weighed 37.5 grams. £200 in 1740 is approximately £23,600 in 2017 figures and gives an idea of the value of the lucrative trade in Canton. *TNA*, 'Currency Converter: 1270–2017', available at <https://www.nationalarchives.gov.uk/currency-converter/>.

[2] A contemporary account describes Mandarin wine as coming from the fruit '*Pausio* [...] reckoned the same with our grapes'. This is likely a misspelling of *pútao*, which is Chinese for grapes (Osbeck, Torren, and Eckberg, *A Voyage to China*, I, p. 315).

[3] In the original diary Fergusson has written 'and' over the first 3 letters of 'against', without crossing out the remaining 4 letters.

[4] Fergusson would have seen this ceremony with his own eyes. According to the *Godolphin*'s logbook, 'the Hoppo came aboard to measure our Ship Saluted him as Customary' on 18 August 1738, after the ship anchored at Whampoa (BL: IOR L/MAR/B/594M(1), entry under heading for 15 August 1739). For the hoppo's role, see above, p. 141, n. 1.

[5] This is the uppermost cabin at the rear, or stern, of a ship.

[6] See above, p. 120, n. 4.

[7] It is unclear what reference Fergusson is using as his basis for the date of Creation. In the first half of the 17th century several European theologians and scientists attempted to calculate the date, the best known of whom was Irish Archbishop James Ussher. He developed an entire chronology of world history based upon Genesis. Using a complicated methodology, Ussher determined the beginning of the world to have occurred midday, Sunday, 23 October 4004 BC, making the Flood having occurred in 2349 BC. Fergusson was well-read and it is very likely that he was aware of some of these scholars' calculations, which did not differ very significantly

or false; So that it is reasonable to believe their Empire is of 4000 years Standing atleast, and this appears more indisputably true from an accountt of an Eclipse that happened 2155 Years before the Birth of Christ, which is registred [*sic*] in their Publick Records, as Several of the missionarys have attested, who had resided in China many years & perus'd their Annals.[1] Notwithstanding the Great antiquity of this People yet it is Said, that from the beginning to this Day, they have continued to follow the Same Laws Customs &.C, excepting the alteration of Some parts of their habit [fasc. 21, f. 1v] since the Tartar Conquest.[2] This Tenaciousness of their antient Customs even in the minutest things, is a Strong argument of the fix'd & constant Temper of the People, and it may probably have proceeded, from their contempt of other nations, which they considered as Barbarians, as indeed the other Eastern Neighbouring Nations may be justly enough esteem'd when compar'd with the Chinese. This has made them fond of their own Knowledge in So much as to undervalue that of other, Nations; But their commerce with the Europeans has of late help'd to remove these prejudices, by observing how much they excell in mathmatical Learning, & Mechanick arts.

The Tartar Conquest happened about 90 Years ago,[3] that People [the Manchus][4] being called in to assist the Chinese who made war upon an oppressive usurper [Li Zicheng of

---

from each other in their timelines. It is thus likely that for Fergusson, two centuries after the Flood was around the 21st century BC. This also conforms with what Fergusson read regarding the history of China, as will become clear below. For an explanation of Ussher's dating system and methodology, see Barr, 'Why the World Was Created in 4004 BC', pp. 575–608.

[1] Fergusson again borrows from Du Halde, who gives the same information and years regarding the origins of China (Du Halde, *The General History of China*, II, pp. 2–3). European missionaries in China, such as the prolific Antoine Guabil (1689–1759), read and translated many Chinese texts, including compendia of astronomical observations, such as eclipses. Many of these were published in European volumes, which were used to confirm the antiquity of Chinese society against their own records. See Souciet, *Observations mathématiques*, p. 30. Today, the history of China is associated with its first written records, which date from the Shang Dynasty, in *c.*1250 BC. Early Chinese historical texts do make reference to an earlier Xia Dynasty, however, archaeological and documentary research have yet to uncover evidence supporting its existence.

[2] Meaning the Manchu invasion, which captured Beijing and formally established the Qing Dynasty as rulers over China proper in 1644.

[3] Fergusson is again drawing upon Du Halde, whose timeline is off by about a decade, for his information. The Manchu invasion was complicated and involved several parties. Fergusson does a rather poor job of paraphrasing Du Halde's version of events, which is just as well as it was not quite right either; see Du Halde, *The General History of China*, II, pp. 3–7. The Manchu invasion took place when the Ming state was beset by financial trouble and facing several internal revolts. Various parties challenged the right of the Chongzhen Emperor Zhu Youjian (r. 1627–44) to rule under the Mandate of Heaven, amongst them the Manchu clan Aisin Gioro, who in 1618 began openly rebelling in the Manchurian territory of Liaoning. After achieving these victories, the leader of the clan, Hong Taiji (1592–1643), proclaimed himself Emperor, establishing the Qing Dynasty in 1636. The chaotic situation continued and, in 1644, Li Zicheng (1606–45), a former Ming official and now leader of the largest peasant rebellion, took the capital Beijing in late April, proclaiming the short-lived Shun Dynasty. It is said that, rather than submit, the Chongzhen Emperor killed himself and most of his daughters as the army approached the capital. Li Zicheng's rule was immediately unpopular and many Ming officials, generals, and soldiers rallied to the Qing, who themselves marched on Beijing in early June, thus ending Shun rule. This established the Manchu dynasty of the Qing as rulers over China proper under Fulin the Shunzhi Emperor (r. 1643–61) and his prince co-regents, Dorgon (r. 1643–50) and Jirgalang (r. 1643–7). Despite this support, opposition remained, and Ming loyalists kept fighting against the consolidation of Qing rule, particularly in the south-east. By 1684 the last sustained resistance was put down.

[4] I have added the names that Fergusson references throughout this section wherever appropriate to assist the reader.

the Shun Dynasty]; So that the Tartar King with 80,000 of his men joining the Chinese malecontents [*sic*] they drove [fasc. 21, f. 2r] out the Chinese Emperor [Li Zicheng], & Setled the Tartarian King [Fulin, the Shunzhi Emperor] upon the throne of China; who being one of great abilities, Secured the Government to his Descendants,[1] by intermixing numbers of Tartars every where with the Chinese, & in time admitting them into the highest Posts; At the Same time making not the least alteration in the Establish'd Laws & Customs,[2] excepting that of obliging all the men to have their Heads Shav'd after the Tartarian Manner. Yet So obstinately fond were Some of that antient Chinese fashion of wearing the Hair, that they Suffered their Lives to be taken rather than Submitt to this New Custom.[3]

By all this it appears that the Chinese fell under the Tarter Government; Not by Conquest; but rather with their own Consent, Chusing a Tartar Emperor.[4] He by artifice rivett'd the Yoke; which however differs So litle from what they were allways accustom'd to, that it's litle felt. [fasc. 21, f. 2v] One thing admirable in the Chinese Constitution is, that none are Capable of being preferr'd to any Post of Power or Trust, but those whose Personal merit Naturally claims it; There is no Such thing as any hereditary Nobleness by Birth; excepting the near Relations of the Emperor or Princes of the blood who are distinguish'd by Some particular titles, but even these depend upon the Emperor's Pleasure.[5] This is a great incitement to Study & application as also to a regular blameless behaviour; for these are the Steps by which alone, People can arrive at any Dignity. For the Candidates for any office or Titular Distinction, are carfully examin'd; and they whose Capacity or learning is greatest are preferr'd, however mean their Extraction may be.[6] 'Tis true the Children of Mandarins & other great men are most frequently preferr'd, but that is not upon accountt of Parentage or Interest; but purely be= [fasc. 21, f. 3r] =cause they are generally better Learn'd & instructed in these Parts of Knowledge that are necessary to Preferment. And this I'm told is So generally observ'd, that even the Emperors very often postpone their first Born Son, and advances another

---

[1] The most notable of the Qing rulers was Xuanye, the Kangxi Emperor (r. 1661–1722). During his long reign the Qing Dynasty consolidated its rule by defeating the last of the Ming loyalists. His governance ushered in a period of economic and cultural revival, and he reversed Ming embargos on foreign trade, making Canton the flourishing marketplace it was when Fergusson arrived. The Kangxi Emperor was officially China's longest-ruling monarch, though his grandson the Qianlong Emperor would have been, had he not abdicated to honour his grandfather's legacy and longevity.

[2] This is not true, as the above note demonstrates.

[3] Another reference to the queue hairstyle observed previously by Fergusson. Adopting this hairstyle was a marker of subjugation to Qing rule and certainly did not indicate a preference for a particular coiffure, as Fergusson will remark. Rather, this was an issue taken very seriously as the oft-quoted Qing slogan indicates: 'Keep your hair and lose your head, or cut your hair and keep your head.' Fan, *Culture, Institution*, p. 104.

[4] Fergusson's statement reflects Du Halde's own silence on the intricacies of the Ming–Qing transition. It seems neither was aware of the difficulties and long military and naval campaigns necessary to secure Qing rule.

[5] This is not quite correct. China did have some titles of hereditary nobility, even under the Qing. Nonetheless, their numbers were much smaller than in Europe.

[6] This is the imperial examination system which became the norm during the mid-Tang Dynasty (AD 7th–10th centuries) and lasted in various forms until the early 20th century. Official posts at all levels of governance were allocated according to one's standing in the examinations creating the scholar-bureaucratic class, which Europeans frequently referred to as Mandarins.

of his Son's who is thought to have the greatest merit.[1] 'Tis true the Emperor generally names his Successor, being esteem'd the most able Judge of a Person Capable of that important & high Trust. Yet there are many Instances in their History, where the Emperors have Sett aside all their own Relations and Nominated some other as more fitt to Succeed Him. Thus it appears that True merit is no where So greatly encouraged & rewarded as in China. Those Emperors ~~who~~ And other great men, who have distinguished themselves remarkably by their great regard for & Paternal Care of the People, are held in the greatest veneration while Living, [fasc. 21, f. 3v] and have a Sacred Regard paid to their memory after their Death. In So much that in most of the Chinese Houses, they have the Picture of one or other of these great Men, before which they burn Incense, & Show other marks of veneration.[2]

As to the Religion of the Chinese I can give no tolerable accountt from my own knowledge or Observation. The not knowing the Language of this people is a great obstruction to one's being able to form just notions of these things from their own observations; for altho' one has the opportunity of Seeing many of their Religious Ceremonys, the not understanding what they Say keeps one a Stranger, to their Nature & Intent.[3] And the Information we recieve upon Inquiring of the merchants who talk English, is So Small & im perfect [sic], that it affords one litle or No Satisfaction in these [fasc. 21, f. 4r] matters. Whether this is owing to Shyness of the People in admitting Strangers into the knowledge of their Religious worship, or to their own Ignorance, I cannot well guess. Tho' it is reasonable to believe that both may have a Share in it.

As to the last it is generally observed, that merchants who are constantly employ'd in the affair of Loss & gain, Seldom trouble themselves with Inquirys into the foundation or reasonableness of any Schemes of Religion. It is for the most part Sufficient with the Busy Bulk of mankind to fall in with the reciev'd forms & Customs without any farther trouble or consideration; And therefore from People of this Stamp, one can expect but Small Satisfaction in these Speculations. When I have ask'd any of them, who appear'd in all respects men of Sense, Why they pay'd their adoration to these Images which [fasc. 21, f. 4v] they call Joss,[4] and did not rather worship God that invisible Being who alone was able to assist them? They answer'd that, it Was to God alone that they address'd their prayers; and that these Images were only design'd for the Common People, who could not So well concieve the Existence of the Invisible God, and therefore would be apt to forgett all Religion; And that Since these things had been establish'd by long Custom, it

---

[1] This is certainly true, particularly because the Chinese imperial household was much larger than their European counterparts. Chinese emperors frequently married more than one empress, and also had several imperial consorts as well as concubines. For example, the Qianlong Emperor was the fourth son of his father the Yongzheng Emperor (r. 1722–35), who was married to two empresses, had five consorts, and one official concubine.

[2] There is no way of accurately knowing what Fergusson is describing with the information he offers. Chinese religion operated under a diverse set of practices and beliefs, especially in a cosmopolitan place like Canton, where overlapping complex systems of local and regional deities were worshipped. The picture Fergusson refers to could be of a deity or ancestor, to either of which offerings would be made.

[3] Fergusson did not speak South Asian languages either, however, in Madras he had a *dubashi* to serve as an interpreter. In Canton, such things were not available to European sailors.

[4] *Joss* is a Chinese Pidgin English word referring to objects and statues of idols representing deities. It is derived from *deus*, the Portuguese word for god.

was necessary to comply with them. How far this account is just I cannot Say; Yet it is a general observation made by those who have had the best opportunitys of knowing it, that there is No Country in the world where Religion has done So litle harm as in China. Their Bonzes[1] or Priests Live meanly, have no power or authority, and are not much regarded except by those of the meanest People & a few others; They live mostly near their Temples, occupied in the multifarious Ceremonys relating to their Idols, & living partly by the [fasc. 21, f. 5r] offerings of the Devout to the Idols, or the voluntary Donations given to themselves; But I know not if they have any revenue Setled upon them by the authority of the Government. Thus it appears that where the clergy are trusted with the least pow'r Religion how bad So ever in itself, is capable of doing the least hurt. Whereas it is too obvious, by the fatal Experience of many nations, that where the power of the Clergy is greatest, there the People are most miserable; Lett the Profess'd Religion be of whatever kind. This may appear Strange, that those who from their office are called the messengers of Peace, Should become the ministers of misery & oppression. But the Romish Clergy & others, are manifest confirmations of this melancholy Truth, which ought to teach all nations that love the native Liberty & privileges of mankind, to keep this Sett of men Strictly within the Bounds of their office; allowing them no Jurisdiction of any kind over the People; For it has been allways observ'd, that in proportion to the advancement of [fasc. 21, f. 5v] their power, encreases the Slavery of the People, & that of the worst kind, a Slavery in which Poverty & want, are but the least of its evils; where the Free minds of men are bound fast in the inextricable Fetters of absurdities & Ignorance.

The principle Idol that I have Seen in all their Temples, is the Image of a man, most commonly of clay but finely painted & adorn'd. This is what they Call Joss, & he is commonly Made of a Fatt bulky Size, for the Chinese esteem most, men of this Shape as the Handsomest, contrary to what happens in Europe.[2] At one Side of this Image is commonly plac'd Another Image of a Woman well Drest; And Sometimes One Sees the Image of a Child. The Woman We commonly call Joss's Wife & the other his Son.[3]

Before these Idols the Bonzes & others prostrate themselves, & perform the other Ceremonies of Devotion. There is almost at all time keept A [fasc. 21, f. 6r] Lamp burning before them, & you See constantly standing the Censerfull of ashes, where is burnt their Incense & various perfumes. In every House Yea in every Boat, they have one or mo[r]e Images of this kind, which may very properly be called their Household

---

[1] From the Japanese *bonzô*, meaning priest and introduced into European languages via the Portuguese (*bonzo*), meaning a Buddhist monk, particularly from East Asia.

[2] This sounds like the deity Budai, however, Fergusson's further description of being represented sometimes with a 'wife' and 'son' calls this into question. If it is Budai, this is the figure commonly referred to as the Laughing Buddha, commonly represented as a heavyset man in a sitting posture who is smiling or laughing. The actual origins of Budai are obscure, however, he is said to have been a 10th-century Buddhist monk. His popularity spread to all parts of China where he is revered as a deity representing abundance and contentment.

[3] There are more than 200 deities in the Chinese pantheon, and from Fergusson's description it is again difficult to know exactly which ones he saw. One possibility is that he is describing the goddess Guanyin, who is sometimes depicted with a child or child consorts. Guanyin is a bodhisattva and the protector of women and children representing compassion and love. However, Fergusson could also have seen Tudigong, the Lord of the Earth, who is often depicted as somewhat heavyset, and sometimes with his wife, Tupido. Another possibility is detailed in the following note.

Gods.[1] And Such I take it were these that Rachel Stole away from her Father Laban's House, but 'tis likely made of more valuable materials than Painted Clay.[2] Something of this kind 'tis probable were the Penates & Lares of the antients.[3]

The Chinese I find have Religious festivals annually; One of the Most considerable happened in the Month of October. This Europeans called the Feast of Lanthorns, I suppose from the Many Lanthorns with which the streets are every night illuminated at this Time.[4] For tho' all houses of Distinction have two lighted Lanthorns every Night hung up at their Entry; Yet now the whole Street is Hung So full that they are in Most places touching one another. This Festival [fasc. 21, f. 6v] lasts for near a month. During which are perform'd many peculiar Ceremonys of Processions &.C. The ordinary habit of the Bonzes is a kind of loose Gown of Dark Gray Stuff Made in the Same Shape as I have observ'd Some of the Sects of Friars of the Romish Church wear, in So much, that at first I took them for Priests of that Religion; They go bareheaded, their Hair being all cutt, which distinguishes them from the Laity who are all oblig'd to wear a plaited Lock. But the Bonzes in these Processions, & while they perform their religious Ceremonys, wear Small Coronets upon their Heads, exactly of the Shape that our Kings Crowns in Europe are. During these Ceremonys at proper Intervalls, musik of Several kinds is us'd. And their processions are allways preceeded with a band of musick. Not only in the Publick Temples, at this Time are their adorations &.C. made; But in numbers of Peoples Houses which are keept open, adorn'd with [fasc. 21, f. 7r] all kinds of Gewgaw ornaments,[5] & the Images Sett up with uncommon Ceremony, in these places of the House that open to the Street, I Suppose for this Reason, that all that please may have the benefit of this extrordinary [sic] Devotion. In these places they continue constantly for 2 or 3 Days to attend their Idol entertaining it with Musick, perfumes &.C. besides offerings of Fruit, bak'd cakes, & other kinds of the nicest victuals which are plac'd before it. At Sett Times the Bonzes enter with their usual Robes & Ensigns of Devotion, which they perform in conjunction with other Laymen. But I observ'd that the Prayers or ~~addresses~~ Verbal addresses to their Deity were only made by the Bonze, the Laymen only joining in the Kneelings & various prostrations. During all this, there were various litle circumstances observ'd by a person appointed for that Purpose, of removing Lamps & Candles, Censers &.C. from this to that place; taking one Book from & bringing another to the Priests, & Many others needless & [fasc. 21, f. 7v]

---

[1] The most important of the Chinese domestic gods is Zào Jûn, the Kitchen or Stove God, who is often represented with his wife. Almost every family in China had images of these deities in their homes, to whom they would make offerings such as incense, for protecting the household.

[2] Fergusson is referencing Genesis 31:19, wherein Rachel takes her father's idols from his house and conceals them in a camel saddle.

[3] Lares and Penates were a collection of deities in the Roman pantheon that protected the household and state. Roman families each had their own *Lar familiaris* that was given offerings in the home's shrine to ensure that the family line would not die out. Penates were originally gods of the pantry, later becoming guardians of the household.

[4] This is not what is commonly known today as the Feast of the Lanterns, which takes place in Spring within the first month of the Chinese lunisolar calendar. What Fergusson is describing is the Mid-Autumn Festival, also known in English as the Moon or Harvest Moon Festival, and officially in Cantonese as the *Jūng-chāu Jit*. This festival takes place every autumn during the 8th month of the Chinese lunar calendar and is now known for its lantern lighting and the preparation and eating of mooncakes, a thin-crusted pastry filled with lotus seed or red bean paste.

[5] A gewgaw is a showy thing, like a bauble or trinket.

nauseous to mention.¹ During this Festival were exhibited many Shows, but especially many Plays that were acted not only in Private houses, but on Stages built in Several parts of the Streets. This acting of Plays is what is most common in China; The Entertainments of all the great men commonly ending with it.² They are much of the Same nature with the Dramatick Performances in Europe atleast the manner of acting is of the Same Kind. They Seem to give great Delight to those who understand the language; and the Dress, action &.C. of the actors often gives entertainment to those who know not what they Say. Betwixt the acts are Interludes of musick; & Sometimes, are exhibited Dancing, Harlequin Tricks & other Common amusements.

It appears that of these Strollers³ there are considerable many Companys, For I have known, within a Small Bounds of the Suburbs, 4 or 5 Plays acting at the Same time in different Parts.

[fasc. 21, f. 8r] This is all that from my own observation I could learn of the Religion &.C of this People. There are I'm told in Several parts of China great numbers of Christians that were converted by the missionarys who During the Reign of the late Emperor Cang ti,⁴ had a good deal of respect Shown and liberty allow'd them; but his Successor the Present Emperor, has banish'd the most of them from China, as I'm inform'd, looking upon it as dangerous to allow these Emissarys to practise too much upon the minds of his Subjects.⁵ This had oblig'd many of them to retire to Maccaow,⁶ & others to Ship themselves for Europe. It is observable, that to none other of the Eastern Countrys, have Such a Number of Missionarys & those men of abilities been Sent as to China; But the reason is plain; for few Countries have Such pow'rfull allurements, as this

---

¹ While customary practices are always in flux, celebrations such as the Harvest Moon Festival described here have changed radically as a result of the end of imperial China. For example, 190 years after Fergusson was in Canton, the new republican government hung banners where lanterns should have been for the Harvest Moon Festival. On the banners were slogans declaring 'Eradicate superstition to make Guangzhou an exemplary city!' and instead of eating mooncakes and celebrating, many people instead attended an anti-superstition rally (Wah, 'Refashioning Festivals', p. 199). Today the Harvest Moon Festival is one of the most famous and celebrated in China and retains its mythical association with figures such as the moon goddess Chang'e, but it has lost much of its religious symbolism that Fergusson described.

² Chinese theatre, or opera, has a very long heritage stretching back to at least the Zhou Dynasty (c.1046–256 BC), and probably earlier. Actors formed private and public troupes who performed plays for elite private audiences, or by the late 1600s, the general public. As Fergusson earlier alluded with actors in Europe, there was a certain sexual promiscuity associated with those who took to the stage.

³ A stroller is an itinerant actor. Most actors in the Qing were professionals who had undergone a long apprenticeship, sometimes up to 8 years.

⁴ Fergusson means the Kangxi Emperor, who initially was open to regulated European missionary activities. However, from the mid-1600s on debate brewed over what kinds of cultural practices Chinese Christians could continue to engage in, in what was known as the Chinese Rites Controversy. Pope Clement XI (1649–1721) issued a decree in 1704 condemning Confucian rites such as honouring ancestors as idol worship and un-Christian. Several Jesuit missionaries working in China protested at this decision and many were sent in embassy to Rome to lobby for overturning the decree. The Pope remained resolute and forcefully settled the issue in 1715 by issuing an even stronger edict against Chinese cultural practices. As a result, the Kangxi Emperor banned Christian missionaries in China.

⁵ Fergusson is forgetting the Yongzheng Emperor, who ruled between the Kangxi and Qianlong Emperors. It was under the Yongzheng Emperor that anti-Christian policies were intensified, beginning with the removal of all foreign priests followed by prohibiting Catholicism in 1724, which set off a series of Christian persecutions continuing into the reign of the Qianlong Emperor.

⁶ Macao.

Delightfull Rich & plentifull Country China, where Godly Conversions could not but be attended with great Gain.

[fasc. 21, f. 8v] Before I make an end of my acco*un*tts of the Chinese Religion, it is proper to take notice, What Pere Du Halde has wrote concerning it.[1] For, Says He, altho' the Mandarins and men of Learning Sometimes may Seem to comply with the Idolatrous worship of the Common People, Yet they have a System of Religion very different, which they embrace and practise. This is no other than the Religion of Nature, first illustrated & taught in the greatest perfection by their most celebrated antient Philosopher Confutzee or Confucius,[2] of whom & his Tenets I Shall Sett down the following Short Extract taken from the above Pere Du Halde who relates it from Several missionarys who from their residing many years as the chiefs of the missionarys in China, acquir'd a Perfect knowledge of their Language, & perus'd many of their Books. And we have no reason to Suspect Jesuits of Partiality in favour of any Religion different from their own.

[fasc. 22, f. 1r] Confucius was born in a town of the Kingdom of Lou which at present is the province of Chang Tong,[3] 551 Years before the Christian Era, and 2 Years before the Death of Thales the Greecian Philosopher.[4] He was contemporary with the famous Pythagoras;[5] and Socrates[6] appear'd Soon after China had lost this Philosopher. He gave very early proofs of his Noble Talents, applying himself betimes to the Study of the most famous antient authors of his nation, and furnishing his mind with maxims the most proper to regulate the heart, and inspire people with the Love of Virtue. His Integrity, extensive knowledge, and the Splendor of his Virtues Soon made him known. He was offered & invited to Several high offices in the magistracy, which he often refus'd with a view of propagating his Doctrine and reforming mankind. It was an uncommon Sight to behold a Philosopher, who after he had gain'd the [fasc. 22, f. 1v] admiration and Esteem of the Publick in the highest and most honourable offices of the Kingdom, return of his own accord to the private functions of a Sage intirely devoted to the Instruction of the People, and on this acco*un*tt undertaking Continual & painfull journeys; His Zeal extended to people of all ranks, to the Learn'd and Ignorant, to Peasants & Princes.

---

[1] Du Halde, *The General History of China*, III, pp. 53–5.

[2] Confucius, or more appropriately Kǒng Fūzǐ (551–479 BC), is the best-known Chinese philosopher. He was born into a middle-class family in Lu, a tributary kingdom of the Zhou Dynasty and worked his way up into local government, becoming for a time the governor of a small town and later the minister of crime, all while developing a following with his teachings and moral philosophies. Disappointed in not having his teachings and advice put into practice by the rulers he served, Confucius exiled himself from Lu for 23 years. During this time, he wandered between various states developing his teachings and gaining more followers. Toward the end of his life he returned to Lu, transmitting the knowledge that would become known as the Four Books and Five Classics, the foundational texts of Confucianism.

[3] This is today's province of Shandong (alternatively Shantung).

[4] Thales (*c.*624–545 BC) of Miletus was a Greek philosopher, mathematician and astronomer from Ionia in what is today Anatolia. He is considered as one of the first of the philosophers in the Greek tradition and influenced later thinkers such as Aristotle.

[5] Also from Ionia, Pythagoras (*c.*570–*c.*495 BC) of Samos was another influential Greek philosopher, mathematician and astronomer. He is perhaps best known today for his eponymous theorem in the field of geometry and is often referred to as the first pure mathematician.

[6] Socrates (*c.*470–399 BC) was an Athenian philosopher who is generally considered to be one of the founders of the Western philosophical tradition. Concerned with moral and ethical philosophy, he was influential in his own lifetime and counted Plato amongst his students. Due to his teachings, he infamously ran afoul of Athenian powerholders and was put on trial, then forced to drink poison, thus ending his life.

He gain'd numbers of Proselytes, & among these were three Thousand of his Disciples, of whom 5 hundred bore the Highest offices in the Empire. But they reckon 72 who were Still more distinguish'd than the rest by the practice of virtue. His Zeal even inspir'd him with a Desire of crossing the Sea, to propagate his Doctrine in the most distant Countries. Even tho' in travelling thro' the Different Kingdoms Subject to this vast Empire of China, he was reduc'd to the greatest Indigence without laying aside his greatness of Soul and usual Constancy.[1]

[fasc. 22, f. 2r] The whole Doctrine of this Philosopher tended to restore humane Nature to its former Lustre, and that first Beauty it had reciev'd from Heaven, and which had been Sullied by the Darkness of Ignorance and the Contagion of Vice. The means he propos'd to attain it, was to obey the Lord of Heaven, to honour and fear Him; to love our Neighbours as ourselves; to conquer irregular inclinations, Never to take our Passions for the rule of our conduct, to Submitt to Reason, to listen to it in all things, to do nothing, to Say nothing, to think nothing contrary to it. As his actions never belied his maxims, and as by his gravity Modesty, mildness, Frugality, contempt of earthly enjoyments, & a Continual watchfullness over his actions, he was in his own person a pattern of the preacepts [sic] which he taught in his writings and Discourses. The Kings endeavour'd to Surpass each other in encouraging Him to come into their Dominions.

[fasc. 22, f. 2v] Having ended his philosophical Labours he died in the 73d year of his age. They built his Sepulch're on the Banks of the river Su where he us'd to assemble his Disciples, which having been encompass'd with walls is to this very Day resembling a Small City.[2] He was lamented by all the Empire especially by his Disciples who went into mourning bewailing his loss as tho' he had been their Father. These Sentiments full of veneration which they had for him, have been encreasing every~Day Since, and he is look'd upon at this Day as the greatest Doctor of the Empire.[3] The Books he wrote are esteem'd as oracles, and his Doctrine and Precepts are those by which the Emperors mandarins & men of Letters in general Since have regulated their Sentiments of Religion and morality. Tho' Some of them have Seemingly comply'd with the Ceremonys of Some prevailing Idolatrys. Besides what has been Said above [fasc. 22, f. 3r] The High veneration that Confucius has [had] paid to his memory ever Since his appearence [sic] down to the present times, is evidently conspicuous by the peculiar Dignities that have constantly descended to his posterity by their Birth,[4] contrary to what happens to any other in China

---

[1] This brief introduction to Confucius's life is taken, as Fergusson said, from Du Halde, who likely borrowed from well-known Chinese texts, such as Sima Qian's (c.145–c.86 BC) *Records of the Grand Historian*, often considered to be the foundational text of the Chinese historiographical tradition (Du Halde, *The General History of China*, I, pp. 329–31).

[2] Confucius's tomb still lies on the banks of the Sì River in the town of Qūfù and is the second largest temple complex in the country after the Forbidden City, with which it shares many architectural characteristics having been remodelled in the same (late Ming) period. Fergusson never went to Qūfù, if he had he surely would have noted the most recent renovations to the tomb complex, finished in 1730.

[3] Fergusson is again following Du Halde who wrote, 'The *Chinese* pay the greatest Veneration to the Memory of this Philosopher; they look on him as the Master and Doctor of the Empire' (Du Halde, *The General History of China*, I, p. 331).

[4] The descendants of Confucius have indeed been honoured and privileged by every dynasty with titles and lands. While the modern Chinese state does not recognize such hereditary titles, still the ancestors of Confucius enjoy a degree of cultural capital and social prestige. There continue to be official family trees and lineage charts published by the Confucius Genealogy Compilation Committee, the last edition of which was published in 2009.

of what rank So ever, the Emperors family alone excepted, which however soon evanishes after a few Generations. But the Honour & Nobility of the Family of Confucius alone has lasted and been continued for above 2000 Years.

His works Still remain and are in the highest Esteem by the Chinese. Of them there are principally four, to which two others are added. Those who would have a perfect notion of these works will find it in the Latin Translation of *Pere* Noel printed at Prague 1711.[1] This Father is one of the most antient missionarys,[2] of his [Confucius's] 4 principal Books I Shall here give a Short account.

[fasc. 22, f. 3v] Confucius his first book is called Tahio or the grand Science because it was Chiefly design'd for Princes & Grandees who ought to learn to govern their people Wisely.[3] It is what Beginners ought to Study first, because it is as it were the Porch of the temple of wisdom. It treats of the Care one ought to take in Governing oneself, that we may be able afterwards to govern others, and of perseverance in the chief Good, which according to him, is a conformity of our actions to right reason.

The whole Science of Princes and Grandees of a Kingdom, Says Confucius, consists in Cultivating and perfecting the reasonable Nature they have recieved [*sic*] from Tien, (or God) and in restoring that Light and primitive clearness of Judgment, which has been weakned [*sic*] or obscured by various passions, that it may be afterwards in a Condition of labouring to perfect others. To Succeed then we Should begin at ourselves, and to this End [fasc. 22, f. 4r] it is necessary to have an insight into the Nature of things, and to gain the knowledge of true Good & Evil; to fix the will towards the Love of this Good, and the hatred of this Evil; to preserve integrity of heart, & to regulate the manners according to right reason. When a man has thus renewed himself, there will be no difficulty of renewing others, and by this means one likewise Sees concord & Union reign in Families, Kingdoms governed according to the Laws, and all the Empire enjoy a profound peace and tranquillity.

These are the Doctrines taught in this first Classical or Cannonical [*sic*] Book of Confucius, upon which an excellent commentary is wrote by one of his followers.[4]

[1] European readers had been introduced to Confucius 100 years earlier with the publication of Nicolas Trigault's *De Christiana expeditione apud Sinas suscepta ab Societate Jesu* in 1615. This text introduced the Chinese philosopher through the work of the well-known Jesuit missionary Matteo Ricci (1552–1610). François Noël was one of Europe's foremost experts on China, and his *Sinensis imperii libri classici sex* introduced Europeans directly to 6 classical works of Confucian thought published together in one volume containing (in their common English titles): *The Great Learning*; *Doctrine of the Mean*; *Analects*; *Mencius*; *Classic of Filial Piety*; and *Lesser Learning*. The first 4 are collectively known as the Four Books of Confucianism, the first 3 of which are in Legge, *The Chinese Classics*, I, pp. 12–44. For Mencius's writings, see Legge, *The Chinese Classics*, II, pp. 123–385. He also translated the *Classic of Filial Piety* into English in Müller, ed., *The Sacred Books*, III, pp. 449– 88. Selected contents and analysis of *Lesser Learning* text may be found within, Virág, 'Moral Psychology and Cultivating the Self', pp. 33–55. Noël was also instrumental in the aforementioned Chinese Rites Controversy (see above, p. 160, n. 4) as he was one of the ambassadors who tried unsuccessfully to convince Pope Clement XI both in letters and in person to allow Chinese Christian converts to continue with rites associated with the veneration of ancestors.

[2] Since Noël (1651–1729) was his contemporary, Fergusson probably meant longest-serving by his use of the word 'antient'.

[3] This work is now transliterated most commonly as *Daxue*, or the *Great Learning*. It is one of the celebrated Four Books of Confucianism and has been a foundational textbook of scholarship and learning in China throughout the dynastic period and remains a classic. See also p. 161, n. 2 and n. 1, above.

[4] The *Great Learning* is a short text with a subsequent 10-chapter commentary by Zeng Shen, better known as Zengzi (505–435 BC), who was one of Confucius's disciples and is revered as one of the Four Sages of Confucianism. See also p. 161, n. 2 and n. 1, above.

The Second Classical or Cannonical Book of Confucius is Called Tchong Yong, or the Immutable Mean.[1] It was publish'd by his Grandson and treats of that mean which ought to be preserv'd in all things. [fasc. 22, f. 4v] He undertakes to prove that Every wise man ought to follow this rule which is the Essence of virtue. He enters on his Subject by defining Human Nature & its passions. Then he brings Several Examples of Virtue, and amongst others of Piety, Fortitude, Prudence and filial respect, which are given as Patterns to be imitated in keeping the mean.

In the next place he Shows that this mean and the practice of it, is the right and true path which a wise man ought to pursue in order to attain the highest virtue.

This Book is divided into 33 articles.

In the First, he Says That the Law of Heav'n is imprinted in the Nature of Man; that this is the right way he Should follow in his actions, and is the Rule of a wise and virtuous Life; that we must never forsake this way, but constantly watch over our Heart and our Passions, to restrain and moderate them So that they may Still be keept Conformable [fasc. 22, f. 5r] to reason, by which Man observes that right way, that mean which is the Source and principle of virtuous actions.

In the 2d article and the following to the 12th, he deplores the wretched State of the greatest part of mankind, of which there are So few that observe that Mean, which is the essence of virtue. He then gives an account of Some virtues, and explains the Mean of Prudence, Piety & Fortitude, He confirms his Doctrine by examples of the ancient Emperors and Some others.

In the 12th & 13th articles, he proves that this Science of the mean, is Sublime, difficult and Subtile in Speculation; but that in practice it is common and easie, extending to the most ordinary actions of Life.

In the 14th he Shows that in keeping the mean a man confines himself to the Duties of his Employment, and never minds other Bussiness [sic]; that whatever changes may happen in his fortune, he is allways equal, [fasc. 22, f. 5v] always Master of himself, preserving the same Steddy temper in the hurry of bussiness, and in the tranquillity of a private Life; that he is never proud nor haughty in an exalted Station, as he never does any thing low or groveling in the meanest circumstances.

From the 15th to the 21, he gives Some examples of Princes, who both understood and practis'd this Science of the Mean &.C.

In the 20th he Shows that in order to govern others well we must learn to govern ourselves; that the regulation of our manners depends chiefly on 3 Virtues Viz. Prudence, Love of Justice & Fortitude; that Prudence is necessary to discover that Just mean we are Speaking of; a Natural Love of Equity to pursue it, and fortitude to persevere in the pursuit of it. After this he mentions Several virtues which Should meet in an Emperor.

In the 12 following articles he Shows That Virtues do not deserve this ami= [fasc. 22, f. 6r] =able name, if they are not real and free from all disguise; that truth is the life of evry [sic] virtue; that a wise man who would follow this mean which constitutes virtue Should diligently apply Himself to the Study of Truth; that Virtue dwells in the Heart of its true votaries, and is outwardly Seen in their actions; that when we have once acquired it, our views and cares are extended to all Events, and we foresee things to come,

---

[1] The *Doctrine of the Mean*, or *Zhōngyōng* is another of the Four Books. It is attributed to another of the Four Sages, Zisi (né Kong Ji, *c*.481–402 BC), who was Confucius's grandson. The text mainly deals with the principles of conducting oneself with moderation and sincerity. See also p. 161, n. 2, and p. 163, n. 1, above.

as if they were actually present; in Short that he who has acquir'd the perfection of true virtue if he enjoys the Sov'reign authority, can make no Laws but what are wise and usefull for publick Good.

Lastly in the 33d article he proves that to attain this perfection or mean of virtue, we need not do any thing painfull & difficult, or that requires extrordinary abilities; It is Sufficient to apply ourselves carefully to it, which tho' intirely Secret and hidden in our hearts, quite imperceptible to human Eyes, will nevertheless Show itself, be Shown and admir'd. He concludes all with the Example of Some Illustrious Emperors.

[fasc. 22, f. 6v] The other Books contain various maxims ~~on virtue~~ concerning virtue with precepts religious & moral resembling these before mentioned.

The Philosopher of greatest repute in China next to Confucius, is Montzee or Mentius who liv'd Some time after Him, following his Steps and recommending the Doctrines of Confucius, as also adding some of his own.[1] Thus for Du Halde.[2]

Hence it appears, how prevalent the Principles of that first & most excellent Religion are with the wise in all nations, I mean the Religion of Nature; A Religion arising from the nature of things and discoverable of its Self by all reasonable Beings; A Religion previous to & us'd as the foundation of all others, whose worth or merit is only estimated in proportion as they are consonant to or recede from this the only Rule of Good & Bad, of Right & Wrong; A Religion obvious to and embrac'd by all, whose minds have [fasc. 22, f. 7r] not been perverted & poisoned by Early[3] Prejudices, & untimely prepossessions in favour of Some other absurd & Inconsistent Systems. This is that Great Law of God & Nature, not improperly Said to be engraven on every Rational Soul, to whose Dictates if we firmly adhere, we Shall be preserv'd from these Enthusiastical Delusions & extravagant Superstitious Fancys, that have made Such Distraction in the Universe, tyrannizing over & enslaving the Free Minds of Intelligent Beings; A deplorable State into Which the Bulk of Mankind is led by the Base Impostures & Cunning Machinations of a few, invented & propagated from Sordid Selfish views.

In China I do not find that there are or has been any Laws enforcing conformity to a Particular System of Religion, they being left at Liberty in this matter to think for themselves without Restraint.[4] This is confirm'd by the above mentioned Author,[5] who [fasc. 22, f. 7v] gives accountt of Several Idolatrous Systems, different from and opposite One to another, which prevail'd in China; In all which the People were left to their native & infringible Liberty of judging & choosing for themselves in Religious

---

[1] Mengzi (372–289 BC), commonly Latinized as Mencius, is the second-most important Chinese thinker after Confucius and one of the Four Sages. He studied under Zisi, and like Confucius he held a series of government postings and also spent a significant time wandering and teaching, gathering a significant following. He is the eponymous author of the *Mencius*, a seven-chapter book of sayings that reflect on the nature of humankind, and other aspects of moral philosophy. See also p. 163, n. 1, above.

[2] Meaning as described by Du Halde, who asserted that Mengzi 'is esteem'd the wisest of the *Chinese* after *Confucius*' (Du Halde, *The General History of China*, I, p. 335).

[3] Fergusson might have meant 'Earthly', as he split the word between two lines and may have omitted the 'th'.

[4] Aside from the early 18th-century Chinese Rites Controversy that led to the limiting and then banning of foreign missionaries in China, religion was indeed open under the Ming and early Qing dynasties. China had a diversity of faiths and belief systems, including Confucianism, Daoism, Buddhism, and Islam. See also p. 160, n. 4.

[5] Again, Du Halde's *The General History of China*.

Matters. This Happy Priviledge of the People must in my Opinion have ow'd its preservation in a great measure to the noble Principles of that Religion that is profess'd by the Emperors, Mandarins & Men of Letters in whom all the authority of the Government resides.

If ever they have been disturb'd in this matter, it has been by Some weak ~~Bigotted~~ Emperor, bigotted to Some one or other of these Idolatrous Systems, In which it is worth observing as in all the other ridiculous Systems that are profess'd in many parts of India, that they all pretend to have had their Origin from Revelation; The first Broachers and Propagators of them allways affirming, that the Doctrines were communicated to them by a Spi= [fasc. 22, f. 8r] =rit or Angel, or in Some other miraculous manner. In confirmation of which many pretended miracles are affirmed to have been wrought by these first Institutors, & are firmly believ'd by the deluded votaries. These things cannot but be matter of melancholy reflexion to Every unprejudic'd Person who has had opportunitys of knowing & Seeing So many of these monstrous & Extravagant Religious Systems. Whereas it must afford uncommon Satisfaction to all those who have learn'd to think & judge for themselves, to observe that amicable System of Natural Religion embrac'd by the few & wise of all nations however Distant, and differing in other things, Yet in this uniformly agreeing in all its Essential Precepts. A Sure demonstration of its fix'd invariable nature and of its Intrinsick Excellence!

To conclude my observations upon the Chinese it might be proper to give a Summary character of the People, But the small opportuni= [fasc. 22, f. 8v] ties, we have of knowing, by being able to converse with none but a few merchants, hinders me from being able to give any just or tolerable character of them from mine own Knowledge. These merchants like the generality of others, Seem to Study a low Cunning in order to over reach another in a Bargain, & to take other advantages in Trade. At this the Chinese are very alert, which putts Strangers much upon their Guard in their Dealings with them. In address they have a very becoming Politeness in their air & deportment. Their Manner of Salutation is by joining the Hands which they raise up equal to the upper part of the Breast, and making with them thus join'd, Small quick motions up & down, they express Chin Chin,[1] two or three times. This is their ordinary manner with their acquaintance; But upon meeting with Some Friend that they had not Seen for a long time, they meet them bowing with their join'd hands to the Ground & other marks of joy & respect.

[fasc. 23, f. 1r][2] In Short they are generally esteem'd the most Polite, & Knowing People of the Eastern world. All kinds of mechanick Trades flourish there in great Perfection; and there is no machine how curious So ever, brought them, but upon a very Short Survey, their artificers can imitate it to great perfection. As to astronomy & other parts of Natural Philosophy they have Studied these from their most early times; But their Knowledge in the Mathematicks is deem'd but Superficial, when compar'd with the late Improvements made in these Sciences in Europe.[3] Yet their Moral Philosophy

---

[1] An archaic expression of salutation that is usually hyphenated.

[2] On the inside front cover of this fascicle Fergusson has written, 'Journals of my Voyages & Manifesto 1767' (see Figure 3, p. 34).

[3] Indeed, Fergusson was writing at a time when Europe was just beginning to emerge as a world centre for science. Isaac Newton's *Principia Mathematica* was published only 50 years before Fergusson's last voyage.

we find has been in the greatest Perfection taught & followed by all the Learned for ~~more~~ those 2000 Years, and probably longer. As an effectual Demonstration of the esteem that the Chinese have allwise had for Arts & Sciences, we Need only consider what has been taken [fasc. 23, f. 1v] notice of before, Viz. That the only means of advancement to Dignity or Power, were Knowledge in these Particulars, which is the Source of all Nobleness, Grandeur & Preferments.

The Last Day of Octo*ber* 1738. The Supracargo's Capt*ain* &.C. left Canton, & came aboard of the ship at Ouampo, from whence we Sail'd the 2d of Nov*ember*;[1] & on the 5th in the morning passing through the Tygers, [*sic*] Mouth, Where one of the Hoppo Boats coming off, took ashore, the two Hoppo men who had remain'd aboard of us from our first arrival. The Same night we putt ashore the Pilot opposite to Maccow; and having a Brisk Gale all night, we were out of Sight of the Ladroons in the morning, when it blew fresh with a pretty large Sea. This forenoon we mett with a very Surprising accident, which for Some minutes made [fasc. 23, f. 2r] all onboard look for immediate Death; for very unexpectedly the largest Sea that had ever been Seen Ship'd by the oldest Sailor aboard, broke over us from the Weather bow[2] in a full body, So as to break Down all our Booms with Spare Masts Yards &.C. which it broke in pieces, and carried the Longboat which had been hoisted upon the Leeside of the Deck, quite over the Gunwall[3] into the Sea, Smashing our Small boats that were on the Booms all in pieces.[4] It was Surprising Beyond all Imagination, that none of our People were wash'd over board or Kill'd by the fall of the Booms, they being all at that time on Deck. But what exceeded all the rest was the floating of our longboat over the gun wall without any Stop, She tearing up all the Gangway, & other obstructions in an Instant; By whict [*sic*, which] it is plain that our Lee Gun wall must have been at least 8 foot under Water. This considering how deep loaded [fasc. 23, f. 2v] we were, was thought more than Sufficient to have founder'd us without Delay. And indeed the Ship remain'd for a few minutes So motionless in the water that all of us imagin'd She was going down. However everything was instantly done that could be thought necessary for our Safety. The Long boat that continued towing alongside by the foresheet which had been belay'd or fastened to her, help'd to wear the Ship before the wind,[5] upon which, the Long boat was presently cutt away. While others immediatly [*sic*] gott the Chain Pumps fitted & Sett to work, by which we soon gott clear of the Water which by the Hatches not beeing [*sic*] tarpoling'd & batton'd down had gott in vast quantities into the Hold. By these means in alitle time we were reliev'd of our Fears, & continued our Course. But Such was the weight & violence of that Sea, that it broke two of our Strongest Stan= [fasc.

---

[1] According to the *Godolphin*'s logbook, the supracargo came aboard on 2 November (BL: IOR L/MAR/B/594M(1), entry for 2 November 1738).

[2] This is the frontside of the ship from which the wind is blowing.

[3] Properly the gunwale, this is an added rim along the top edge of the hull above the deck.

[4] What Fergusson is describing is being swamped unexpectedly by a large wave crashing over the entire deck. As the wave came from the windward side it would have rolled the ship far over to the side. As it did, the wave took spare masts, booms, sails, and boats with it, smashing and sending them into the sea.

[5] Wearing a ship before the wind means to point the bow of the ship into the wind, thus bringing it to standstill in the water. As Fergusson is about to describe, this enabled the crew to stabilize the vessel and clear away any damaged rigging.

23, f. 3r] =dards[1] betwixt Decks, & broke or Drew the thickest Iron Bolts of Some others; and partly by the Longboat & weight of water the Lee Gunwall[2] was torn about an Inch from the Upper Deck. Our Ship at the Same time having Sprung a Leck,[3] which obliged us to keep one of the Hand Pumps going the most of our Passage to Malacca: where having discovered the Leck it was easily Stopp'd within board to our great joy, being apprehensive that we Should be oblig'd to unload & heave down[4] the Ship, & consequently not have time to gett home that Season. Thus have we been twice plung'd into the most imminent Danger, & happily delivered without losing or much hurting one man. A Surprising matter to all who were present, who ought with gratefull Hearts to revere & adore the Kind Providence of Heav'n.

November 13th. we Saw Pouly Sapata an Island or rather a Large high Rock[.] [fasc. 23, f. 3v] The Day following we had Sight of Pouly Condore,[5] & next Day having had gales of wind & Foul weather which continued three Days more, we were oblig'd at times to lay the Ship to under a Ballast Mizen.[6] By the Current we were unexpectedly carried within a few Leagues of the Anambas,[7] a parcell of Small Islands & Rocks very dangerous to come near. This happened the 17th But the weather turning easier & more clear we Soon gott clear of them, and gott into the Mouth of the Straits of Malacca the 19th, and the 24th we arriv'd at Malacca; From whence after having watered & refresh'd &.C. we Sail'd the 30th. Having pass'd through the Straits, we gott in Sight of One of the Andeman Islands[8] the 15th of Dec*ember*. These are Islands well inhabited, that lie from 9 to 12 or 13 Degrees of N*orth* Lat*itude*. The Land of that I saw is very levell, & I'm told they are generally fruitfull, & possess'd by Natives of very humane Tempers.[9]

---

[1] A standard in this sense is a support piece of a ship, also known as a knee, which braces and provides stability and strength between the frame and deck of a ship.

[2] Also gunwale. This is the uppermost edge of a ship's side.

[3] Archaic form of leak.

[4] This means to careen or lay the ship on its side.

[5] See above, p. 136, nn. 3–4.

[6] To 'lay a ship to' is essentially to bring it to halt in the water. The weather was so poor that Fergusson tells us that the crew had to further stabilize the ship by taking down all the sails save the mizzen, and shifting the ship's ballast, or weight in the hull, to balance out the effects of the wind. In other words, they had to trim the ship to account for the weather.

[7] These are a group of small islands comprising the most north-westerly grouping of the Riau Archipelago, lying between the Malay peninsula and Borneo. Today they are a part of Indonesia.

[8] The Andaman Islands are in the eastern Bay of Bengal north of the Nicobar Islands, which the *Godolphin* passed on its journey to Malacca (see above, p. 130). According to the *Godolphin*'s logbook, they spotted the 'Little Andeman's', lying to the south of the main cluster of islands (BL: IOR L/MAR/B/594M(1), entry for 15 December 1738).

[9] The experience of the last 300 years appears to have changed the attitude of 'natives' toward outsiders. The first foreign settlement of the islands came with European imperialism when they were used as a penal colony for British South Asian territories. This meant the appropriation of land, exploitation of resources, and abuse of indigenous peoples, many of whom fled into the jungles and more remote areas and islands. See Sen, *Savagery and Colonialism in the Indian Ocean*, pp. 90–126. Today, several islands are still inhabited by indigenous groups such as the Jarawa, who continue to experience exploitation by unscrupulous tourism operators, despite coming under the protection of the Indian government. Attempts to contact some of the remotest groups have resulted in violence, most notably with the death in November 2018 of an American

[fasc. 23, f. 4r] **On the 24th of December.**[1] we arriv'd in Madras Road about 10 in the forenoon; and soon after I accomapnyd [*sic*] the Capt*ain* and Supracargos ashore, where I mett with that hospitality & friendship I had allways experienc'd at Fort St George.

After having finish'd our affairs there by unloading our over burthend [*sic*] Ship, and taken in a new loading for Europe &.C.,[2] We left Madras Road on Monday Morning the 29th of Jan*ua*ry 1738/9, and after an agreable passage Saw Land Near the Cape of Good Hope bearing North about 18 Leagues distance on the 10th of April; and on the 16th gott round the Cape; Soon after which we saw 2 Ships to Windward of us, One of which the *Prince of Orange* Capt*ain* *Charles* Hudson bore down to us, by whom We learn'd that the other Ship was the *London* Capt*ain* Robert Bootle two of the Ships we had left in Canton River. The *Prince of Orange* & our Ship keept [*sic*] Company to St Helena [fasc. 23, f. 4v] where we arriv'd the 1st of May about one after Noon.

We were Surpris'd not to find there The *London*, who being a better Sailor we imagin'd would have been there a day or two before us.

Our surprise encreas'd at her not arriving a day or two after, and we began to apprehend that some Accident had befallen Her; But in 3 Days after us She arriv'd having Nearly miss'd the Island, by imprudently Steering too long on a Rhomb[3] or Streight Line from the Cape ~~before they thought of~~ and not keeping Sufficiently to the Eastward until they gott into the Latitude of the Island, & then running upon it in a direct west course; as is done by all Prudent Sailors.

Luckily for Them the man at the Mast Head Saw the Island to the N*orth* E*ast* 20 or 25 Leagues distant, which made them immediatly [*sic*] alter their Course & haul up on the wind, by which means they with difficulty gott into the Road[.] Thus the old Proverb was Strongly verified Viz. That Those who make [fasc. 23, f. 5r] the greatest haste, have not allways the best Speed.

There we putt ashore 12 or 14 of our People who were Sick of the Scurvey, Some of whom were not able to walk one Step; but were So emaciat'd & breathless, as Scarce to bear being carri'd in a Hammock from the Landing place to their lodgings; & one of them died the morning ashore; Of Some the greatest part of their Gums were rotten & came off, they had livid yellow Swellings on their joints & other parts of their limbs with ulecer's [*sic*] where they happen'd to meet with any hurt; & which Sometime broke out of themselves; from which Such a fatid Humour[4] ran as flows from putrid carcasses. Their breath emitted also a most intolerable putrid Stench. In Short their whole Body appear'd quite putrified [*sic*] and ready to dissolve with putrefaction.

---

missionary, who travelled illegally to North Sentinel Island to evangelize amongst the Sentinelese. Generally considered one of the last uncontacted people in the world they shot arrows and killed the missionary soon after he landed on the island.

[1] The *Godolphin* actually arrived in Madras two days earlier (BL: IOR L/MAR/B/594M(1), entry for 22 December 1738).

[2] Mainly the crew occupied themselves with repairing the damage done to the *Godolphin* since leaving Canton, while also loading saltpetre, water, and fresh victuals.

[3] A rhomb, or rhumb, is a parallel point marked in front from a compass direction used to keep steering on course.

[4] Meaning fetid bodily fluid.

But, as has been observ'd in the preceeding Voyages,[1] Such was the astonishing Effects of change of Air & Diet that in a few days they were all Sensibly better; and in a week So much recovered as to be able to walk Some miles up the Steep Hills, & Soon grew perfectly Well.

[fasc. 23, f. 5v] The Diet prescrib'd for Them was Broth made of Fresh Beef in which was boil'd wild Purslane & Sallary which grows in great Plenty in the Island. They had boil'd yams or Rice for their Bread, and Fresh Beef, and Fowls to eat. They were allow'd Punch made of arrack with Plenty of the Juice of Oranges & Lemons that grow on the Island. And they eat the Purslain & Sallary by way of Sallet, with the juice of Oranges and Sugar.

Their Sores & Swellings were fomented with Decoctions of Fresh Herbs Viz. Rosemary, Wormwood, agrimony &.C. into which was putt Some Spiritous Liquor.[2]

By this plain Simple Diet in a few Days, all their Complaints gradually vanish'd, and their extenuated Pale Stinking Bodys, resum'd again their lively healthfull Look & Smell so that in 12 or 14 days they were restor'd to their usual State of health, which no Power of Medicines us'd while at Sea could produce in the Smallest Degree. In Short this look'd More like a risurrection [sic] than Recovery. [fasc. 23, f. 6r] This Wonderfull Change produc'd So Suddenly by Such Simple means, gives the most convincing proof of the Efficacy of a proper regimen in the Cure of Chronical Diseases, and of the attention that ought to be given by Physicians & others who undertake the Care of Peoples health, to discover that Method of Cure that the peculiar nature of Each different Disease requires; which no theory can discover, but a judicious & patient observation of what does hurt & what does good in the affective Dissorders, [sic] agreably [sic] to the Plan followed & prescrib'd by Hippocrates[3] the Great Father or Founder of true Physical Knowledge in the Cure of Diseases; in whose Footsteps had his Successors tread ever Since, & not been miss led [sic] by the Ignis Fatuus[4] of Syllenus[5] and Theorys. Physicians at this time had Not betray'd so Much Ignorance [fasc. 23, f. 6v] in their attempts to Cure Diseases.

On the 16th of May we left St Helena, and after a pleasant healthy passage gott into Soundings of 120 Fathom in the chops of the Channell [sic] on the 8th of July; and on the 11th gott off Portsmouth where we were boarded by a Tender[6] from Sir John Norris's

[1] See p. 62 for Fergusson's previous experience treating scurvy on the island. Voyage 3 contains Fergusson's observations on St Helena's geography and political and social happenings.

[2] See p. 62 for how these herbs were used medicinally.

[3] Hippocrates (c.460–c.370 BC) is still referred to as the 'Father of Medicine', and today medical doctors still take a form of the Hippocratic oath, obliging them to uphold certain ethical principals in the conduct of their professional practice. Hippocrates is said to be the first person to put forward the notion that diseases were the result of natural phenomena and not due to gods or superstitions. He also developed the humoralist system of medical treatment, which in various forms was still the predominant method for treating ailments well into the 18th century.

[4] Literally a foolish fire in Latin, this is more commonly translated as a will-o'-the-wisp, an atmospheric phantasm seen at night over marshes or bogs.

[5] Silenus was a companion of the Greek wine god Dionysus. It was held that when drunk, which he often was, Silenus was capable of prophecy, which attracted the attention of King Midas, who in one version had him captured and plied with drink in order to learn his secrets.

[6] A tender is a boat or other vessel that services and supports ships, often by carrying crew or supplies to and from shore or other ships.

Ship The *Namur*[1] who lay with other Ships of War at Spithead.[2] His Lieutenant who came on board being a prudent man, and finding our People unwilling to be press'd, and threatening to Stand on their Defence, applied to Our Capt*ain* & represent'd the dangerous consequence of such a Design in the Sailors; who tho' they might be able to repell His Tender, would Soon be Sorrounded [*sic*] by others, by the time they reach'd the Downs [fasc. 23, f. 7r] where Admiral Lestock[3] lay with Several Men of War.

Our Capt*ain* who pitied his poor Sailors who had behav'd well during the voyage and were thus to be forc'd away in Sight of their native Country after So long a voyage from their Familys & Friends without so much as Seeing them; having done all he could Safely to Save them, atlast call'd them together, and told them how unavoidable their being press'd Seem'd to be; and that they had only this Choice to agree to go with the Lieut*ena*nt of the *Namur* on board Sir John Norris, or be press'd by Adm*iral* Lestock on the Downs. They preferring Sir John to Lestock, consent'd to go with the Lieut*ena*nt on his promising to use his Interest with Sir John to procure liberty for their going 10 or 12 days to See their Friends. And the Lieut*ena*nt promis'd our Capt*ain* that he would attend the Ship with his Tender Until She came to the Nore;[4] & then would take the men.

[fasc. 23, f. 7v] To all this the Poor Fellows atlast consent'd, Seeing no hopes of Escaping; and in the Evening we arriv'd in the Downs, where the Admiral [Lestock] knowing we were from China Came on board, and Seem'd much dissappointed [*sic*] to find Sir John Norris's Lieut*ena*nt on board, who address'd him by telling Him that the men were all engag'd to go with Him; at which Lestock Seem'd not to be well pleas'd.

Our Capt*ain* treat'd the Admiral Civilly offering Him Wine Punch &.C. litle of which he car'd to take. And the Lieut*ena*nt having told Him that the Admiral's Lady was on board his Ship with Him, whose rapacious Temper was well known as well as her tyranny over her Husband, He was resolv'd to dissappoint her Schemes & Hopes; For tho' the Admiral[,] first by Insinuations & when that prov'd fruitless, by plain Words told our Capt*ain* that he would [like] [fasc. 23, f. 8r] to carry a few Cattys[5] of Fine Tea & alitle

[1] Sir John Norris (1670–1749) was an officer in the Royal Navy and served as a Whig MP for Rye and Portsmouth. Beginning as a captain's servant, he rose high in the ranks of the Admiralty. He was knighted in 1705 for meritorious service during the War of the Spanish Succession (1701–14) and went on to become Senior Naval Lord in 1727. Over the next decade he became Admiral of the Fleet, and eventually Vice-Admiral of Great Britain. He was off Portsmouth aboard the *Namur*, a second-rate ship of the line of 90 guns, built in Deptford in 1729, as the Commander-in-Chief of the Channel Fleet. The timing of the *Godolphin*'s return to England could not have been worse for the sailors on board. The ships gathered in Portsmouth were Norris's fleet being sent out against Spain in the War of Jenkins' Ear (1739–48). Indeed, it was only the day before on 10 July that King George II gave the Admiralty authority to sail against Spain, creating an immediate demand for impressed sailors.

[2] Spithead is the body of water just outside the mouth of Portsmouth harbour where the large estuary of the Solent meets the Channel. It is named after a sandbank known as the Spit.

[3] Richard Lestock (1679–1746) would later become embroiled in a scandal after being suspended by his superior Admiral Thomas Mathews for failing to engage the enemy in battle during the disastrous Battle of Toulon (1744) during the War of the Austrian Succession (1740–48), which saw severe losses to Britain's Mediterranean Fleet. Lestock in turn accused his accuser of 'treachery' and 'rashness', leading to an investigation by the House of Commons and eventually a court martial in the Admiralty. Lestock was acquitted of all charges while Mathews 'was adjudged incapable of serving in the Royal Navy for the future' (Entick, *A New Naval History*, pp. 788–96).

[4] The Nore is a sandbank laying at the mouth of the Thames estuary, which in 1732 was marked with a lightship.

[5] A catty is a Chinese unit of measurement commonly used for weighing food and grocery items and is equivalent to 1.33 lbs. (604 grams). It is thought to be the origin for the word tea caddy, the storage receptacle used when tea was first becoming popular in Europe.

good China, with a piece or two of Silk for his Lady who wished for these things; for which he would Satisfy Him; The Captain very politely told Him, that he durst not venture, having the Kings officers on board, to break the Laws which were very Severe, and that he apprehend'd a transaction of this Sort might prove of ill consequence to the Admiral if it came to be known, as it necessarily must.

By Such means, tho' the Admiral promis'd to indemnify Him from all Risks, our Captain dissappoint'd the Virago[1] who we guess'd would vent Her Fury on the poor old man, who had prov'd So unsuccessful in his Embassy.

Having taken our Pilot onboard in the Downs we next day Sail'd for the River [Thames], and gott to our Moorings the Day following. From whence I Soon afterwards went to London on the 15th July 1739.

[fasc. 23, f. 8v] N. B.[2] Cicero in the 5th Book of his *Tusculan Questions* takes notice of the custom of Wives burning themselves with their deceas'd Husbands in the following beautifull passage.

Dolor esse videtur accerrimus virtuti adversarius; is ardentis faces intentat; is fortitudinem, magnitudinem animi, patientiam Se debilitaturum minatur. Huic igitur Succumbet virtus? Huic beata Sapientis & Constantis viri vita Cedet? Quam turpe? O dii bone! Pueri Spartiatæ non ingemiscunt verberum dolore laniati. Adolescentium Greges Lacedemone vidimus Ipsi, incredibili contentione certantes pugnis Calcibus unguis, morsu denique, ut exanimarentur, priusquam Se victos faterentur. Quae Barbaria India vastior aut agrestior? In ea tamen gente primum ii, qui Sapientes habentur, nudi ætatem agunt, & Caucasi nives hyemalemque vim perferunt Sine dolore. Cumqz ad flammam Se applicuzrint [*sic*], Sine gemitu aduruntur. Mulieres vero in India, cum est cujusqz Earum vir mortuus, in certamen judiciumqz veniunt, quam plurimum ille dilexerit: plures enim Singulis Solent esse nuptæ: Quæ est victrix, ea læta, prosequentibus Suis, una Cum marito, Rogo imponitur; Illa victa mæsta decedit.[3]

---

[1] From the Latin meaning female warrior or heroic maiden, its more modern usage, even in the 18th century connotated a shrew, or domineering, violent woman.

[2] Abbreviation for *Nota bene*, or 'note well' in Latin.

[3] It is not known from which edition of Cicero that Fergusson took this. Nonetheless, it is from section XXVII of Book 5, 'Whether Virtue Alone be Sufficient for a Happy Life', in *The Tusculan Disputations*. A modern translation of the passage follows: 'pain seems to be the sharpest adversary of virtue: that it is which menaces us with burning torches; that it is which threatens to crush our fortitude, and greatness of mind, and patience. Shall virtue then yield to this? Shall the happy life of a wise and consistent man succumb to this? Good Gods! how base would this be! Spartan boys will bear to have their bodies torn by rods without uttering a groan. I myself have seen at Lacedæmon, troops of young men, with incredible earnestness contending together with their hands and feet, with their teeth and nails, nay even ready to expire, rather than own themselves conquered. Is any country of barbarians more uncivilized or desolate than India? Yet they have amongst them some that are held for wise men, who never wear any clothes all their life long, and who bear the snow of Caucasus, and the piercing cold of winter, without any pain: and who if they come in contact with fire endure being burned without a groan. The women too, in India, on the death of their husbands have a regular contest, and apply to the judge to have it determined which of them was best beloved by him; for it is customary there for one man to have many wives. She in whose favour it is determined exults greatly, and being attended by her relations is laid on the funeral pile with her husband: the others, who are postponed, walk away very much dejected' (Cicero, *The Tusculan Disputations*, trans.Yonge).

BIBLIOGRAPHY

UNPUBLISHED SOURCES

British Library, London, UK.
India Office Records, EIC Factory Records (IOR G)
   17/2, Letters and Accounts from Mocha, 1728–40.
India Office Records, Marine Department Records (IOR L/MAR)
   B/17A, Journal of the *Royal George*, 1737–39.
   B/285A, Logbooks and Ledgers of the *Britannia*, 1732–34.
   B/285B, Logbooks and Ledgers of the *Britannia*, 1735–37.
   B/594M, Ledger of the *Godolphin* 1737–39.
   B/594C, Journal of the *Godolphin*, 1737–39.

Guildhall Library, London, UK.
City Livery Company Records
   Ms 8206/2, Society of Apothecaries, Freedom Registers 1725–85.

Maharashtra State Archives, Mumbai, India.
Bombay Public Department Diaries, vol. 10, 1736–37.

National Archives, The Hague, Netherlands.
Dagregister, VOC 2415.

National Maritime Museum, Caird Library, London, UK.
Logs, 81, G. Parr, Surgeon's Journal on the HEICS *Ocean*, 1798–1800.
Journals and Diaries, 289/1 and 289/2: A. Coventry, Journal of the Proceedings (1) and Medical
   Journal (2) on the HEIC ship *Warren Hastings*, 1833–34.
TRN 37, Grantham family of West Thurrock, Essex. Extracts from the journals of East India
   Company ships *Sydney*, *Craggs* and *Britannia* 1698–1734, commanded by Caleb Grantham.

The Centre of South Asian Studies, University of Cambridge, Cambridge, UK.
Ferguson [*sic*] Papers.

The National Archives, Kew, London, UK.
Board of Stamps: Apprenticeship Books
   IR 1/13, Register of Duties Paid for Apprentices' Indentures, 1710–1811.

PUBLISHED SOURCES

Africa Check, "'Gay Baboon Rapes men in African Village" Story just Money-Making "Hogwash"',
   30 January 2019. Available at: <https://africacheck.org/fbcheck/gay-baboon-rapes-men-in-
   african-village-story-just-money-making-hogwash/>. Accessed 26 May 2020.

Anon., *A Faithful Narrative of the Capture of the Ship Derby*. London, 1738.

—, 'British Medicine in India', *The British Medical Journal*, 1(2421), 1907, pp. 1245–53.

—, *Historical and Ecclesiastical Sketches of Bengal, from the Earliest Settlement, until the Virtual Conquest of that Country by the English in 1757*, Calcutta, 1831.

—, 'The Overland Route to India', *The Friend: A Religious and Literary Journal*, 32, 1859, pp. 26, 42, 53, 67.

Arnold, D., *Colonizing the Body: State, Medicine, and Epidemic Disease in Nineteenth-Century India*, Berkeley, CA, 1993.

—, *Science, Technology, and Medicine in Colonial India*, Cambridge, 2004.

Arrowsmith-Brown, H., *Prutky's Travels to Ethiopia and Other Countries*, London, Hakluyt Society, 2nd ser., 174, 1991.

Baer, M., 'Death in the Hippodrome: Sexual Politics and Legal Culture in the Reign of Mehmet IV', *Past & Present*, 210, 2011, pp. 61–91.

Bailey, P., 'Voltaire and Confucius: French Attitudes Towards China in the Early Twentieth Century', *History of European Ideas*, 14, 1992, pp. 817–37.

Barendse, R. J., *Arabian Seas, 1700–1763*, 4 vols, Leiden, 2009.

Barr, J., 'Why the World Was Created in 4004 B.C.: Archbishop Ussher and Biblical Chronology', *Bulletin of the John Rylands Library*, 67, 1985, pp. 575–608.

Basu, R. S., 'Ideas, Memories and Meanings: Adi Dravida Interpretations of the Impact of the 1857 Rebellion', in B. Pati, ed., *The Great Rebellion of 1857 in India: Exploring Transgression, Contests and Diversities*, Milton Park, Oxfordshire, 2010, pp. 161–78.

Bivins, R., 'Expectations and Expertise: Early British Responses to Chinese Medicine', *History of Science*, 37, 1999, pp. 459–89.

Blussé, L., 'Chinese Trade to Batavia During the Days of the V.O.C.' *Archipel*, 18, 1979, pp. 195–213.

Bristow, W., 'Enlightenment', *Stanford Encyclopedia of Philosophy*, 2017. Available at: <https://plato.stanford.edu/archives/fall2017/entries/enlightenment/>. Accessed 21 May 2020.

Brooke, T. H., *A History of the Island of St. Helena, from its Discovery by the Portuguese to the Year 1806*, London, 1808.

Bruce, J., *Travels to Discover the Source of the Nile*, 5 vols, Edinburgh, 1790.

Bruijn, I., *Ship's Surgeons of the Dutch East India Company: Commerce and the Progress of Medicine in the Eighteenth Century*, Leiden, 2009.

Burke, E., *The Complete Works of Edmund Burke*, 9 vols, Boston, MA, 1839.

Burke, J., and Burke, J. B., *A Genealogical and Heraldic Dictionary of the Landed Gentry of Great Britain and Ireland*, 2 vols, London, 1847.

Burke, P., Classy, L., and Fernández-Armesto, F., 'The Global Renaissance', *Journal of World History*, 28, 2017, pp. 1–30.

Burton, R. F., *Personal Narrative of a Pilgrimage to El-Medinah and Meccah*, 3 vols, London, 1855–36.

Calanca, P., 'Piracy and Coastal Security in Southeastern China, 1600–1780', in Antony Reid, ed., *Elusive Pirates, Pervasive Smugglers: Violence and Clandestine Trade in the Greater China Seas*, Hong Kong, 2010, pp. 85–98.

Cheng, Z., *New Dimensions of Confucian and Neo-Confucian Philosophy*, Albany, NY, 1991.

Churchill, W. A., *Watermarks in Paper in Holland, England, France, etc., in the XVII and XVIII Centuries and their Interconnection*, Amsterdam, 1935.

Cicero, *The Tusculan Disputations*, trans. C. D. Yonge, eBooks@Adelaide, Adelaide, 2014. Available at: <https://ebooks.adelaide.edu.au/c/cicero/tusculan-disputations/index.html>. Accessed 20 August 2019.

Clarke, S., *A Discourse Concerning the Being and Attributes of God, the Obligations of Natural Religion, and the Truth and Certainty of the Christian Religion*, Glasgow, 1823.

Colley, L., *The Ordeal of Elizabeth Marsh: How a Remarkable Woman Crossed Seas and Empires to Become Part of World History*, London, 2008.

Cope, *A New History of the East-Indies. With Brief Observations on the Religion, Customs, Manners and Trade of the Inhabitants*, London, 1754.

Crawford, D. G., 'The Legend of Gabriel Crawford', *The Indian Medical Gazette*, 44, 1909, pp. 1–7.

Currie, J., *The Complete Works of Robert Burns*, Halifax, 1855.

Darwin, J., *After Tamerlane: The Global History of Empire since 1405*, London, 2008.

Doniger, W., *On Hinduism*, Oxford, 2014.

Downing, C., *A Compendious History of the Indian Wars*, London, 1737.

Du Halde, J. B., *Description géographique, historique, chronologique, politique et physique de l'Empire de la Chine et de la Tartarie chinoise*, 4 vols, Paris, 1735.

—, *The General History of China: Containing a Geographical, Historical, Chronological, Political and Physical Description of the Empire of China, Chinese-Tartary, Corea and Thibet*, 3rd edn, 4 vols, London, 1741.

Elliott, D. L., 'The Politics of Capture in the Eastern Arabian Sea, *c.* 1700–1750', *International Journal of Maritime History*, 25, pp. 187–98.

Elliott, D. L., and Prange, S., 'Beyond Piracy: Maritime Violence and Colonial Encounters in Indian History', in M. Mann and I. Phaf-Rheinberger, eds, *Beyond the Line: Cultural Narratives of the Southern Oceans*, Berlin, 2014, pp. 95–119.

Entick, J., *A New Naval History: or, Compleat View of the British Marine*, London, 1757.

Fan, C. S., *Culture, Institution, and Development in China: The Economics of National Character*, Milton Park, Oxfordshire, 2016.

Ferguson, J. and Fergusson, R. M., eds, *Records of the Clan and Name of Fergusson, Ferguson, and Fergus: Supplement*, Edinburgh, 1899.

Firminger, W. K., 'The Massacre of Jiddah, 1727', *Bengal: Past and Present*, 13, 1916, pp. 156–76.

Foster, W., *John Company*, London, 1926.

Galletti, A., Van der Burg, A. J., and Groot, P., eds, *The Dutch in Malabar: A Translation of Selections Nos. 1 and 2 with Introduction and Notes*, Madras, 1911.

Gerstner, J. N., *The Thousand Generation Covenant: Dutch Reformed Covenant Theology and Group Identity in Colonial South Africa, 1652–1814*, Leiden, 1991.

Gill, C., 'The Affair of Porto Novo: An Incident in Anglo-Swedish Relations', *English Historical Review*, 73, 1958, pp. 47–65.

Gordon, S., *The Marathas 1618–1818*, Cambridge, 1993.

Gray, A. and Bell, H. C. P., eds, *The Voyages of François Pyrard of Laval: To the East Indies, the Maldives, the Moluccas and Brazil*, 3 vols, London, Hakluyt Society, 1st ser., part II, 76, 77, 80, 1887–89.

Grose, J. H., *A Voyage to the East Indies*, 2 vols, London, 1772.

Grove, R., *Green Imperialism: Colonial Expansion, Tropical Island Edens and the Origins of Environmentalism*, Cambridge, 1996.

Hamilton, A., *A New Account of the East-Indies*, 2 vols, London, 1739.

Hardy, C., *A Register of Ships Employed in the Service of the Hon. the United East India Company, from the Union of the Two Companies in 1707, to the Year 1760*, London, 1800.

—, *A Register of Ships in the Service of the Hon. the United East India Company, from the Year 1760 to 1819*, ed. H. C. A. Hardy, 3rd edn, London, 1820.

Hardy, P. D., *The Holy Wells of Ireland: Containing an Authentic Account of those Various Places of Pilgrimage and Penance which are Still Annually Visited by Thousands of the Roman Catholic Peasantry*, Dublin, 1840.

Harvey, K., *The Little Republic: Masculinity and Domestic Authority in Eighteenth-Century Britain*, Oxford, 2012.

Holmes, R., *The Hottentot Venus: The Life and Death of Saartjie Baartman*, London, 2016.

Jackson, E. L., *St. Helena: The Historic Island from its Discovery to the Present Date*, New York, 1905.

Jacobsen, S. G., 'Chinese Influences or Images? Fluctuating Histories of How Enlightenment Europe Read China', *Journal of World History*, 24, 2013, pp. 623–60.

Janisch, H. R., ed., *Extracts from the St. Helena Records*, St Helena, 1885.

Jolly, J., trans., *The Minor Law Books: Part I Nârada: Brihaspati*, Oxford, 1889.

Joyce, L. E. E., ed., *A New Voyage and Description of the Isthmus of America by Lionel Wafer*, London, Hakluyt Society, 2nd ser., 73, 1934.

Kentley, E., 'The Masula: A Sewn Plank Surf Boat of India's Eastern Coast', in S. McGrail, L. Blue, E. Kentley, and C. Palmers, eds, *Boats of South Asia*, London, 2003, pp. 120–66.

Lane, J., 'The Role of Apprenticeship in Eighteenth-Century Medical Education in England', in W. F. Bynum and R. Porter, eds, *William Hunter and the Eighteenth-Century Medical World*, Cambridge, 1985, pp. 57–103.

La Roque, J. de, *A Voyage to Arabia Felix through the Eastern Ocean and the Streights of the Red-Sea, being the First Made by the French in the Years 1708, 1709 and, 1710*, London, 1732.

Lawson, P., and Phillips, J., '"Our Execrable Banditti": Perceptions of Nabobs in Mid-Eighteenth Century Britain', *Albion*, 16, 1984, pp. 225–41.

Legge, J., *The Chinese Classics: With a Translation, Critical and Exegetical Notes, Prolegomena, and Copious Indexes*, 5 vols, Hong Kong, 1861–72.

Leupe, P. A. and Hacobian, M., 'The Siege and Capture of Malacca from the Portuguese in 1640–1641', *Journal of the Malayan Branch of the Royal Asiatic Society*, 14, 1936, pp. i–iii, 1–178.

Levathes, L. *When China Ruled the Seas: The Treasure Fleet of the Dragon Throne, 1405–1433*, New York, 1994.

Levene, A. '"Honesty, sobriety and diligence": Master–Apprentice Relations in Eighteenth and Nineteenth-Century England', *Social History*, 33, 2008, pp. 183–200.

Locke, J. *Two Treatises of Government*, ed. T. Hollis, London, 1764.

—, *The Works of John Locke, in Nine Volumes*, 12th edn, 9 vols, London, 1824.

Longfield-Jones, G. M., 'John Woodall, Surgeon General of the East India Company. Part I: Events Leading to Woodall's Appointment', *Journal of Medical Biography*, 3, 1995, pp. 11–19.

Mani, L., *Contentious Traditions: The Debate on Sati in Colonial India*, Berkeley, CA, 1998.

Marshall, P. J., *Bengal: The British Bridgehead*, Cambridge, 1988.

Merians, L. E., *Envisioning the Worst: Representations of 'Hottentots' in Early-Modern England*, Newark, DE, 2001.

Minns, C. and Wallis, P., 'Rules and Reality: Quantifying the Practice of Apprenticeship in Early Modern England', *Economic History Review*, 65, 2012, pp. 556–79.

Mukund, K., *The Trading World of the Tamil Merchant: Evolution of Merchant Capitalism in the Coromandel*, New Delhi, 1999.

Müller, M., ed., *The Sacred Books of the East*, 50 vols, Oxford, 1879–1910.

Mulvey, K., 'Visual Pleasure and Narrative Cinema', in C. Penley, ed., *Feminism and Film Theory*, London, 2013, pp. 57–68.

Nair, N. K., ed., *Records of Fort St. George: Letters from Tellicherry, 1734–36*, 8 vols, Madras, 1934.

Noël, F., *Sinensis imperii libri classici sex*, Prague, 1711.

Oddie, G., *Popular Religion, Elites and Reform: Hook-Swinging and Its Prohibition in Colonial India, 1800–1894*, Delhi, 1995.

Osbeck, P., Torren, O., and Eckberg, C. G., *A Voyage to China and the East Indies*, 2 vols, London, 1771.

Paterson, J., *History of the County of Ayr: With a Genealogical Account of the Families of Ayrshire*, 2 vols, Ayr, 1847.

Pomeranz, K., *The Great Divergence: China, Europe, and the Making of the Modern World Economy*, Princeton, NJ, 2000.

Qian, S., *Records of the Grand Historian of China*, trans. B. Watson, revised edn, 3 vols, Hong Kong, 1993.

Rabie, P. J., 'The Legacy of George Schmidt (1737–1743): An Appraisal from an Anthropologist', *Kronos*, 10, 1984, pp. 49–57.

Raman, S., *Framing 'India': The Colonial Imaginary in Early Modern Culture*, Stanford, CA, 2001.

Rawlinson, G., *History of Herodotus: A New English Version*, 4 vols, London, 1862.

Rhoads, E. J. M., *Manchus and Han: Ethnic Relations and Political Power in Late Qing and Early Republican China, 1881–1928*, Seattle, 2000.

Richardson, S., *The Apprentice's Vade Mecum: Or, Young Man's Pocket-Companion*, intro. by A. D. McKillop, Los Angeles, 1975.

Rodger, N. A. M., *The Wooden World: An Anatomy of the Georgian Navy*, London, 1986.

Rogers, C., *Genealogical Memoires of the Family of Robert Burns: And of the Scottish House of Burnes*, Edinburgh, 1877.

Rousseau, J. J., *A Discourse Upon the Origin and Foundation of the Inequality of Mankind*, London, 1761.

Schoeman, K., *Twee Kaapse lewens: Henricus en Aletta Beck en die Samelewing van hul Tyd, 1702–1755*, Pretoria, 2013.

Schottenhammer, A., 'Characteristics of Qing China's Maritime Trade Politics, Shunzhi through Qianlong Reigns', in A. Schottenhammer, ed., *Trading Networks in Early Modern East Asia*, Wiesbaden, 2010, pp. 101–54.

Sen, S., *Savagery and Colonialism in the Indian Ocean: Power, Pleasure and the Andaman Islanders*, London, 2010.

Sheppard, F. H. W., ed., 'Appendix 1: Leases of the Principal Streets on the Estate', in *Survey of London: Volume 39, the Grosvenor Estate in Mayfair, Part 1 (General History)*, London, 1977, pp. 172–95.

Souciet, P. E., *Observations mathématiques, astronomiques, geographiques, chronologiques, et physiques, tirées des anciens livres Chine, par les Peres de la Compagnie de Jesus*, Paris, 1729.

Statman, A., 'The First Global Turn in Enlightenment World History', *Journal of World History*, 30, 2019, pp. 363–92.

Steel, D., *The Ship-Master's Assistant and Owner's Manual*, 6th edn, London, 1795.

Stern, P., *The Company-State: Corporate Sovereignty and the Early Modern Foundations of the British Empire in India*, New York, 2011.

Stocqueler, J. H., *The Oriental Interpreter and Treasury of East India Knowledge*, London, 1848.

Stuart, M. M., 'Scots in India 1: With the *Britannia* and the *Hindoostan*', *South Asian Review*, 7, 1974, pp. 315–23.

Subrahmanyam, S., *Europe's India: Words, People, Empires, 1500–1800*, Cambridge, MA, 2017.

Times of India, 'Woman Guard Forced to Dip Hand in Boiling Oil', 29 December 2018. Available at <https://timesofindia.indiatimes.com/city/rajkot/woman-guard-forced-to-dip-hand-in-boiling-oil/articleshow/67293730.cms>. Accessed 31 May 2020.

The National Archives, 'Currency Converter: 1270–2017', 2017. Available at <https://www.national archives.gov.uk/currency-converter/>. Accessed 1 June 2020.

Trigault, N., *De Christiana expeditione apud Sinas suscepta ab Societate Jesu*, Augsburg, 1615.

Tuchscherer, M., 'Coffee in the Red Sea Area from the Sixteenth Century to the Nineteenth Century', in W. G. Clarence-Smith, and S. Topik, eds, *The Global Coffee Economy in Africa, Asia, and Latin America, 1500–1989*, Cambridge, 2003, pp. 50–66.

Um, N., 'Foreign Doctors at the Imam's Court: Medical Diplomacy in Yemen's Coffee Era', *Genre*, 48, 2015, pp. 261–88.

—, *The Merchant Houses of Mocha: Trade and Architecture in an Indian Ocean Port*, Seattle, 2009.

—, *Shipped but not Sold: Material Culture and the Social Protocols of Trade During Yemen's Age of Coffee*, Honolulu, 2017.

Upham, M. G. 'Hell and Paradise ... Hope on Constantia: Jan Grof (died ante 1700) and his Extended Family at the Cape of Good Hope', *Uprooted Lives,* 4, 2012.

Van Dyke, P. A., 'Floating Brothels and the Canton Flower Boats 1750–1930', *Revista de Cultura*, 37, 2011, pp. 112–42.

—, *Merchants of Canton and Macao: Politics and Strategies in Eighteenth-Century Trade*, Hong Kong, 2011.

Van Kley, E. J., 'Europe's "Discovery" of China and the Writing of World History', *American Historical Review*, 76, 1971, pp. 358–85.

Virág, C., 'Moral Psychology and Cultivating the Self', in Zhu Xi, *Zhu Xi: Selected Writings*, ed. Philip. J. Ivanhoe, Oxford, 2019, pp. 33–55.

Virgil, *Georgics: A New Translation*, trans P. Fallon, ed. Elaine Fantham, Oxford, 2006.

—, *The Works of Virgil Translated in to English Prose, As Near the Original as the Different Idioms of the Latin and English Languages Allow*, 4th edn, 2 vols, London, 1763.

Wah, P. S., 'Refashioning Festivals in Republican Guangzhou', *Modern China*, 30, 2004, pp. 199–227.

White, D. L., 'Parsis in the Commercial World of Western India, 1700–1750,' *Indian Economic and Social History Review*, 24, 1987, pp. 183–203.

Wills, J. E., 'Maritime Europe and the Ming', in John Wills, ed., *China and Maritime Europe, 1500–1800: Trade, Settlement, Diplomacy, and Missions*, Cambridge, 2011, pp. 24–77.

Wilson, P. K., 'Exposing the Secret Disease: Recognizing and Treating Syphilis in Daniel Turner's London', in Linda E. Merians, ed., *The Secret Malady: Venereal Disease in Eighteenth-Century Britain and France*, Lexington, KY, 1996, pp. 68–84.

Winterbottom, A., *Hybrid Knowledge in the Early East India Company World*, Houndmills, Basingstoke, Hampshire, 2016.

Woodall, J. *The Surgions Mate*, London, 1617.

Worden, N., 'Slavery at the Cape', in *Oxford Research Encyclopedia of African History*, 2017. Available at <https://oxfordre.com/africanhistory/abstract/10.1093/acrefore/9780190277734.001.0001/acrefore-9780190277734-e-76?rskey=1PsR0B&result=1>. Accessed 1 June 2020.

Yu-Lan, F. *The Spirit of Chinese Philosophy*, trans. E. R. Hughes, Milton Park, Oxfordshire, 2005 [1947].

Yule, H., *The Diary of William Hedges, Esq.*, 3 vols, London, Hakluyt Society, 1st ser., part II, 74, 75, 78, 1887–9.

INDEX

Page references to figures are in bold.